'I cried reading parts of this book. [...] mation that is superbly liberating abc[...] too many of us. Highly recommend.'
Dr. Sonia Henry, *b*

'No one wants to cause burnout in others or be the victim of burnout. Avoiding both calamities requires a much deeper and clearer understanding of what causes burnout and what cures it. This book does precisely that.'

Adrian Piccoli, *Professor, Gonski Institute for Education*

'A must for every senior executive and all HR professionals.'
Warren Hogan, *banker and economist*

'Lawyers need to read this book: burnout doesn't have to mean the end of your career.'

Alice Cooney, *Principal Solicitor, Office of Public Prosecutions Victoria*

Burnout

Burnout: A Guide to Identifying Burnout and Pathways to Recovery is the first complete self-help guide to burnout, based on groundbreaking new research.

Burnout is widespread among high achievers in the workplace, and the problem is becoming more prevalent and profound in its impact. This book contains new evidence-based tools for readers to work out for themselves whether they have burnout and generate a plan for recovery based on their personal situation. Chapters show readers how to recognise their own burnout patterns and how far they may have travelled into burnout territory, and provide research-based management approaches to help them regain their passions and build their resilience.

Offering fascinating new insights into the biology of burnout, and stories from people who have rebounded from it, the book acts as a complete guide for anyone who suspects they may have burnout, for their friends and families, and for health professionals and employers.

Professor Gordon Parker, AO, is a clinical psychiatrist and Scientia Professor of Psychiatry at the University of New South Wales, Sydney. He previously headed university and hospital departments and was founder of the Black Dog Institute. He was the recipient of the Australian Mental Health Prize in 2020.

Gabriela Tavella is a research officer at the University of New South Wales and is completing a PhD on burnout.

Kerrie Eyers, AM, is a psychologist and writer.

Burnout

A Guide to Identifying Burnout and Pathways to Recovery

Gordon Parker, Gabriela Tavella, and Kerrie Eyers

Routledge
Taylor & Francis Group

LONDON AND NEW YORK

Designed cover image: © Getty Images

First published 2023
by Routledge
4 Park Square, Milton Park, Abingdon, Oxon OX14 4RN

and by Routledge
605 Third Avenue, New York, NY 10158

Routledge is an imprint of the Taylor & Francis Group, an informa business

Originally published in Australia by Allen & Unwin 2021

British Library Cataloguing-in-Publication Data
A catalogue record for this book is available from the British Library

Library of Congress Cataloging-in-Publication Data
Names: Parker, Gordon, 1942- author. | Tavella, Gabriela, author. | Eyers, Kerrie, author.
Title: Burnout : a guide to identifying burnout and pathways to recovery / Gordon Parker, Gabriela Tavella and Kerrie Eyers.
Description: 1 Edition. | New York : Routledge, 2023. | Includes bibliographical references and index. |
Identifiers: LCCN 2022034307 (print) | LCCN 2022034308 (ebook) | ISBN 9781032367729 (Hardback) | ISBN 9781032358963 (Paperback) | ISBN 9781003333722 (eBook)
Subjects: LCSH: Burn out (Psychology)
Classification: LCC BF481 .P355 2023 (print) | LCC BF481 (ebook) | DDC 158.7/23--dc23/eng/20221017
LC record available at https://lccn.loc.gov/2022034307
LC ebook record available at https://lccn.loc.gov/2022034308

ISBN: 978-1-032-36772-9 (hbk)
ISBN: 978-1-032-35896-3 (pbk)
ISBN: 978-1-003-33372-2 (ebk)

DOI: 10.4324/9781003333722

Typeset in Times New Roman
by Taylor & Francis Books

Contents

Acknowledgements

Our sincere thanks to the University of New South Wales and the National Health and Medical Research Council for making our research possible, to the Australian Government for providing a Research Training Program Scholarship, and to the Black Dog Institute for their support in advancing our burnout studies. To Dusan Hadzi-Pavlovic, for statistical wisdom and support. To Adam Bayes, for compiling and collating the research material on the biology of burnout. To Elizabeth Weiss, for first commissioning this book and then for providing her advice and wise and deft editorial judgements. To Simone Ford, Pamela Dunne, Tom Bailey-Smith, Grace McDonnell and Tom Bedford, for skilled and perceptive editing of the highest order. To Grace McDonnell for her editorial perceptiveness in producing this international edition. Finally, to the study participants, patients and commentators who so generously shared their personal stories with us: you have inspired this book's creation and brought its content to life.

Introduction

*'The year 2020 started with American physicians, nurses and the whole
healthcare workforce dispirited, in a deep state of burnout. Indeed, this
was not confined to the United States, a global epidemic of burnout has
been diagnosed. But things were about to get considerably worse...'*

Eric Topol[1]

Are you wondering whether the constant exhaustion that you can't
shake off is, in fact, 'burnout'? Not depression, not chronic fatigue, but
the real thing.

You are beyond simply feeling weary: you're world-weary, just scanning when you read and with a loss of feeling and *joie de vivre*. In fact,
any personal and social pleasure has become a vanishing memory. You
are finding it harder to perform in response to the demands you once
thrived on—both at work and home.

Do workdays feel like an eternity? Are you like the ancient king of
Corinth, Sisyphus, endlessly pushing a boulder uphill only for it to roll
back down again? What about your brain power: concentration span
of a gnat? Ever stop to think, and forget to start again? Reading
without retention, scanning without comprehension? Vocab as bad as
like, whatever. Then read on.

This book will not only be helpful for those in the depths of burnout
but also for *families and friends,* those who wonder whether the changes they are observing in someone they care about are a consequence
of burnout—whether the sufferer remains unaware or is trying to keep
it all together by soldiering on.

Our book is also designed for *employers* seeking to create a burnout-
free workplace. Apart from the huge financial costs, the human cost of
burnout is fuelling an increasing awareness of employers' obligations

DOI: 10.4324/9781003333722-1

to provide their employees with a safe and healthy place to work. The marked increase in successful actions undertaken to redress the accidents, suicides and stress-induced illnesses attributed to poor employment practices is a steady drumbeat.

Many of us get our burnout at work: law graduates doing double the work they signed up for in a harsh workplace, academics with year-to-year contracts, teachers struggling daily with difficult environments (and students), doctors buckling under the dictates of the electronic medical record system, and managers snowed under by emails and admin. However, burnout can also be experienced by *carers*. Some years back, the first author saw a woman in his psychiatry practice for treatment of her 'depression'. The life of this woman, let's call her Jane, had been rich and pleasant until she had two children who were severely intellectually disabled. Each slept less than two hours at night, cried for much of the day (and night) and was incontinent. Neither seemed to recognise her. Her husband had left their home altogether, her remaining family visited once a month. Jane relayed her days in an objective and matter-of-fact way, smiled when denying any depressive symptoms, but did admit to complete exhaustion. At that assessment it was clear that she did not have clinical depression and she appeared appreciative to have that diagnosis rejected. But the author was unclear as to what diagnosis was relevant as burnout lay under his radar in those days. How many other times had he failed to detect a true burnout syndrome?

We argue for including this burnout domain occupied by unsung heroes such as Jane who care for disabled children, for ageing and demanding relatives, for partners who are physically or mentally unwell, for the new babe who seems to cry 24/7. Burnout doesn't only smoulder in the workplace, it can also cast a pall over home life.

Despite its prevalence, a diagnosis of 'burnout' is rarely provided by health professionals—be they psychiatrists, psychologists, general practitioners or others—reflecting the topic's absence in training and postgraduate educational programs. In fact, despite its high prevalence and pervasiveness, it is not recognised in the medical world as a formal diagnosis (unlike, say, anxiety or depression). And there is little agreement among even those professionals aware of the condition as to the best management strategies. Most sufferers receive a diagnosis of 'stress' or 'depression' and thus risk a medicalised treatment (such as an antidepressant drug) or a simple homily ('Take a week off and see how you feel'). So this book is also designed for *professionals*, to advance their awareness of the topic, suggest how best to make a diagnosis and provide them with nuanced management recommendations.

If you need help fast, skip the rest of the Introduction, go to Appendix A and complete our burnout questionnaire. Review your score and speed-read Part 3 for management suggestions.

But you will get more out of this book if you take it slowly. Burnout is a bit mysterious, and if you follow the clues with us, you'll understand your own situation better.

So what's provided in the pages that follow?

First, *a richer definition of burnout*. Burnout is informally defined by the World Health Organization (in the organisation's latest disease classificatory manual) as an occupational phenomenon (rather than a medical condition) and comprising: (i) feelings of energy depletion or exhaustion, (ii) increased mental distance from one's job, or feelings of negativism or cynicism related to one's job, and (iii) a sense of ineffectiveness and lack of accomplishment. This builds on a model developed in the early 1980s, which has ever since dominated the literature. In essence, this definition comprises only three symptoms, or perhaps only two (as the third could simply be the consequence of exhaustion). We, however, argue for a more extensive set of symptoms. While our research is ongoing, you will read how we eventually generated a broader symptom set, commencing with obtaining the observations of sufferers and then by undertaking a number of statistical analyses, and we reference our current set of papers published in peer-reviewed journals.

Second, *the Sydney Burnout Measure* (SBM). We include the questionnaire (Appendix A), developed from our research, that quantifies the level or severity of burnout.

Third, *how to distinguish burnout from depression and other conditions*. We look at the implications of a high score on the SBM. Scores in the higher range can also be returned by those with other psychological conditions—especially depression, and those with certain physical states (e.g. severe anaemia) or receiving certain treatments (e.g. chemotherapy). This risk, that a high score can give a false positive 'diagnosis', applies to *all* measures of burnout, though this limitation is generally unrecognised.

Fourth, *the gift of 'clinical reasoning'*. As a consequence of blurred boundaries between burnout and other conditions, and burnout currently lying in an arid zone of medical knowledge, we take you into the world of clinical reasoning in order to give *you* the tools to assess your own symptoms and clinical profile. You may not necessarily have burnout. Alternative physical and psychological diagnoses as well as other causes need to be considered. We maintain that you can engage in this process by employing clinical reasoning, especially to differentiate burnout from depression and other psychological states, and, with the assistance of your doctor, from other medical conditions that we list.

Fifth, we consider *the influence of personality style.* We contend that while burnout is precipitated by work stressors, personality style can supply a strong predisposition, with those who are most dutiful, conscientious and perfectionistic (displaying perfectionist behaviours or tendencies) being at much greater risk. Burnout hits such 'good workers' in particular—and, pssst, now you know why sociopaths never get burnout.

Sixth, welcome to *burnout's history.* One of its ancestors was included in the seven deadly sins—or is it eight? Read Chapter 1 to find out.

Seventh, we examine the reality of *differing burnout patterns.* A medical intern may develop burnout symptoms over a period of just a few months during a demanding term, as can students intensely involved in their final years of school. If the intern has a break at the end of that term—and the student has a holiday after final exams—their burnout symptoms generally rapidly disappear. Like a spring released from pressure, they bounce back to their previous setting. Others may develop minor symptoms in response to chronic work stressors (becoming 'browned off' rather than burnt out) and also recover quickly if those stressors are removed or become manageable. Still others may develop and accrue burnout symptoms slowly, with the slow onset muting their awareness of their altering state. A further pattern is shown by those who experience a rapid and acute onset and even physically collapse (some of the personal stories illustrate this vividly). Then there are those who are unfortunate enough to have completely burnt out and, if still subjected to the relentless pressures that have created their state, feel irrevocably 'broken'. Identifying the pattern helps shape the best management strategy. Just as a flickering candle and one that has completely gone out require differing methods to restore their flame, it is central to concede 'burning out' and 'burnt out' as two differing phases. If burning out, de-stressing strategies may be the priority; if burnt out, restoration may require a new life pattern in addition.

Eighth, we overview the *biological changes that occur in the body and the brain during burnout*. Highly technical, sure, but if you like to look under the bonnet when your car conks out rather than just call for roadside assistance, you should find Chapter 7 fascinating and perhaps even work out what the story is with cortisol (surprisingly, the science is still out on its effects). We detail how burnout's key symptoms link with brain and bodily changes and then detail how such brain and even immunological changes can be reversed by certain therapeutic strategies, often strikingly so.

Ninth, we outline *treatments tailored to the individual's condition* and eschew a 'one size fits all' model. We contend that as burnout is the consequence of differing mixes of predisposing and precipitating factors, it requires nuanced management addressing both realms. While most management options focus on addressing precipitating stressors (workplace factors that fuel the burn) or advocate certain de-stressing techniques—and we cover both—we consider how management should also involve addressing any predisposing personality factors.

Tenth, we detail *the lived experiences* of those who have suffered burnout—principally individuals who have taken part in our studies and several prominent luminaries. Such personal descriptions reach the reader in a way that goes beyond any authorial voice, giving insight and practical wisdom, with many of the recounts marked by grit and wry humour. An individual either on the brink of or well into burnout territory will find a parallel (or should we have said a match?) in someone who has navigated through similar experiences and whose solutions can offer practical compass directions.

Our contributors also provide insights for family and friends on how best to approach a loved one suspected of suffering burnout. We review and critique the evidence-based treatment literature, conclude that it is strikingly limited and so collate and report the most helpful strategies nominated by our contributors. The best of humanity is on view here. Contributors have strived to provide their insights so that you and others might gain from their struggle without having to endure what they did.

Eleventh, *recovery from burnout*. When you read the many positive outcome stories you may suspect that we were selective in our choice of writers. Not so. Given appropriate coping strategies, most people regain their spark. Sure, some get stuck, especially if they cannot escape the flames, and even more so if they also become locked in extended negotiations with employers and HR departments or caught up in protracted legal actions and disability claims. Here, and we invoke Sun Tzu, the 'wise warrior' does best to avoid the battle.

How do so many people do well? A pluralistic model (and the one we advocate) is reflected in so many of the personal stories. People who recover adopt multiple immediate and preventative strategies, and often reinvent themselves as well as their work patterns and success-fully *maintain their new habits*. It's a bit like exercise.

As we prepared this book in 2020—working from home, of course—we read many articles predicting a new post-COVID-19 world and workplace, as people in a more adaptive mental state re-evaluated what provides their life with meaning. The expectation was that people would not return to the 'eat, sleep, work, repeat' grind in the new post-epidemic world. However, this forecast does not accord with human nature. It seems more likely that only a small percentage of the popu-lation will continue working from home while the majority of workers will be required to hop back on the hamster wheel. Workplace burnout will flare again.

To set the scene, we now proceed with three personal stories from people who have experienced burnout or its early symptoms and learned how to deal with it. The factors that caused their burnout symptoms are considered closely in later chapters. All were able to overcome burnout by reworking their life patterns. As a result, they each discovered that their lives were enriched and changed for good.

Three personal stories

Sophie Scott

Sophie Scott is an award-winning journalist who has been the medical reporter for the Australian Broadcasting Commission (ABC) for more than two decades and is the author of Live a Longer Life *and* Roadtesting Happiness.

It was a black-tie dinner for about 500 people. I had been looking forward to hosting it even though it was a busy time for me.

I had been working non-stop on television stories, writing, speaking and hosting health events. My focus was on improving the health and wellbeing of Australians, bringing our audiences the latest scientific research breakthroughs. Somehow, as well, I had become an investigative reporter, uncovering safety scandals that had left so many patients' lives ruined. But I couldn't resist the invitation to fly interstate in the afternoon to host the glittering event that night, honouring health workers.

I felt good in my sparkly dress and high heels as I made my way onto the stage to welcome everyone. When I got to the podium, that's when it hit me. All of a sudden, I felt dizzy and unsteady on my feet and had to hold onto the podium so I didn't fall over. I smiled even more as I could feel my heart pounding harder and harder in my chest.

This wasn't anxiety. I had had that feeling before and this was way worse. I have always had low blood pressure but this was something I had never felt before.

My one consolation, I thought, was that if I fell over in a room full of doctors and nurses, someone would be able to look after me!

In hindsight, I should have seen it coming.

I had been increasingly tired on weekends. I had been working long days during the week and using the weekends to catch up on sleep. Some Sundays, I was so tired I could barely make it along the promenade of my favourite beach when my husband and I took our puppy for a walk. I had to keep stopping on benches for a rest. To the outside world, I was happy. But deep inside, the joy I usually gleaned from my work, from interacting with patients, viewers and readers, had significantly lessened.

After several rounds of medical tests that all came back normal, I found out that my autonomic nervous system had stopped working the way it should. Constant stress and overwork had led to what doctors call 'autonomic dysfunction'.

I was burnt out.

If you think of the body like a computer, the autonomic nervous system is like software that runs silently in the background controlling bodily functions we are not even aware of, such as breathing, blood pressure and digestion. Part of it is the sympathetic nervous system, which prepares your body for stressful or emergency situations. So it increases your heart rate and dilates your airways to make breathing easier. It causes you to sweat, your pupils to dilate and your hair to stand on end. Your body thinks you are facing a serious emergency, so it slows down processes like digestion. My nervous system had been switched to 'on' for so long that my body was constantly primed and ready for attack, leaving me drained and fatigued as a result.

I held onto the podium while I was presenting the awards and sat down, rested and caught my breath in the few moments in between presentations. Somehow, I managed to get through it and back to the hotel without anyone realising what had happened.

My aha moment

On the flight back home, I realised something had to change. I had to find the magic bullet that would give me more energy, more clarity and focus, and calm my switched-on autonomic nervous system. I had to start working differently, not working harder. I didn't want to give up the work I was doing, which I knew was making a difference in people's lives.

My job involves reading scientific papers and interviewing the world's leading medical experts. I had written books on mental health, exercise and living a healthy life. Of all people, I should have been able to fix what I was feeling.

My aha moment was realising I had to listen to that science.

Stress had made my cortisol levels spike so much and for so long that my body just thought that's what I was meant to feel all the time. I knew the impact stress has on the mind and body. Some stress is good for you. Knowing this was a good thing. I had written about the work of American psychologist Kelly McGonigal. She found that if we believe stress is bad for us then being in a stressful situation is more likely to have negative health consequences.

But I was also well aware of the science detailing the effects of prolonged stress. Research clearly shows ongoing stress can lead to inflammation in the arteries and boost your heart attack risk, impact brain and memory function and mess with your hormones, among other things. Like so many other people, I was so over-scheduled, overworked and overcommitted that I had burnt away any reserves my mind and body had left.

And I had no one to blame but myself. No one was piling on the commitments. No one was forcing me to say yes to everything. I had always enjoyed working hard but somehow being motivated and conscientious had morphed into perfectionism, setting unrealistic expectations for myself and focusing on the results, rather than the journey. No one was pushing me into a corner saying your self-worth depends on doing everything, showing up to everything and having nothing left for your family, friends and people you care about.

Small changes

I had to learn that *you can change* and improve how you feel physically, emotionally and mentally. But it wasn't going to be by taking a magic pill. It wasn't going to be one single supplement, one special diet, one enlightened 'expert' or one book. I realised that 'nothing will change unless you do'. Unless I could fundamentally change how I approached living my life, nothing was going to improve.

We all want solutions, quick ones if possible. But I had to wrest the power back from assuming one person or one action was the one simple answer to my problems. I had to focus on rebuilding my nervous system one day at a time. And science could show me the way. Knowledge is power but I realised it was next to useless if you didn't act on that knowledge. That was where the real power for change lies.

Science showed me that even though I was busy and burnt out, there was a way forward, and I didn't have to live my life in the same way I always had. Science also showed me that even small changes could make a difference to my health and wellness. And it wasn't about doing more (thankfully!) and adding to an already over-scheduled life. It wasn't about getting up at 5.30 a.m. to run 10 kilometres (though if that's what you love doing, all power to you). Instead, it was about taking small, simple steps that were achievable.

So it had to be quick. And it had to be easy.

I asked myself: what is the smallest action I can take that will move me forward? I started with eight minutes a day, three times a day. The first was some gentle tai chi in the mornings before work.

I was so tired that I started with a tai chi video for seniors.

The second was a walk in the sunshine to clear my head instead of eating lunch at my desk. Research shows movement can reduce the activity of stress response systems in the body, particularly if it is something you do regularly.

The last was mindfulness meditation just before bed. Shifting my mindset could help me reframe my thinking. In other words, I could acknowledge I was feeling busy and burnt out without being defined by those feelings. Deep breathing can reduce cortisol levels by 25% and reduce emotional exhaustion by bringing down the stress response.

What I found was making those small changes and sticking with them started to make a difference. I was able to shift my mindset from all or nothing to realising that small changes *can* improve how you feel every day. (I called it my 'feel great in eight' strategy.)

What had been blocking me was my all or nothing thinking and picking a massive goal—I wanted to feel full of energy, happy, motivated, productive and successful all the time, as well as calm and relaxed. But if your goal is too big (e.g. start a million-dollar business, have a perfect body), it's intimidating and you don't ever feel like making a start. Instead, by taking small and simple steps, finally, I overcame those feelings of being burnt out and having nothing left.

I was able to set boundaries, saying 'yes' to those things that really mattered while giving a firm but polite 'no' to things that didn't. Finally, I had the energy to take my dog, Sammi, for a walk at the beach. I had the energy to focus on regular connections with my friends and family. I had the mental energy to think clearly about my life and how to be the best mother, partner, friend and colleague.

Staying where I was had consequences on my physical and mental health. I had forgotten what it felt like to be calm, living in the moment and feeling good. Using practices such as mindfulness meditation, gentle movement and adjusting my mindset works. It allows me to enjoy what I am doing, saying no to what isn't bringing me joy and savouring how good I feel. But these practices are just that—'practices', and you have to keep going with such practices, recalibrating them when life, as it will, throws you something unexpected.

Now, when life feels out of control, I can bring myself back to those eight minutes a day each day that I know make a difference: movement, mindset, meditation. Those practices bring me back to the present and help me remember it took only eight minutes a few times a day to turn my life around.

Jayson Greenberg

Dr Jayson Greenberg is an American otolaryngologist (ear, nose and throat specialist) based at the University of Michigan. In January 2020 he published a highly evocative article in the American Medical Association's high-ranking journal JAMA, titled 'A call for help—reflections on burnout, CABG surgery and the Super Bowl'. Here he provides the story of his burnout experience, personalised for this book.

I had experienced anxiety chest pain before, so I assumed the intermittent tingling in my chest was similar. It was probably anxiety related to my new position. I had recently switched to academia after 16 years as a private practice otolaryngologist. I was 48 years old and in good shape. I ate well and exercised regularly. My blood pressure and cholesterol were normal. Regardless, I saw a colleague for an evaluation of my cardiac health. 'We have stressful jobs', he acknowledged, as he scheduled me for further testing the following week. To our consternation, my stress test showed multiple areas of decreased blood flow to my heart, and a coronary calcium test corroborated that I was at very high risk of a heart attack. A cardiac catheter confirmed serious narrowing in many of my heart's supporting arteries.

I am now nearly 18 months out from a successful quintuple bypass (a complicated procedure required when all five arteries to the heart are diseased). Given my genetics, I realise now I was likely destined for a cardiac bypass at some point. However, I knew the extent of the silting up of my arteries went much deeper than genetics. I also knew that statistically I may need a further procedure in the future. Change was critical for me.

Surgical disciplines attract those with certain personality traits: motivated, focused, disciplined, high-achieving and driven by the practice and perfection of their craft. We are intrinsic perfectionists who must reconcile that we will never truly be perfect. Most patients we can help but some we cannot. The human body and outcomes are mostly predictable but not always. Complications happen despite our best efforts.

I had never heard about burnout in residency or even early on in practice. Surgical residency was challenging, but I truly enjoyed those years. I was learning constantly in a supportive team environment. After residency, I transitioned to a community private practice. The area was perfect for my family, and I enjoyed the surgical case load. I was on call for the emergency department ten days a month, but we all covered our own patients... all the time. In essence, unless we were out of town, we were always on call. I knew this situation was not sustainable, but my attempts to propose a more team-orientated approach were unsuccessful.

Early on in practice, I was involved in a devastating complication after a routine surgical procedure. I prayed for that patient every day, but I knew his prognosis was poor. I know that I will never suffer what that family suffered, but I still suffered. Support from the practice and hospital was minimal. Surgeons are supposed to be tough and resilient. I did my best to manage the emotional scars and soldiered on, but the burnout seed had been planted.

I appeared well enough on the outside, but the effects of frequent call demands along with stress from the complication slowly gnawed at me on the inside. I began to catastrophise every patient phone call. My heart would beat out of my chest every time the pager went off as I feared the worst-case scenario. Being on call became unbearable. I was home when on call, but I was rarely mentally present. I began dreading Sundays and the thought of going back to work. Meanwhile, my practice continued to grow. One partner relocated. The recruitment process was unsuccessful and costly, so we chose not to replace him. The quarterly bonus cheques may have eased the burnout progression, but the burnout tree was still growing.

Articles about burnout began to propagate my inbox. I deleted every hospital email regarding physician engagement and began thinking about encore careers. I still cared about my patients. My complication rates did not go up. I did not feel like I was clinically depressed. I was not abusing alcohol, getting divorced or experiencing suicidal thoughts. I'd never heard of nor taken the Maslach Burnout Inventory, and I didn't need to. I diligently tried all the suggestions to address the burnout: meditation, reading, exercise, vacations and starting a side business. I hired a scribe to help with the electronic health record. There were only so many variables I could control. These efforts may have trimmed the branches of the burnout tree but the roots were still growing internally, cracking the foundation.

After 16 years in private practice, I applied for a position at the nearby academic medical centre. My family would not have to move.

The compensation would be less, but I didn't care. Call demands would be less, and there would be residents to teach and assist with patient care. I would be part of a team of talented colleagues who worked to support each other. I was hopeful the culture change would slowly eradicate the burnout tree at its roots. Unfortunately, the damage had already been done.

I had spent my career helping and healing patients. Needing help for myself and asking for it was a foreign concept. Medicine is a calling to help and heal others, but I needed to learn to help and heal myself. For so many years I had clung to the outdated mantra from residency that asking for help is a sign of weakness. 'Don't complain. Don't explain', senior residents frequently told us. The burnout tree grows slowly over time. If not recognised, the roots grow and plaque accumulates. It took a diagnosis of coronary artery disease and a quintuple bypass before I finally realised that asking for help is a sign of courage and strength, not weakness.

Bo Schembechler, the late legendary American college football coach at my institution, was famous for his saying 'The Team, the Team, the Team'. The path to wellness is different for everyone, but you cannot successfully walk that path alone. Change requires a supportive team environment. I could not create the environment I needed in my previous private practice, so I ultimately switched to a position in a system that had a supportive culture already in place.

Beating burnout requires a deep root cause analysis including paying attention to symptoms (mental and physical) and having them evaluated. Beating burnout involves recognising when feeling unhappy or overworked and examining reasons as to why. Some issues can be controlled, others cannot. My previous work environment, with increasing patient loads, continued on-call demands and an early catastrophic complication, combined with my responses to those stressors, was an ideal fertiliser that allowed the burnout tree to sprout and grow. I tried to make modifications along the way, but these only slowed the progression.

It was only in a new position with a new team that wellness and positivity began to thrive. Work and call demands are less, and help is all around me if I need it. More importantly, I am no longer afraid to ask for it. I still eat well and exercise regularly, but I have added a few cardiac medications to my daily regimen. I am grateful for the second chance and reinforce those feelings and thoughts daily in my gratitude journal. The shift in my demeanour is palpable. I am more in the moment and mindful. I am not on edge all the time. The result is a better husband, father and physician.

The wellness formula includes multiple variables, but there are a few constants. Our bodies and minds will usually tell us when something is wrong or out of alignment, and those signs will keep getting louder until they are recognised and addressed. Wellness works better in a supportive team environment. Everyone needs a little help now and then. As noted earlier, asking for it is a sign of strength, not weakness. Wellness is a journey. Anxiety and stress are obstacles that can be mitigated and managed through careful analysis, change and help from yourself and the team you surround yourself with.

My mind and arteries are more open now. Keeping them clear is the challenge.

Anne-Marie Rice

Anne-Marie Rice is an award-winning conflict resolution expert based in Brisbane, Australia. She teaches at one of Australia's leading law schools and has worked in legal dispute resolution for over 20 years. She is a highly sought after mediator, trainer and speaker whose work centres on the notion that conflict can be resolved without combat.

I've never visited the town known as Burnout. I've never wanted to. But I know where it is on the map and I've even seen it shimmering on the horizon. Once, my body received an invitation to a party at that tragic oasis—that was enough to scare me into working out how to put the map away and resume control of the vehicle.

I'm an intelligent, educated woman who came of age in the early 1990s. I'm a product of my generation and the opportunities it represented. The narrative of my life was that I could have it all if only I worked hard enough (and wasn't too greedy in wanting 'it all' at the same time). But that narrative was dangerously naïve. It taught me nothing about who I really am and what I needed to feel fulfilled or to sustain the many hats I would come to wear. It prepared me for none of the challenges in the inevitable collision of my personal and professional roles.

I am a mother and I cherish that role and my children and my husband. I am also a woman whose work matters—to me, to those I work with and to the clients I work for. I believe in the importance of that work and I feel I have much to contribute to it. I recognise that my vocation is bigger than me and I have been eager to progress in a profession where women remain under-represented in positions of leadership and longevity. I am a lawyer. Sort of.

It has been said that being a lawyer is easy. It's like riding a bike. Except that the bike is on fire. You are on fire. Everything is on fire. And you are in Hell. I have been working in the law for over 20 years and for the second half of my career I have spent a lot of time wondering why I have so often felt like I was on fire. And what I could do to put that fire out.

After a decade of questioning, soul-searching, incubating and thinking about what it means to be 'a mother in the law', I worked something out: it only takes everything you've got.

Being a lawyer is, of itself, plain hard work. It requires mental and, in its own strange way, physical stamina. It requires commitment and ambition and attention to detail and the shouldering of great responsibility and risk. And being a mother takes none of that responsibility away. And none of the need for commitment. And none of the need for precision. And none of the risk. And none of the hard work. In fact, it just doubles down on all those things—they are now ever present both at work and at home. Like so many professions, the law is populated by perfectionists and imposes deadlines that the individual strives to meet but can never really control. Conflict does not keep office hours.

Being a mother is the hardest, most important thing I've ever done. Perhaps it could be said that being a mother in the law is very much like being permanently stuck on that bike. Everything feels on fire. And while you can joke about it in a professional sense, you are not supposed to feel that way about being a mother.

Many of the skills I honed in being a lawyer—precision, focus, timeliness, judgement, control—are precisely the opposite of what is needed to parent. Lawyers and small children can be seriously incompatible bedfellows. I suspect I am not the only new mum who recorded breastfeeding regimes with the precision of a detailed file note, or who perversely relished the new level of mayhem that comes with combining babies and toddlers because then at least there was always plenty to do—some order to be brought to the chaos and less time to think about what was really happening. While the exhaustion, isolation and discombobulation that come with being at home alone with a baby were immediate, it took years for me to become comfortable with the pace of parenting and to work out how to transition to and from the pace of the office.

For me, the most acute stress was not associated with either work or with parenting per se, it was with the collision of those two parallel universes: when I came home still palpably riled from the day and the kids stood back watchfully and did not run to my arms; when I had to compose technical correspondence from the side of the playground while making sure no one fell from anything; or when I had to engage the electronic babysitter (again) so that I could take a call that I convinced myself could not possibly wait one day or be interrupted by sounds that resembled something as audacious and unprofessional as a life outside the office. I was never not working. Weekends presented delicious opportunities for catching up. On work.

My toddlers have marched in the background of phone calls shouting, 'My mum is always on the phone, always talking, but never to me', and invented games where I am the babysitter so they can go to work in a flurry of pretend high heels, computer bags and messages of 'Here's the baby, she'll need to be fed, I've got a big meeting, I'm not sure when I will be back'. I've 'laughed' with other lawyer mums about the places we have had to lock ourselves into to take work calls on days we should have been 'at home', about the parenting fails and #motheroftheyear moments. We've shared stories of how some days, many days, all you've needed after a big day at the office, managing looming deadlines, was for the dinner-bath-bed routine to be miraculously quick so you could get back to work as soon as possible and be in bed sometime before the 2 a.m. feed.

And I have administered plenty of doses from the unending supply of self-judgement after seeing the faces and hearing the gasps of others who have not had to resort to those extremes. I know I've fallen short of my own mothering expectations. I've felt the shame and the grief of that, and I've let that take a toll, because I'm not a person who fails. At anything. Ever. It's what has made me good at my job. Toughing it out has been rewarded. 'If you can keep your nerve when all about you are losing theirs and blaming it on you', and all that.

And even though I was told I could have it all, and in the beginning I had the energy to believe that I could, and to pretend it was fun, and achievable, I was steadily failing at being all things to all people at all times. I've wondered aloud to my husband about whether I had any hope of teaching my children something other than how to work hard. And I have wept from the frustration and from the exhaustion of trying to make it all work and from trying to see where to even begin to find balance.

I once heard a child psychiatrist say that one of her adolescent patients, who was self-harming, told her 'my mother is everywhere and nowhere all at once'. That hit home. So I put a 'BE HERE NOW' note on my fridge, but I changed nothing. I was determined to 'lawyer well' and I did. I was determined to 'parent well' and I did, but I felt stretched and brittle and reactive and internally inconsistent and frustrated. And *exhausted*. But I changed nothing. I didn't know how. And then my body got that invitation. And I laughed at it and said, 'We're not going to that party'. But still, I changed nothing, because I didn't know how, and I thought that's what a lawyer did: toughed it out in the face of unrelenting responsibility.

And then when things didn't miraculously settle into a manageable groove, I looked in the mirror properly and let myself see who I had become. And then I really stopped pretending. Because in the midst of all the juggling and plate spinning and striving and caring, I've also lingered, blinking, unmoored, over the bedtime story and snuggle that has felt like a sublime bubble on the rare evenings where there is no work to be done as soon as sleep is secured. And I've made time to talk meaningfully to my young son about why my work matters to me when he's asked why I can't go to school events 'like other mums'. And the kids and I have stopped and, awe-struck, watched a butterfly hatch from a chrysalis found on the washing line. And I've had many, many moments of embracing all that it is to be a mother and, at the other end of the spectrum, all that it is to be a good lawyer. And I became determined to work out how to be spread less thin.

To do less, well.

I started to pay careful attention to the things that were impacting profoundly on me. And after a while and utterly unexpectedly I found both the capacity and the opportunity to put it into words.

In October 2018 I had the wonderful honour of being named the WLAQ Leneen Forde AC Woman Lawyer of the Year and made a short speech at the awards dinner. It was not lost on me that the speech was almost exactly six minutes long. It was the most powerful billable unit of my professional life.

It earned a standing ovation and, almost as soon as I had given it, the speech was posted on social media and generated the most extraordinary response. The transcript and recording went viral in legal circles and beyond. It was tweeted by ABC journalist Annabel Crabb. It led to a television interview with Australia's SBS's *Insight* host, Jenny Brockie. It has appeared and reappeared in the most unexpected places. I've given speeches and made media appearances and podcast interviews with hosts from all over the country and I received countless wonderful emails and other messages of support. One of my favourite responses came from North America: 'I didn't know whether to fist pump or cry'.

That speech struck a chord with professional women (and men) around the world and started a most significant conversation about how close to the wind we sail and how little we know of what to do about it. Here it is:

Thank you to the judges and to the sponsors—it's particularly lovely to receive an award sponsored by my alumnus, the University of Queensland, a place where I now teach and indeed am taught.

I would like to thank a few who are here with me tonight. First of all my mother, whose name, confusingly, is Dorte. Yes, my mother, Dorte. I am Dorte's daughter. She is everything a Danish Viking should be: brave, beautiful, strong and willing to frock up at a moment's notice.

To the totally amazing women who made and supported my nomination, thank you. To know that I have in some small way encouraged and inspired you is a gift in itself. And I am glad I didn't have to die before you wrote such nice things about me!

Also here with me tonight are two barristers who I joined in 2002 as finalists in the category of Emergent Woman Lawyer of the Year. And so to tonight's Emergent finalists I say: we are what 16 years and seven children will do to you. But that we are all still in this game and able to be here together tonight means a great deal and says much.

But, ladies and gentlemen, I have a confession to make.

I am tired.

I am tired because I am 44 years old, self-employed and the mother of two primary school-aged children. Tired goes with the territory.

I am tired because as well as being a mother, I am a wife, daughter, sister, friend, colleague, mentor, teacher, contributor to my personal and professional communities, and I take those opportunities seriously and I give them my all.

I am tired because I am a lawyer and the law is a jealous mistress.

But most of all I am tired from 20 years of doing a job through a prism that is inconsistent with who I am. A lens that I find fundamentally one-dimensional and inherently aggressive. It is inherently masculine. The way the law is largely practised invites lawyers to solve problems by first making them bigger and then aggressively holding a position until a decision is imposed or a compromise based on brinkmanship is reached.

I don't naturally think like that but I have been taught that's how my job is done. And I have learned how to excel at it. But I am tired.

I am exhausted from walking that walk. It affects who I am. It dims my light. And looking around this room, I know I am not the only one who feels it.

But it also affects those who are not in this room. The women who have left the profession. Not having retired after a full and fulfilling career but who have opted out. Early.

I get it. Law was historically a man's game and the pace of cultural change is glacial. But, ladies, at least as graduates and junior lawyers we have been here, en masse, for decades. But we are not here in numbers in the roles that require longer service. We know that. We drop out for many reasons—not least because we become tired.

I think that has much to do with the fact that law, business, sport, family lives still operate so much through a lens that is not ours. It's not even equal, which would be better still.

I used to think in my moments of feeling tired, exhausted and overwhelmed that my role in the profession didn't matter. That I am not a trailblazer like Leneen Forde, Agnes McWhinney or Margaret McMurdo. That the doors for women's entry to the law were now wide open and no one would care if I raised the white flag and opted out to run the school's second-hand uniform shop.

But I can see now that I (and the women of my generation) matter just as much as those upon whose shoulders we stand. The responsibility for the change to make professional life sustainable for women is mine. It's ours. The responsibility to stop pretending that a flourishing legal career and a committed parenting (or other) role is at all easy, realistic, healthy or sustainable is mine. It's ours.

We lie loudest when we lie to ourselves. But worse, I think, we lie to the generations to come. To the women and men who will benefit from the opportunity to enjoy a deeply thoughtful, multi-dimensional professional life.

The time to think about and then work out how to practise as a problem-solver, not a gladiator, is upon us. And it's so terribly exciting that it makes me forget about the tired.

We all know that Ginger Rogers did everything Fred Astaire did, but that she did it backwards and in high heels. But puzzle me this: what might have happened if Ginger Rogers had been invited to turn around?

Postscript: I've stopped working as a gladiator. Slowly, and with great discipline, I taught myself to stop thinking like one. I re-imagined what it would be like to do my job and live my life through a different lens. I've allowed myself to be the multidimensional person I truly am: the mother, the wife, the friend, the person, the professional. I had to give up much to do that. And it took a long time and it hurt greatly and was deeply confusing and confronting.

It's been five years since my body received the party invitation from destination Burnout. And what surprises and comforts me most about that journey is that it feels almost impossible for me to now truly rekindle those feelings of brittle exhaustion. Just as, back then, it felt almost impossible to imagine how things could be different.

I've turned around. And if you are also in need of doing that then know this: it only takes everything you've got. But it's infinitely easier to dance when you can see where you are going, when you recognise the tune and when you choose the path. And where that path takes you can be utterly surprising in its unpredictability.

Note

1   E.J. Topol, 'Topol: US betrays healthcare workers in coronavirus disaster', *Medscape*, 30 March 2020, <www.medscape.com/viewarticle/927811>, accessed September 2022.

Part 1

What is burnout?

Chapter I

Burnout

Forerunners and variants

'I did not die, yet nothing of life remained'.
Dante, as quoted by Graham Greene in *A Burnt-Out Case*

It was not until the mid-1970s that burnout, as a psychological phenomenon, emerged as a hot issue. It was defined in the early 1980s as a syndrome with three principal but variably described symptoms: exhaustion, decreased empathy and decreased professional accomplishment. This begs the question: is burnout a modern phenomenon that reflects a real change in our psychological environment? If so, can we blame this on the work environment being tougher than it has ever been previously, or are we just less resilient than previous generations? Or is the current burnout wave simply a rediscovery of an age-old human condition with a facelift? In this and the next chapter, we dip into history to look for the answer.

The biblical prophet Elijah, following great successes and miracles, broke down 'in the face of impending defeat, plunging into deep despair and falling into a deep sleep',[1] with that state subsequently described by priests as 'Elijah's fatigue' and judged by many commentators as a burnout state. Some commentators also view Moses as having suffered from burnout—in becoming disillusioned during the flight from Egypt as his people demanded ever more from him, and he was warned that doing work that was 'too heavy' for him would eventually 'wear [him] out' (Exodus 18:17–18). Shakespeare, too, created recognisable characters ground down by circumstance, like Hamlet: 'How weary, stale, flat, and unprofitable/Seem to me all the uses of this world!' (act 1, scene 2).

But were these figures from the past describing what we now know as burnout?

DOI: 10.4324/9781003333722-3

Key forerunners of the modern burnout syndrome

Acedia

We are on firmer ground when we examine the concept and history of 'acedia'. As detailed by Schaffner, the core indicators of acedia described by the ancients included mental and physical exhaustion—weariness, torpor, apathy, lethargy, non-productive activity, as well as sleepiness, irritability, cognitive impairment and feelings of hopelessness—a pattern of symptoms highly consistent with some contemporary definitions of burnout.[2]

In an evocatively titled paper, 'Disgust with life in general', psychiatrist Robert Finlay-Jones noted the list drawn up by the monastic saint John Cassian detailing the multiple temptations faced by monks in the fifth century AD as they meditated in the Egyptian desert.[3] Acedia was one such temptation, described earlier by the Greeks as a state of 'non-caring', being marked by an absence of interest and a disinclination to exertion. It captured the lassitude of some monks and their doubt as to whether 'there was any point in it all... [preventing them] from doing anything useful' (p. 150). After decades of caring for their flocks, monks (especially the ones most faithful, assiduous and attentive to their prayers and duties) might wake one day and view the blue sky as grey, find that nothing gave them pleasure and wonder whether there was any meaning to life. Finlay-Jones summarised the syndrome as 'disgust, or rather a-gust, no taste, for life in general'.

As further described by Pascal Chabot: 'Monks who had never doubted, who seemed to be on their way to sainthood, one day found themselves tired of God. For that is what they were experiencing: spiritual fatigue. Soon, the Our Fathers just wouldn't come; the sufferer would genuflect and find he had no strength to rise. Then came the forgotten Ave Marias and, in the middle of the morning service, a diabolical urge to sleep'.[4]

What was the matter? In essence, nothing mattered. And Cassian's remedy for acedia? Manual labour and physical activity. So, basically, punishment, because acedia was viewed as sloth and a cardinal vice. In addition, the impact and potential infectiousness of acedia was a threat to the monastic community, particularly when sufferers began to doubt the existence of God. Luckily for us, this judgement of acedia as a spiritual and moral failing (and thus a 'sin') is quite at variance with current conceptualisations of burnout, which do not invoke any moral connotation.

While you are probably aware of the seven deadly sins—and you may even be able to roll them all out—you may not know that in the fourth century AD there were eight deadly sins. As listed by the Greek monk Evagrius Ponticus (or Evagrius the Solitary to many of his colleagues), they were: gluttony, lust, greed, pride, wrath, vainglory (aka vanity), tristitia (sorrow, hopelessness and depression) *and* acedia.

In the sixth century Pope Gregory the Great recast this list and combined tristitia with acedia. Why combine the two? Did this simply reflect the intriguing phenomenon that seven has long been viewed as the 'magic number'? (Seven examples: seven seas, seven continents, seven days of the week, seven notes on a musical scale, seven colours of the rainbow, seven ages of man and seven dwarfs squiring Snow White.)

Those with acedia were judged then, however, as more 'mopish' than those with tristitia (essentially, depression), because they tended to complain more about not finding anything useful, having blunted senses and feeling detached from people, things and pleasant activities. However, in joining tristitia and acedia, Gregory initiated a debate that continues to this day: are depression and burnout one and the same? We will take up this hot debate later.

If the concept of acedia captures burnout then we can conclude that there is nothing new under the sun. But let's pursue the solar image. Let's briefly shine a light on the 'Noonday Demon' (aka Noonday Devil and Meridian Demon). Evagrius Ponticus (the solitary monk again) associated acedia with this demonic figure, who attacked at midday when the heat was harshest and the days insufferably long. The fiend, referenced in Psalm 19, drove a monk to exhaustion, listlessness and the belief that he had lost the love of his brethren, and caused him to hate life itself. Intriguingly, one of the most detailed and praised contemporary books on clinical depression is titled *The Noonday Demon*, which again illustrates the long-queried overlap between acedia/burnout and depression.[5]

The definition of acedia diffused over the centuries, with David Michael tracing how acedia moved beyond a personal experience to a cultural manifestation, arising in particular (according to Aldous

Huxley in his 1923 essay titled *Accidie*) from disillusionment following World War I.[6] Acedia has been a topic for many writers (including Dante, Chaucer, Kafka and T.S. Eliot) and playwrights (Chekhov and Beckett). However, the theme common to these works seems more about existential angst and despair than the more pristine and personal symptom state of acedia (actually well captured in Graham Greene's 1960 book of fiction *A Burnt-Out Case*) and has moved away from acedia's essence. We judge that acedia, as originally described, closely parallels contemporary descriptions of burnout.

Neurasthenia

The next possible condition viewed by some as a forerunner of modern burnout is 'neurasthenia', a diagnosis consolidated in the 1860s by the American neurologist George Beard. Beard's publications detailed key symptoms—fatigue, anxiety and depression—as well as physical symptoms that included headaches and heart palpitations. Beard judged neurasthenia as reflecting 'exhaustion' of the energy reserves of an individual's nervous system. He observed that neurasthenia was over-represented in the elites and achievers, and was most commonly due to overwork, and to technological advances such as steam power, the periodic press and the telegraph. Neurasthenia became a common diagnosis in the late nineteenth century, nicknamed 'Americanitis' and viewed as a disease of civilisation. It also became a highly popular and culturally acceptable diagnosis in China at this time, where it was viewed as reflecting depletion in 'vital energy'. Researcher Patrick Kury overviewed relevant literature to suggest that neurasthenia provided a catchall diagnostic and explanatory link between a stressful life and previously vague and unclassifiable expressions of ill health, which would have included a burnout syndrome.[7]

Regardless, the acceptability of neurasthenia as a less stigmatising diagnosis than other psychiatric diagnoses led to it being provided by health professionals and offered by patients as an explanation for any number of psychiatric, psychosomatic and even physical conditions. Effectively, if you had a burnout syndrome back then, a diagnosis of neurasthenia would have commonly been made—but only a proportion of those with a diagnosis of neurasthenia would have had a true burnout syndrome.

Chronic fatigue syndrome

Also known as myalgic encephalomyelitis, post-viral syndrome and, more recently, systemic exertion intolerance disease (SEID), chronic fatigue syndrome (CFS) has been viewed by some as a forerunner of burnout as a diagnostic term. While CFS has its historical antecedents in neurasthenia and related states, it moved centre stage after an outbreak in London in 1955 of a polio-like illness and is most commonly positioned as a post-viral state. The US Centers for Disease Control and Prevention (CDC) have published criteria for CFS and weight the following: (i) decreased activity levels, (ii) post-exertional malaise (where individuals describe feeling exhausted), and (iii) sleep problems. Common accompanying symptoms include cognitive problems (i.e. difficulties with memory and concentration), a worsening of symptoms when standing upright, pain and a panoply of somatic symptoms. Another feature weighting a diagnosis of CFS is disproportionate exhaustion after concentrating on mental tasks.

So there is some overlap between symptoms experienced by those with burnout and those with CFS (especially a profound sense of exhaustion). However, shared symptoms and features (especially causes) are few. Only a very small minority of those with CFS will be misdiagnosed as having 'burnout'. More commonly, those with burnout may receive a CFS diagnosis and then undergo extensive immunological investigations—generally without any specific findings emerging.

Adrenal fatigue

This diagnosis was coined some two decades ago by naturopath and chiropractor James Wilson.[8] The adrenals (there are two) are perched on top of the kidneys and produce several hormones including cortisol, which is released when we are under stress. The hypothesis here is that exposure to prolonged and severe stress exhausts the adrenals and so leads to a low cortisol state, causing exhaustion, brain fog, depression, sleep disturbance and a range of physical symptoms. There have now been some 60 studies by medical researchers examining the 'condition', with all effectively concluding that it has no scientific basis. If adrenal fatigue does exist, it remains unclear whether it is synonymous with burnout or possibly affects a small subset of those with a severe burnout syndrome.

What about compassion fatigue?

The term 'compassion fatigue' is most commonly used to describe the indifference or seeming disregard shown by many when exposed to manifold disasters involving others, with excessive and repeated exposure causing people to emotionally 'tune out' on their compassion register. It is relevant to consider given that one of burnout's defining features is a loss of empathy.

Compassion fatigue as we understand the concept today appears to have first been used in the early 1990s by English nurse Carla Johnson, who studied the phenomenon in nurses working in emergency departments and who she observed as exhibiting a 'loss of the ability to nurture'.[9] Over the years the term has been used interchangeably with others, including 'secondary traumatic stress', 'vicarious traumatisation' and 'empathy fatigue', and suggests exhaustion of the carer's compassion ration.

The theory supposes that our 'compassion bank' can be emptied by exhaustion, lack of appreciation from those we give to and/or lack of self-care. Listed symptoms commonly include numbness, helplessness, irritability, withdrawal, sleep disturbance, depression, impaired concentration and impaired performance. Those at most risk are more likely to be overly conscientious, perfectionistic, self-giving, empathetic and compassionate (similar to those who develop burnout, as detailed later). Compassion fatigue has been variably viewed as equivalent to burnout, a single component of a burnout syndrome, and as a separate, distinct entity. Those arguing the last view suggest that, compared to burnout, compassion fatigue is tied to trauma (while burnout is tied to chronic workplace stress), that it has a rapid onset (while burnout develops over time), has a faster recovery pattern and (unlike burnout) creates secondary trauma in the helper. Our view is that while compassion fatigue can reflect adaptive desensitisation in certain circumstances, and as such is a defence mechanism adopted by many health practitioners, it is a common component of a diffuse burnout syndrome, being part of a broader 'inability to feel' or lack of *joie de vivre* that constitutes one facet of burnout.

So, which of the possible forerunners corresponds best with what is now known as burnout? Our view is that the ancient descriptions of acedia align more closely with today's burnout syndrome than the more recent diagnostic categories of neurasthenia and CFS. However, prior to burnout being defined and recognised, those with a burnout syndrome would have been highly likely to receive either of these rather specific diagnoses—or receive a non-specific diagnosis such as 'nervous breakdown' or 'stress reaction'. As for adrenal fatigue, if it does exist, it is unclear whether it is implicated in a subset of those with a severe burnout syndrome. And, finally, we view compassion fatigue as an independent state in some instance, or, at times, only one aspect of a burnout syndrome that is characterised today by a broader array of symptoms, with these symptoms described in more detail in later chapters.

Notes

1 W.B. Schaufeli, 'Burnout: A short socio-cultural history', in S. Neckel, A.K. Schaffner & G. Wagner (eds), *Burnout, Fatigue, Exhaustion: An interdisciplinary perspective on a modern affliction*, Palgrave Macmillan, Cham, Switzerland, 2017, pp. 105–27.
2 A.K. Schaffner, 'Pre-modern exhaustion: On melancholia and acedia', in S. Neckel, A.K. Schaffner & G. Wagner (eds), *Burnout, Fatigue, Exhaustion, An interdisciplinary perspective on a modern affliction*, Palgrave Macmillan, Cham, Switzerland, 2017, pp. 27–50.
3 R. Finlay-Jones, 'Disgust with life in general', *Australian and New Zealand Journal of Psychiatry*, 1983, vol. 17, pp. 149–52.
4 P. Chabot, *Global Burnout*, Bloomsbury Academic, New York, 2019, p. 14.
5 A. Solomon, *The Noonday Demon: An atlas of depression*, Simon & Schuster, New York, 2001.
6 D.J. Michael, *Pale King or Noonday Demon?*, master's thesis, Lund University, Sweden, 2012, <lup.lub.lu.se/luur/download?func=downloadFile&recordOId=2861758&fileOId=2861759>, accessed May 2020.
7 P. Kury, 'Neurasthenia and managerial disease in Germany and America: Transnational ties and national characteristics in the field of exhaustion 1880–1960', in S. Neckel, A.K. Schaffner & G. Wagner (eds), *Burnout, Fatigue, Exhaustion, An interdisciplinary perspective on a modern affliction*, Palgrave Macmillan, Cham, Switzerland, 2017, pp. 51–73.
8 J. Wilson, *Adrenal Failure: The 21st century stress syndrome*, Smart Publications, New Jersey, 2001.
9 C. Johnson, 'Coping with compassion fatigue', *Nursing*, 1992, vol. 22, no. 4, pp. 116, 118–19, 120.

Chapter 2

Burnout

Its modern history

> 'Burnout was our greatest challenge until we changed our mission statement'.
>
> Company chief executive

The term 'burnout' is used these days across domains as diverse as physics through to motor sports. Its initial use as a description of a psychological state, however, occurred only as recently as 1974. It was the year in which Richard Nixon was the first US president forced to resign, ABBA won the Eurovision Song Contest with 'Waterloo', Stephen King published his book Carrie, and the world population was a slim four billion people—but bulked up by the first known sextuplets to survive after birth.

So, when did we actually start using the term 'burnout'?

The American psychologist Herbert Freudenberger is credited as first using the term 'burnout' to describe a psychological syndrome.[1] In his history of burnout, Wilmar Schaufeli recounts that Freudenberger adopted this term which had long been used to describe the impact on volunteers who worked at a home for drug addicts and the homeless in New York.[2] These volunteers progressively became emotionally depleted, amotivated and less committed. Freudenberger admitted to experiencing such symptoms himself. He had been working from 8 a.m. through to 2 a.m.—18-hour stretches—for an extended period, and one day when he was about to go on holiday he was unable to get out of bed. He subsequently slept for three days straight. He detailed his diagnosis to rapid acclaim by his professional colleagues and was further acknowledged with several awards for his self-exposing frankness.

DOI: 10.4324/9781003333722-4

During that same period, Christina Maslach, a social psychology academic at the University of California, Berkeley, was interviewing employees in the human services sector about the emotional toll of their jobs. Several interviewees related strongly to the word 'burnout' as a descriptor of how they felt. Maslach and colleagues consequently developed a self-report measure of burnout, the Maslach Burnout Inventory (MBI), which is reviewed in the next chapter.[3]

Burnout, when first recognised as a psychological phenomenon, was generally considered only in relation to those employed in the 'caring professions', for instance, health workers, educators and law enforcement employees. The apparent epidemic of burnout in such employees at that time was attributed to structural and cultural changes that had occurred across the US in the previous decade. Such changes included increased bureaucratisation that compromised workers' idealism, the diminished prestige accorded to such professionals by the community, and the development of a more narcissistic and entitled office culture.

Is burnout a global phenomenon?

Since the 1970s, however, recognition of burnout has spread and it has been identified across nearly all occupations. One theory behind the syndrome's proliferation is that burnout is a by-product of the capitalist preoccupation with personal achievement and *individualism*, in contrast to *collectivistic* cultures where achievement is viewed as the result of group efforts. In theory then, burnout is likely to be a more distinctly western phenomenon. Schaufeli observed that 'it seems that the concept of burnout is restricted to modern, industrialised, and urbanised societies'.[4] However, this view may not hold. Research in Africa, South America and Asia has in fact reported very high burnout prevalence rates.[5]

And what about those not in the 'formal' workforce?

> *'My boss is four months old'.*
>
> New mum

Does burnout occur in settings outside formal employment? This is a largely neglected issue. Although stressors outside the workplace were recognised early on as adding to the impact of workplace burnout, little recognition has flowed to people in the community who are not in formal or paid work. The strain endured by women isolated at home, new mothers and fathers depleted by the relentless needs of a premature baby, elderly partners caring for a dementing spouse, carers with a family member who requires constant assistance, as well as 'sandwiched carers' who are looking after both their children *and* their elderly parents at the same time, surely breeds similar symptoms to those spawned by the relentless demands of the workplace.

We don't know how prevalent burnout is among these caregivers, whether their burnout scenarios differ from those employed in formal positions or whether support for such caregivers should be based on strategies found to help those in formal employment. Until now, most research and recommended corrective strategies have focused on people in work settings.

Is burnout an 'official' psychological condition?

A formal diagnosis requires that the relevant psychological condition be recognised and listed in the World Health Organization's *International Classification of Diseases* (ICD) manual[6] or its American equivalent, the *Diagnostic and Statistical Manual of Mental Disorders* (DSM).[7] Burnout was first listed in the 2015 tenth edition of the ICD (ICD-10), which defined burnout briefly as a 'state of vital exhaustion'.

The ICD-10 definition was expanded in 2018 in its eleventh edition (ICD-11), where burnout is described as a syndrome resulting from chronic workplace stress not successfully managed. It lists three descriptive 'dimensions' or symptoms:

i Feelings of energy depletion or exhaustion.
ii Increased mental distance from one's job, or feelings of negativism or cynicism related to one's job.
iii A sense of ineffectiveness and lack of accomplishment.

Importantly, in both ICD-10 and ICD-11, burnout is positioned as an occupational phenomenon and not a medical condition. To quote the ICD-11, burnout 'is not in itself a current illness or injury'.[8] In addition, burnout has never been included in any American DSM issue.

Thus, it is not regarded as a formal psychiatric disorder or condition, a position consistent with the views of sufferers who see burnout as a 'normal' rather than pathological reaction to work stressors. The perceived *normality* of burnout (so allowing people to talk about their experience quite comfortably) compared to other psychological conditions is a striking phenomenon.

Despite its non-clinical status in ICD-11 and its absence from the DSM, a burnout syndrome is accepted as an occupational disease in many countries, including Denmark, Estonia, France, Hungary, Latvia, the Netherlands, Portugal, Slovakia and Sweden. It now ranks among the most commonly diagnosed psychological conditions in those regions, and in at least five of these countries sufferers can be awarded financially compensated sick leave and receive insurance benefits. Such formalised status is in contrast to countries like the United States, the United Kingdom and Australia, where burnout has not yet been recognised as a formal diagnosis.

As positioned in ICD-11, burnout is viewed as relating to a formalised work environment and as generally reflecting a mismatch between the workload and available resources. We argue that burnout is not limited to those employed in formal workplaces but that it can occur (and with the same symptom pattern) in those who have excessively demanding family caring roles.

The dominant model focuses on precipitating factors within the workplace and ignores any factors that predispose the worker. We will argue against that focus and instead suggest that managing burnout involves attending to both work conditions and to what the worker (whether in formal employment or as a carer) may bring to the mix, including some predisposing personality traits.

Why the current public interest in burnout?

Diagnostic issues aside, public interest in burnout is at an all-time high and still rising. Media outlets across the globe are proclaiming a burnout 'epidemic'. Currently, informal prevalence rates of around 30% are reported across the workforce, but elevated rates are reported in industries with famously high work demands, especially the health professions. In an article in the American medical journal *JAMA* published over a decade ago, Tait Shanafelt observed that 'Numerous global studies involving nearly every medical and surgical specialty indicate that approximately 1 of every 3 physicians is experiencing burnout at any given time'.[9] Burnout engenders an immense cost, not just for individual sufferers at increased risk of low wellbeing and associated mental and physical illnesses, but also for society as a whole. In 2016 the World Economic Forum estimated the cost of burnout to the global economy to be £255 billion (approximately US$332 billion) per year.[10] Such costs accrue from 'absenteeism' (being unable to turn up to work), 'presenteeism' (turning up at work but unable to function adequately) and premature retirement, as well as the indirect costs of treating mental and physical health impacts.

So why does burnout seem to be at an all-time high? Is it simply a result of increased awareness of the syndrome compared to previous decades? Certainly, high-profile individuals are more open nowadays about their experiences and so increase community awareness. Australian women's tennis player Ashleigh Barty (first ranked as number one in the world in 2019) has shared with media her personal experience of developing burnout. Fearing 'mental exhaustion', she decided to step away from professional tennis before she 'flamed out completely'.[11] Luckily for Barty (and tennis fans worldwide), time out doing a business degree and playing cricket saw her passion rekindle, and she was able to (very) successfully make it back out onto the tennis court 'feeling like a champion'.

Burnout in sporting figures is not a new phenomenon. In 2019 journalist Gideon Haigh recorded how Australian cricket icon Sir Donald Bradman's unavailability for the 1930s 'Bodyline' series against England was officially described as a consequence of him being 'run down'.[12] Bradman later described how a Sydney consultant physician had ordered him to rest completely. In an issue of *The Psychologist*, a monthly publication of the British Psychological Society, authors Jamie Barker and Matt Slater note the prevalence of burnout in elite athletes and pinpoint its origins as reflecting their pressing commitments, performance nuances and the greater likelihood of them being perfectionistic.[13] Testimonies from Barty and other luminaries, such as Arianna Huffington, co-founder of the *Huffington Post*, have raised our awareness of how widely distributed burnout is, highlighting that even the most accomplished among us can succumb and possibly be more vulnerable to the syndrome.

The globe, the web, digitalisation and fragmentation

It's not only the gruelling schedule associated with celebrity that is fuelling the increasing burnout blaze. Today's globalised and digital work culture provides plenty of tinder for burnout. One element is our '24/7' online presence. The new tribe of digital natives is constantly available online and we are no longer able (or permitted) to switch off or turn down the burners at the end of the already extended working day. Arianna Huffington described her own rapid onset of a burnout syndrome (after working 18 hours per day, seven days a week) in her book *Thrive.*[14] Four brief vignettes described by Huffington in her book capture the impact of this societal tempo: how her own mother became angry when observing Arianna reading her emails while simultaneously talking to her children; the observation by a senior executive that, as a consequence of having developed a dependence on technology, she had stopped looking into her children's eyes; Carl Honoré (promoter of the Slow Movement) contemplating 'one-minute bedtime stories' for his two-year-old son; and a writer becoming aware that his hands started twitching if he was away from his phone for more than 30 seconds, and that he couldn't even take a pee without getting bored.

Looking back at Schaufeli's contention, are westerners—who are, because of current societal norms, becoming increasingly socially fragmented—more prone to burnout than those from non-industrial, non-urban, collectivist cultures? This issue is a hot topic for political economists and, increasingly, for philosophers. One of the latter, Pascal Chabot, has written that: 'Burnout is a disease of civilization. And civilization is bleeding the earth dry'.[15] Chabot suggests that we were offered new technologies and informed that they would relieve the burden of work, but ultimately 'the civilization of leisure was, in reality, a Trojan horse' as now our 'communications monopolize our time' (p. 3). We have become enslaved to our computers.

Cultural factors complicate conclusions about features of burnout outside the western framework. 'Death from overwork' is a well-recognised phenomenon in Asia, being termed *karoshi* in Japan, *gwarosa* in South Korea and *guolaosi* in China, and with premature deaths generally due to a heart attack or a stroke. The importance of hard work is a deeply held belief in Asia, attributed partly to

Confucian values, high levels of competition for limited education and career opportunities, and the merit attached to getting ahead and seeking a better life. Then there are the organisational settings where hierarchy and peer pressure are dominant plus the importance and ensuing demands of foreign investment, which encourage deregulation to increase competitiveness.

On the other hand, burnout as experienced in Asia might simply reflect excessive workloads and technological imperatives. In some collectivist cultures, all workers are required as a given to labour in arduous conditions for intolerable hours to provide the most basic sustenance for self and family. In this context, their expectations may shape their perceptions and responses and provide extra resilience— with no welfare net, their only alternative to drudgery is deeper poverty. As such, working conditions may be judged in a relative rather than an absolute way if the vast mass of the population work under these conditions. Consequently, such workers may be protected to some degree from developing burnout or, if present, view it as 'normal'. There are too few studies as yet to be sure.

It seems more likely, however, that burnout in non-western populations is simply labelled differently, not recognised or not admitted. Exploring the impact of culture is not only of intrinsic interest but could provide important insights that point to protective factors and management strategies.

Notes

1 H.J. Freudenberger, 'Staff burn-out', *Journal of Social Issues*, 1974, vol. 30, no. 1, pp. 159–65.
2 W.B. Schaufeli, 'Burnout: A short socio-cultural history', in S. Neckel, A.K. Schaffner & G. Wagner (eds), *Burnout, Fatigue, Exhaustion: An interdisciplinary perspective on a modern affliction*, Palgrave Macmillan, Cham, Switzerland, 2017, pp. 17, 105–28.
3 C. Maslach & S.E. Jackson, 'The measurement of experienced burnout', *Journal of Organizational Behavior*, 1981, vol. 2, no. 2, pp. 99–113.
4 W.B. Schaufeli, 'Burnout: A short socio-cultural history', in S. Neckel, A.K. Schaffner & G. Wagner (eds), *Burnout, Fatigue, Exhaustion: An interdisciplinary perspective on a modern affliction*, Palgrave Macmillan, Cham, Switzerland, 2017, pp. 17; 105–28.
5 F.J. Carod-Artal & C. Vásquez-Cabrera, 'Burnout syndrome in an international setting', in S. Bahrer-Kohler (ed.), *Burnout for Experts: Prevention in the context of living and working*, Springer Science+Business Media, New York, 2013.
6 World Health Organization, *International Classification of Diseases for Mortality and Morbidity Statistics* (ICD), 11th revision, Geneva, 2018.

7 American Psychiatric Association, *Diagnostic and Statistical Manual of Mental Disorders* (DSM), 5th edn, Arlington, VA, 2013.

8 World Health Organization, *International Classification of Diseases for Mortality and Morbidity Statistics* (ICD), 11th revision, Geneva, 2018, QD85/QD8Z.

9 T.D. Shanafelt, 'Enhancing meaning in work: A prescription for preventing physician burnout and promoting patient-centered care', *Journal of the American Medical Association*, 2009, vol. 302, no. 12, pp. 1338–40.

10 World Economic Forum, 'Workplace burnout: Can you do anything about it?' 2016, <www.weforum.org/agenda/2016/10/workplace-burnout-can-you-do-anything-about-it>, accessed July 2020.

11 R. Hinds, 'Ash Barty had the strength to walk away from a promising career before she burned out', *ABC News*, 11 June 2019, <www.abc.net.au/news/2019-06-11/ash-barty-break-from-tennis-pays-off/11195866>, accessed June 2020.

12 G. Haigh, 'Cricket grapples with the human toll as Will Pucovski steps away', *Weekend Australian*, 15 November 2019, <www.theaustralian.com.au/inquirer/cricket-grapples-with-the-human-toll-as-will-pucovski-steps-away/news-story/62e89f571c1b5e0354b59d19d8b51821>, accessed June 2020.

13 J. Barker & M. Slater, 'It's just not cricket', *The Psychologist*, 2015, vol. 28, pp. 552–57.

14 A. Huffington, *Thrive*, W.H. Allen, London, 2015.

15 P. Chabot, *Global Burnout*, Bloomsbury Academic, New York, 2019, p. 3.

Chapter 3

Defining and identifying burnout

'All truths are easy to understand once they are discovered: the point is to discover them'.

Galileo Galilei

'Burnout' is generally defined as a negative psychological syndrome that develops in response to chronic stressful work demands (please remain conscious, an oxygen mask will drop shortly). Its definition (and measurement) rests on three key symptoms as described in the World Health Organization's ICD-11 manual:

i   Energy depletion and exhaustion.
ii   Increased mental disturbance from one's job, or feelings of negativism and cynicism related to one's job.
iii   A sense of ineffectiveness and lack of accomplishment.

The ICD definition was shaped by the current dominant measure of burnout, the Maslach Burnout Inventory or MBI.[1] The MBI was developed in the early 1980s by Californian social psychologist Christina Maslach and her then-graduate student, Susan Jackson.[2]

So let's overview the MBI, the most widely used measure of burnout.

The origins and development of the MBI

In Maslach's interviewing of people (human service workers with 'emotionally stressful jobs'), one interviewee used the word 'burnout'. Maslach judged there was something about that term that resonated with people.

She and her colleagues then sought to develop a measure that assessed such an experience in a more scientific way. Analyses of their provisional

DOI: 10.4324/9781003333722-5

and refined measures identified three 'factors' or symptom constructs that they judged were in tune with the reports of their interviewees, and thus the MBI came into being. It was rapidly accepted and has continued to dominate the way burnout is defined and measured. For example, as observed by Schaufeli and colleagues, by the end of the 1990s, the MBI was the measure used in more than 90% of journal articles measuring burnout.[3]

The MBI

The MBI was grounded theoretically in the view that burnout is a psychological response to aspects of an individual's daily experiences at work. Initially designed for employees in human service occupations (for instance, health workers, teachers, police officers), this version is commonly referred to as the MBI Human Services Survey or MBI-HSS.

Features of the MBI-HSS

The MBI-HSS has 22 descriptors (or 'items') generating scores on three scales:

1   An *emotional exhaustion* scale—its nine descriptors aim to capture an individual's feelings of fatigue, being emotionally drained, their frustration with their job and being at the end of their 'tether'.
2   A *depersonalisation* scale—its five descriptors cover an individual's increasing tendency to callousness or lack of care and empathy towards recipients.
3   A *personal accomplishment* scale—its eight descriptors assess the individual's judgement about how energetic, effective and accomplished they judge themselves to be at work.

The degree of burnout is quantified by higher scores on the first two scales and lower scores on the third scale.

The MBI General Survey (MBI-GS)

A more general version of the measure, the MBI General Survey, was then developed for use outside of the human services sector—with two tweaks.

First, the depersonalisation scale was called a 'cynicism' scale to capture negative attitudes towards work itself rather than towards service recipients. Second, the personal accomplishment scale was replaced by a 'professional efficacy' scale to assess an individual's judgement of their effectiveness as a worker. (Academic aside: the individual items in both these scales differ very little from those in the MBI-HSS measure.)

Criticisms levelled at the MBI

Although dominating the definition and measurement of burnout, the MBI has attracted criticism, and we now summarise some of the key concerns raised over time—and add several of our own.

- A three-pointer: (i) the MBI is insufficiently grounded in clinical observation and theory, (ii) its items were selected on an 'arbitrary' basis, and (iii) if a broader set of symptoms (e.g. depression, anxiety, sleep disturbance) had been included and evaluated, the resulting MBI-based definition of burnout might have been quite different.[4]
- The measure is 'circular'. That is, the MBI was developed to measure 'burnout' and then burnout came to be defined by the MBI triadic model.[5]
- While higher MBI scores indicate more severe burnout, the MBI does not deliver a yes/no decision as to whether an individual is actually burnt out or not, as it has no designated burnout cut-off score. Some researchers have subsequently imposed their own MBI cut-off scores for diagnostic purposes, but none have clearly established the accuracy of such cut-offs. Importance? Dimensional scores can risk 'over' or 'under' diagnosis and so also artificially inflate or deflate prevalence rates.
- It is unclear how the three scale scores generated by the MBI should be used. If someone obtains a high score on one scale but lower scores on the other two scales, are they burnt out or not?
- The MBI was designed for those in formal/paid employment. However, burnout occurs across a much wider sphere. An immense number of sufferers are unpaid caregivers, a sector overlooked in the design of the MBI.

- The MBI may not distinguish sufficiently between burnout and (i) job dissatisfaction or (ii) occupational stress. Other researchers have shown that MBI scores and scores on depression measures are strongly associated, suggesting equivalence or overlap.[6,7] Some individuals also show symptoms of both clinical and non-clinical depression alongside their burnout symptoms.[8,9] However, burnout is not the same as depression, and we examine this issue more closely in Chapter 6.
- Finally, those with other psychological conditions (e.g. depression, anxiety, stress) return high scores on all burnout measures (including the MBI), risking 'false positive' burnout diagnoses. This is a problem in itself but is also likely to drive spuriously high prevalence rates of 'burnout' in epidemiological studies.

Is burnout simply exhaustion?

'I'm so tired, my tired is tired!'

Anon

There is a view that burnout may simply be another name for exhaustion, leading to the development of 'burnout' tools that measure exhaustion as its sole feature. For example, Ayala Pines and Elliot Aronson's Burnout Measure (BM) is made up of a single scale that has items assessing 'physical, emotional and mental exhaustion'.[10] Similarly, the Copenhagen Burnout Inventory (or CBI) measures a single burnout construct: fatigue/exhaustion.[11] Items weight tiredness, physical and emotional exhaustion, and feeling worn out.

However, if burnout is just exhaustion, the term 'burnout' would be redundant. The world of lost wellbeing would be robbed of a richer explanation and of a diagnostic syndrome that captures the extra dimensions of burnout as reported by sufferers and identified in other burnout measures. No, folks, burnout is not simply exhaustion.

Do burnout symptoms emerge simultaneously?

The initial MBI model and other models assume that the three key features of burnout emerge simultaneously. Others suggest that burnout develops in stages.

Clinical observation suggests that the sufferer commonly notes exhaustion first and then experiences a leaching of pleasure from previously enjoyed activities and a lessening of care for other people. This leads to lower engagement in activities and an increasing retreat to what they see as a 'comfort zone' (in reality, more of a psychological cave). Other symptoms may emerge simultaneously or at a later stage.

Initially the individual may construe these changes as normal accommodations or perhaps the process of ageing. As part of the developing burnout syndrome—or accompanying it—they become apathetic, asocial and withdrawn, feel helpless and judge that life has lost much of its meaning. Our research has identified additional symptoms or markers of burnout as well as an expanded range of settings in which burnout becomes more likely, as we have overviewed in two recent publications[12,13] and detail in the next two chapters.

Notes

1 C. Maslach, S.E. Jackson, M.P. Leiter, W.B. Schaufeli & R.L. Schwab, *Maslach Burnout Inventory*, 4th edn, Mind Garden Inc., Menlo Park, CA, 2016.
2 C. Maslach & S.E. Jackson, 'The measurement of experienced burnout', *Journal of Occupational Behavior*, 1981, vol. 2, pp. 99–113.
3 W.B. Schaufeli, M.P. Leiter & C. Maslach, 'Burnout: 35 years of research and practice', *Career Development International*, 2009, vol. 14, pp. 204–20.
4 W.B. Schaufeli, 'Past performance and future perspectives of burnout research', *SA Journal of Industrial Psychology*, 2003, vol. 29, no. 4, pp. 1–15.
5 T.S. Kristensen, M. Borritz, E. Villadsen & K.B. Christensen, 'The Copenhagen Burnout Inventory: A new tool for the assessment of burnout', *Work & Stress*, 2005, vol. 19, no. 3, pp. 192–207.
6 R. Bianchi, C. Boffy, C. Hingray, D. Truchot & E. Laurent, 'Comparative symptomatology of burnout and depression', *Journal of Health Psychology*, 2013, vol. 18, no. 6, pp. 782–7.
7 D.C. Glass & J.D. McKnight, 'Perceived control, depressive symptomatology and professional burnout: A review of the evidence', *Psychology & Health*, 1996, vol. 11, pp. 23–48.
8 L.N. Dyrbye, M.R. Thomas, F.S. Massie, D.V. Power, A. Eacker, W. Harper et al. 'Burnout and suicidal ideation among US medical students', *Annals of Internal Medicine*, 2008, vol. 149, pp. 334–41.
9 M. Takai, M. Takahashi, Y. Iwamitsu, N. Ando, S. Okazaki, K. Nakajima, S. Oishi & H. Miyaoka, 'The experience of burnout among home caregivers of patients with dementia: Relations to depression and quality of life', *Archives of Gerontology and Geriatrics*, 2009, vol. 49, no. 1, pp. e1–e5.
10 A. Pines & E. Aronson, *Career burnout: Causes and cures*, Free Press, New York, 1988.

11 T.S. Kristensen, M. Borritz, E. Villadsen & K.B. Christensen, 'The Copenhagen Burnout Inventory: A new tool for the assessment of burnout', *Work & Stress*, 2005, vol. 19, no. 3, pp. 192–207.

12 G. Parker & G. Tavella, 'Burnout: Modeling, measuring, and managing', *Australasian Psychiatry*, 2021, vol. 29, pp. 625–7.

13 G. Parker & G. Tavella, 'The diagnosis of burnout: Some challenges', *Journal of Nervous and Mental Disease* 2022, vol. 210, pp. 475–8.

Chapter 4

The Sydney studies

'The important thing in science is not so much to obtain new facts as to discover new ways of thinking about them'.

Sir Lawrence Bragg

If burnout is to be properly diagnosed and managed, its accurate definition and diagnosis are vital. If you are itching to find out whether or not you have burnout, you may wish to complete our questionnaire in Appendix A now. Then we recommend you return to these next two chapters.

In the previous chapter we noted some limitations to the dominant measure of burnout—the Maslach Burnout Inventory (MBI). Our experience with clients suggested a broader range of symptoms, and so we embarked on our own research. We refer to this research as the Sydney studies, as it was undertaken at the University of New South Wales in Sydney, Australia.

We found that burnout is a constellation of symptoms that goes beyond the three domains long emphasised as defining the condition. We also found that burnout is not just limited to those in formal work positions. Importantly, we were also able to link a heightened risk of burnout to those with a particular personality style.

Respondents with self-judged burnout (Study 1)

For our first study we recruited a sample of more than a thousand adults (1019 to be precise) who judged that they were currently experiencing burnout[1,2] We didn't limit entry to those in formal work positions but also included people caring for children or others and those no longer working. Participants were asked to nominate

DOI: 10.4324/9781003333722-6

symptoms supporting their view that they were experiencing burnout. They also completed a 106-item questionnaire covering a wide range of symptoms that (i) captured MBI constructs and our clinical observations, (ii) included symptoms of other psychological states, and (iii) added items assessing responsibility and dutifulness.

Our participants reported a wide range of symptoms which we have grouped under 12 key headings.

The 12 main symptoms volunteered by subjects about their burnout syndrome[3]

- **Exhaustion** (nominated by 69% of the sample)—experienced as fatigue, tiredness, lethargy and feeling drained.
- **Anxiety** (51%)—feeling stressed, worried and overwhelmed, unable to relax or switch off, ruminating about work when not there, experiencing a sense of dread and feeling fidgety or restless.
- **Indifference** (47%)—experienced as a lack of empathy and interest or pleasure in work or activities outside of work, cynicism, apathy, disengagement, lack of feeling and instead just 'going through the motions.'
- **Depression** (38%)—low mood and sadness, hopelessness and helplessness, lowered self-worth, self-doubt and even (albeit rarely) suicidal thoughts.
- **Irritability and anger** (35%)—with the most frequent descriptors being irritability, impatience, agitation, frustration, anger and resentment.
- **Sleep disturbance** (34%)—with either lack of sleep or excessive sleep being reported.
- **Lack of motivation or passion** (33%)—experienced as a lack of satisfaction in life and/or work, feelings of not making any difference at work or that work lacked purpose, or reduced passion for their job.
- **Cognitive problems** (32%)—components included concentration, attention and memory problems, 'brain fog' or cloudy thinking, difficulty in planning or making decisions as well as feeling confused.
- **Impaired performance** (26%)—evidenced by lower productivity, reduced quality of output, making more mistakes, avoiding responsibilities and procrastinating.
- **Becoming asocial** (25%)—effectively cocooning themselves and withdrawing from family, friends, colleagues and clients.

- **Physical symptoms** (25%)—aches or headaches, eating and appetite changes, nausea and low libido.
- **Emotional lability** (16%)—fragile emotions, increased sensitivity, emotional outbursts and being more tearful.

Characteristics of burnout described by our sample

Assuming that our respondents truly had a burnout syndrome, the spontaneously nominated symptoms and their frequency enabled some initial conclusions:

- Exhaustion was the dominant symptom—no surprise there.
- Anxiety, depression, irritability, anger, having trouble sleeping (despite sufferers being exhausted) and physical symptoms were commonly reported. These findings invite questions as to which symptoms might be attributable solely to burnout and, if so, do they aid in defining the syndrome? And which ones are secondary features that might be expected to accompany *any* distressing psychological state?
- The MBI construct of 'depersonalisation' (usually defined in psychiatry as feeling detached from oneself) or 'loss of empathy' might better be viewed more broadly, going beyond 'compassion fatigue' and reflecting a more general 'inability to feel' associated with a lack of engagement with others and usual activities.
- The MBI construct of 'low accomplishment' at work was supported but nominated by only a quarter of our respondents—most likely because people who are burnt out or are burning out often keep working at their hardest.
- Impaired cognitive functioning emerged and is a burnout construct that has largely gone under the radar (and certainly is not included in the MBI measure), although it was a well-described feature of acedia (see Chapter 1). Patients rarely spontaneously report it but, if asked, commonly affirm disabling impairments in memory, concentration and attention, and a tendency to scan rather than absorb written material. Some women observe that it is akin to

'baby brain', a phenomenon reported by up to 80% of women in the last trimester of pregnancy.

Word cloud of burnout descriptors

We also generated a 'word cloud' of the descriptive words most commonly nominated by our participants. Each word's position and size reflects its relative frequency, with the most frequently reported words in the centre and in larger font. Something unexpected emerged: the word 'lack' dominates and is a revealing descriptor. Essentially, people with burnout are highly likely to report a *lack* of certain qualities. A *lack* of vigour, pleasure, *élan vital* or passion; a *lack* of interest in people or things; a *lack* of sleep; a *lack* of emotion, motivation and passion; a *lack* of cognitive clarity; their performance is *lacking* and accompanied at times by a *lack* of emotional control.

Figure 4.1 Burnout descriptors word cloud

Symptoms most often judged as present by our respondents

The prevalence rates reported earlier reflected symptoms volunteered by participants and thus, being unprompted, were essentially off the top of their heads. When, however, subjects were provided with a list of 106 potential burnout symptoms and asked to judge their presence, a somewhat different symptom pattern emerged. Items affirmed by more than 90% of participants were:

1 'I lack energy across the day' (affirmed by 98%).
2 'I feel emotionally drained and exhausted' (98%).
3 'I am viewed as a highly responsible person' (97%).
4 'I constantly feel tired or fatigued' (97%).
5 'I feel less satisfied with life' (95%).
6 'I can't get distance from my responsibilities' (94%).
7 'I have to re-read things because I wasn't concentrating the first time' (94%).
8 'My attention is less' (94%).
9 'I'm more cynical about things and people in general' (94%).
10 'I find it hard to concentrate on the task at hand' (93%).
11 'My capacity to remember things is not as good as it was' (93%).
12 'I feel agitated constantly' (92%).
13 'My word is my bond and I'm somewhat perfectionistic' (92%).
14 'I tend to scan when I read, rather than focus' (91%).

In summary, exhaustion and impaired cognition items dominated, while there was only one 'lack of empathy' item in this top set. Note that two of the most commonly affirmed items captured a dutiful and responsible, and possibly perfectionistic, personality style.

The statistics

We wanted to know whether responses to each item enabled us to identify 'domains', zones where similar features cluster together.[4] Using what is termed a 'bifactor approach', we identified a *general factor* (made up of items essentially defining the overall condition). Component items comprised exhaustion, lack of energy, fatigue, worrying, an inability to relax, insularity (or cocooning), depression and impaired concentration.

Hanging off that 'frame' defining the general syndrome were three largely independent factors:

- An 'inability to feel' factor, with its items reflecting a loss of empathy for others, a lack of general feeling and social withdrawal or insularity. This factor label appeared to be broader (and have a less critical tone) than a stand-alone 'loss of empathy' or 'compassion fatigue' descriptor. How do we explain its independence from the main frame? In essence, while a key feature of burnout, it would also appear to be a consequence of burnout, or perhaps a characteristic that only develops when burnout has reached a certain level of severity.
- A 'compromised work performance' factor, and which we view as (i) a consequence of burnout, (ii) burnout reaching a certain level of severity, and/or (iii) being secondary to impaired concentration and memory.
- A 'work-focused' factor, with high scores indicating that the individual views work as important or essential, is driven to meet responsibilities, and enjoys work and taking responsibility. The tone here was of someone with a dutiful if not perfectionistic personality. And our explanation of its independence from the main frame? That it is not a characteristic of the syndrome or condition but a *predisposing personality* factor and so interlinked.

Overall, our analysis adjusted some of the three MBI constructs and added new elements.

We also asked all participants to report what they considered to be their primary occupation (even if such an 'occupation' was not related to formal/paid employment). The fourth most commonly nominated occupation was being responsible for home or care duties, indicating that burnout does not just occur at work but also in the home. This interpretation aligns with Tage S. Kristensen and colleagues' model: burnout can be 'work-related', 'client-related' or 'personal'.[5] The last obviously refers to the burnout experienced by individuals outside of a formal work environment, hence a stay-at-home parent with unremitting tasks experiences 'personal' or 'carer burnout' but not 'work-related' burnout.

One study led to another. Our initial questionnaire had relatively few items capturing symptoms such as depression, anxiety and irritability.

The MBI measure doesn't cover depression and we wanted to find out whether the two are linked.

Respondents with self-judged burnout (Study 2)

To work out whether burnout and depression are synonymous, we recruited a second sample comprising 622 individuals who judged that they were experiencing burnout.[6] They completed a questionnaire evaluating 137 *symptoms* only (rather than including any items assessing predisposing personality traits), with this list of symptoms including depression and anxiety items.

Analyses refined the item set to 34 items, which included several sets of symptoms capturing: (i) cognitive dysfunction, (ii) exhaustion, (iii) empathy loss, (iv) decreased work performance, and (v) social withdrawal.

Importantly, we didn't find a prominent 'depression' symptom cluster, although some individual depression items (e.g. feeling 'sad') emerged, along with several other psychological symptoms (e.g. anxiety, worry and frustration/irritability)—but not as central features. This finding rejects any suggestion that burnout is depression. If present, depression (and some other psychological symptoms) is either associated with or a consequence of burnout.

Our analyses also indicated that the degree of burnout was best measured by summing the scores on all 34 items, which we therefore have compiled into a single scale called the *Sydney Burnout Measure* (SBM). In Appendix A, we have provided the SBM, which is structured around the symptom clusters. As noted in the previous chapter, the MBI generates three scale scores but does not have rules for considering how each can be interpreted in relation to the others. By contrast, the SBM generates a single score, the 'total' burnout score. There is a problem with the SBM that we acknowledge: as for all burnout measures, it is a dimensional one (reflecting burnout being mild, moderate or severe) and thus there is no formal cut-off for concluding absolutely that any individual has or does not have burnout.

What does the Sydney research add to the MBI?

While the MBI has dominated the burnout field and essentially underpins the World Health Organization ICD-11 definition of burnout, our studies, resulting in the Sydney Burnout Measure, have extended the definition of burnout beyond that provided by the MBI model. So what have we confirmed and what have we added?

- Yes, *exhaustion* is a central component.
- Yes, there is a *loss of empathy*, but for many people this symptom is experienced more broadly as a general inability to feel or a loss of *joie de vivre*, and generally accompanied by the sufferer becoming asocial and insular.
- Yes, there is *compromised work performance*, though what under-lies it is still to be determined. Performance is likely to be decreased by pervasive exhaustion, exacerbated by decreased motivation and/or impaired concentration. We suspect that all three explanations are in play.
- *Impaired cognition* emerged as a central characteristic of burnout in our studies. Though not considered by the MBI, cognitive pro-blems have been identified in other research studies as well—and, as we detailed in Chapter 1, were included by the ancients in their definition of acedia and in some other measures such as the Burnout Assessment Tool (or BAT).[7] Items probing for cognitive impairment in such measures include an inability to think clearly, trouble concentrating and staying focused, and being forgetful and distracted. Other researchers have asked whether, if not argued that, cognitive impairment should be included as one of burnout's 'cardinal symptoms'.[8]
- Cognitive impairment in our respondents included features such as: difficulty in concentrating, needing to re-read things because of failing to capture the meaning the first time, lowered atten-tion span, poor memory, distractibility and, when reading, tending to scan rather than being able to focus. In a later chapter we overview the biological changes that occur as a consequence of burnout, including those that explain impaired memory and attention. In later chapters, too, we explain the benefits of cer-tain stress-relieving therapeutic approaches that can reverse such cognitive changes.
- *Burnout and depression are not synonymous.* Our second study findings argue against the proposition that burnout and depression are the same, in that when multiple depressive items were

evaluated, 'depression' did not make a distinct contribution to the general burnout factor or emerge as an additional symptom construct. While many of our participants did have depressive symptoms (along with other psychological symptoms), we judge such symptoms as being 'downstream' or secondary consequences of burnout as can occur in other psychological states (e.g. depressed people commonly have anxiety symptoms, those with anxiety states commonly have depressive symptoms). This issue is looked at more closely in Chapter 6 as it has considerable clinical implications.

- *Perfectionism heightens the risk of burnout.* Perfectionism is a personality style. Perfectionistic individuals set very high standards for themselves and they are self-critical when they perceive that they have 'failed'. As they are usually highly dutiful and reliable, they cope with pressure by working harder and harder. Other researchers have also highlighted perfectionism's potential contribution to burnout. Pascal Chabot notes 'unsustainable perfectionism' leading to 'running out of steam' as a key contributing factor.[9]

- *The likelihood that burnout can be modelled as a 'diathesis–stress' condition.* 'Diathesis', when used as a medical term, describes a person's predisposition or vulnerability to developing a particular condition. The 'diathesis–stress' model, widely used in psychology and psychiatry, stipulates that people develop certain conditions when predisposing diathesis factors (usually internal—genetic, developmental or personality factors) interact with a precipitating stressful event/s (usually external to the person, such as getting fired). In the same way a seed will not grow unless planted in fertile soil, neither may a psychological condition develop after exposure to a stressful event in those without an inherent predisposition. The link has important management implications, covered in the following chapters.

This model suggests that management of burnout should not only involve reducing stressors and their impact but also requires addressing any predisposing personality contribution (especially perfectionism). Escape from work or caregiving pressures may relieve *some* of the burnout symptoms, but failure to identify and modulate any personality contribution will not allow burnout to be so readily managed, while also increasing the risk of relapse.

The SBM is provided in Appendix A. Those who are experiencing a burnout syndrome will return a distinctive score. The measure has high 'sensitivity', that is, it detects *true* cases. However, a high score does not by itself confirm a burnout syndrome—the measure (as for all burnout measures) is not 'specific'. This is not uncommon in clinical situations. For example, a thermometer may measure that an individual has a temperature but it will not inform as to whether the fever is due to pneumonia, meningitis or any other condition causing a fever. Clinical reasoning is the next required diagnostic step. This means that people with other conditions, including depression, may also return significant SBM scores—so-called 'false positives'—and clarification is required.

Such a reality is generally unrecognised or ignored in relation to the use of all burnout measures but certainly contributes to the high rates of burnout reported in prevalence studies. But we do not leave you in such a 'no man's land'. We shortly take you into the world of 'clinical reasoning', a skill that will assist in confirming whether an SBM score indicates a true burnout syndrome.

Notes

1 G. Tavella & G. Parker, 'A qualitative re-examination of the key features of burnout', *Journal of Nervous and Mental Disease*, 2020, vol. 208, pp. 452–8.
2 G. Tavella, D. Hadzi-Pavlovic & G. Parker, 'Burnout: Re-examining its key constructs', *Psychiatry Research*, 2020, vol. 287, article 112917.
3 G. Tavella & G. Parker, 'A qualitative re-examination of the key features of burnout', *Journal of Nervous and Mental Disease*, 2020, vol. 208, pp. 452–8.
4 G. Tavella, D. Hadzi-Pavlovic & G. Parker, 'Burnout: Re-examining its key constructs', *Psychiatry Research*, 2020, vol. 287, article 112917.
5 T.S. Kristensen, M. Borritz, E. Villadsen & K.B. Christensen, 'The Copenhagen Burnout Inventory: A new tool for the assessment of burnout', *Work & Stress*, 2005, vol. 19, pp. 192–207.
6 G. Tavella, D. Hadzi-Pavlovic & G. Parker, 'Burnout: Redefining its key symptoms', *Psychiatry Research*, 2021, vol. 302, article 114023.
7 W.B. Schaufeli, S. Desart & H. de Witte, 'Burnout Assessment Tool (BAT)—development, validity, and reliability', *International Journal of Environmental Research and Public Health*, 2020, vol. 17, article 9495.
8 R. Bianchi, I.S. Schonfeld & E. Laurent, 'Burnout-depression overlap: A review', *Clinical Psychology Review*, 2015, vol. 36, pp. 28–41.
9 P. Chabot, *Global Burnout*, Bloomsbury Academic, New York, 2019, pp. 4, 31.

Chapter 5

What burnout is *NOT*

'Neurosis is the inability to tolerate ambiguity'.

Sigmund Freud

This chapter and the next aim to put *you* in the driver's seat. The information you will acquire is designed to help you clarify whether you are likely to have burnout or not.

In Chapter 4 we invited readers wondering if they had burnout to complete the SBM (Appendix A). You would have hoped that your overall score and sub-scale scores would allow you to firmly conclude whether burnout is present and, if so, its severity. However, a caveat: a high score on the SBM does not 'prove' you have burnout. Many symptoms defining burnout (especially lack of pleasure in life, inability to feel, drop in work performance)—as well as stress symptoms such as worrying—are not unique to burnout; they also occur in other physical and psychological conditions. So a high score does not establish that your symptoms are necessarily due to burnout, as individuals with other primary psychological conditions (such as depression and anxiety) would return high scores on our measure and on all other measures of burnout, as might occur if an individual had a primary medical condition like (say) severe anaemia or was receiving a fatiguing physical treatment (e.g. chemotherapy).

Measuring psychological states: Sensitivity versus specificity

Measures of burnout at best have high 'sensitivity' (i.e. they pick 'true' cases of burnout with high accuracy) but have lower levels of 'specificity' (i.e. they can generate 'false positive' diagnoses of burnout). The latter problem has two significant implications, both rarely conceded

DOI: 10.4324/9781003333722-7

by researchers. Firstly, and as noted, such measures may produce spuriously high prevalence rates of 'burnout' in surveyed populations. Secondly, if we wish to diagnose burnout accurately, we cannot rely solely on a burnout measure. Self-report questionnaires are really a first step towards becoming more self-aware, and are not diagnostic in and of themselves, as noted in the last chapter.

Let us return to the thermometer analogy. Imagine it's the flu season, and you've started to feel seedy and, well, fluey. If you went to your GP and he/she simply: (i) took your temperature, (ii) observed, 'Yes, your temperature's up, and there's a lot of flu going round', and (iii) suggested you take aspirin for a few days, you would/should walk out uninspired. The thermometer reading has high sensitivity (i.e. it picks up you are febrile) but minimal specificity (i.e. its raised level is to be expected if you have the flu, but it could also be raised for multiple other reasons). Considered by itself, it is non-specific. In such circumstances, you'd want your doctor to take a history, do a physical examination (to exclude other causes of infection) and order any relevant tests to determine your most likely diagnosis. The thorough practitioner would also consider any 'differential diagnoses' (i.e. other disorders that look similar) and then initiate a condition-specific treatment.

It is typically much easier to diagnose medical as opposed to psychological conditions as there are generally more specific data for a physical disorder or disease—such as a distinct symptom or sign, or an abnormal blood test. However, that's not so for psychological conditions. They lack precise and specific symptoms. Stress-related psychological conditions often present with 'fuzzy' symptom patterns, have soft boundaries with other conditions and there are usually no helpful laboratory tests. If you give a depressed patient a depression measure, they will return a high score, but often, too, they will also return a high score on an anxiety measure and vice versa. So, as said, self-report measures should not be viewed as providing definitive and conclusive diagnoses.

Entering the labyrinth

> 'There are moments when, if one rejects the simple and obvious promptings of duty, one finds oneself in a labyrinth of complexities of some quite new kind'.
>
> Iris Murdoch

And so we enter a labyrinth of differential diagnoses which can lead to a 'false positive' diagnosis of burnout.

An example of the 'low specificity' problem is Florence Nightingale, the famous founder of professional nursing. Her methods and insights, particularly during the Crimean War, changed the face of public hygiene and provided a foundation for our response to the COVID-19 pandemic in 2020. On her return to England, this heroic and erstwhile vigorous figure collapsed, and took to her bed for 30 years. If Nightingale had completed a burnout measure at the time, she would have returned a stellar score. The question, however, is *did* she actually have burnout as some have concluded? Or had she developed some other condition?

Historians have generated a potpourri of diagnoses for Nightingale such as brucellosis, spondylitic pain, syphilis (which can be caught from open sores), senile dementia, bipolar disorder and post-traumatic stress disorder. We'll never know which of these diverse diagnoses was accurate for Nightingale, and this shows that a seeming burnout diagnosis made at first glance may not always be accurate. There are many other medical and psychological conditions that need to be considered before one can settle on burnout with some confidence.

The gift of clinical reasoning

If the fields of psychology and psychiatry were pure sciences then a well-programmed computer could substitute for the best clinician in generating a diagnosis. In reality, however, there is imprecision that is inherent to making psychological diagnoses because there is an intrinsic 'fuzziness' to psychological/psychiatric symptoms. There is the additional possibility of co-morbidity (two or more conditions being present at the same time). Psychological and psychiatric conditions are commonly defined by sets of symptoms with the diagnostic model being that if x or more symptoms are present then the individual has the listed condition. This is akin to painting by numbers and risks a range of diagnostic errors.

A skilled and accurate diagnosis goes beyond merely ticking boxes. It takes into account the complete picture by employing *clinical reasoning* underpinned by a *pattern analytic* approach.

Pattern analysis is beautifully described in the book *Thinking, Fast and Slow* by the Nobel Prize winner Daniel Kahneman.[1] In medical practice, pattern analysis involves identifying meaningful symptoms and signs, then weighting and assembling them in order to produce a 'most likely' diagnosis and updating the probability of that diagnosis as more evidence becomes available or is sought by specific questioning. Non-medical examples include speech recognition systems and fingerprint analyses. Pattern analysis commonly first employs the 'fast brain' and functions quickly and without effort. It seeks to 'categorise' by constructing the best possible story or diagnosis, overlooking ambiguity and suppressing doubt, focusing on existing evidence and ignoring absent evidence. In the flu example it looks like this: 'The patient reported flu symptoms, there is an epidemic of flu, he has a temperature—it must be the flu'.

There are, of course, downsides of the 'fast brain'—gullibility for one. Kahneman gives a wonderful non-medical example of the hazard of simply trusting your fast brain: if a bat and a ball cost $1.10 and the bat costs a dollar more than the ball, how much does the ball cost? Most people will quickly offer the answer as ten cents. But is that really the right calculation? (Answer shortly.)

A clinician employing clinical reasoning would then wisely move to a second phase, activating their 'slow brain'. The slow brain is lazy and reluctant to invest more effort than is strictly necessary, but it needs to be called into action both to check if the initial intuitive 'spot' diagnosis is accurate and to evaluate the probability of any alternative diagnoses.

If you returned a positive score on a measure of burnout, you (or a health professional) might diagnose burnout. That would be equivalent to a 'fast brain' decision, and it could be a 'false positive'.

A clinical reasoning approach would consider some 'pseudo-burnout' diagnoses before judging that burnout is your most likely condition.

Physical conditions

Following an infection or physical injury, an 'acute sickness response' may be triggered through activation of the immune system.[2] This can result in a disturbed mood, impaired concentration, a lack of pleasure, and other symptoms akin to those observed in a burnout syndrome. A Google search for the medical causes of 'fatigue' or 'exhaustion' might leave you at risk of developing burnout merely reading the extensive list of conditions and states returned (including pregnancy!).

The first step is to rule out a physical condition. If your symptoms are caused solely by a physical condition, you *do not* have burnout. Get your medical practitioner to give you a check-up.

If nothing shows on physical examination, all tests come back as normal and your doctor judges that any physical cause is unlikely, then consider the next diagnostic stage: is your condition burnout or some other psychological state? This will be difficult for the doctor to judge. Burnout is a diagnosis that is quite recent. It has not been defined clinically to any clear degree, and it is not included in most educational curricular for health professionals, so your doctor's judgement (if burnout is considered at all) is generally an educated guess.

Physical and/or psychological conditions

Before we consider clear-cut psychological syndromes (like anxiety), we have to acknowledge two states that blur the line between the physical and the psychological.

Chronic fatigue syndrome?

True chronic fatigue syndrome (CFS), as mentioned earlier, is an ill-defined somatic illness marked by extreme fatigue and a host of non-specific physical symptoms such as joint pain and headaches. Exhaustion is prominent in both CFS and burnout, and both conditions clearly compromise work performance. There are few studies seeking to clarify how best to differentiate burnout from CFS. One review concluded that the main difference was causal, with CFS attributed to underlying physical issues such as viral infections, and burnout more often attributed to psychological causes such as chronic work-induced stress.[3]

More importantly, for CFS, mental fatigue (e.g. after studying or concentrating for a while)—in addition to the CFS-defining post-exertion physical fatigue—is usually the key diagnostically specific symptom, and this is rarely described by those with burnout. In other words, exhaustion in CFS is usually experienced in peaks and troughs, whereas exhaustion in a burnout state is more persistent and constant, rather than peaking after concentration or study.

In late 2020 it became apparent that many people who recovered from COVID-19 displayed a pattern of profound physical and mental exhaustion as well as marked cognitive impairment (for instance, some being only able to read one page of a book in a day, and with difficulty) together with other common burnout features. Did they have burnout? Unlikely. Far more likely to be a post-viral syndrome akin to CFS.

Exhaustion?

Exhaustion can be physical, mental or emotional. As noted, it is often assumed that burnout is simply a state of exhaustion and/or extreme stress. If it is not solely that—as we contend—then how do you distinguish between the two states? If burnout is early in its trajectory—and exhaustion and compromised work performance are the only symptoms to date—then burnout is predictably difficult to distinguish from an exhaustion/extreme stress reaction. However, once the circumstances are better established and the crucial markers of (i) cognition/concentration/memory problems, and (ii) a loss of feeling for and connection to others are factored in, a burnout syndrome becomes more probable. An additional clue is that someone who is simply exhausted (and might even state that they are feeling 'burnt out') is likely to feel restored after a short break in activities and/or a good night's sleep, while someone with a true burnout state is less likely to be restored so rapidly or so completely.

Psychological conditions

There are several well-established psychological conditions that your doctor should (but may not) consider before arriving at a diagnosis of burnout. We now list several candidates and, after providing their defining features, specify how they can be differentiated from a true burnout state. In doing so, we again seek to assist your 'clinical reasoning' to arrive at the correct diagnosis.

Anxiety?

How can burnout be distinguished from a state of extreme anxiety? Central features of anxiety include a pounding heart, clammy hands, loose bowels and symptoms like feeling apprehensive, edgy and wound up, often compromising appetite and sleep. In extreme cases, those with an anxiety disorder have a sense of losing control and 'going mad'. When anxiety has no obvious reference or focus, we describe it as 'free-floating'. If it is focused on particular situations (e.g. a morbid dislike of heights or dogs), we are more likely to describe it as 'fear' or even 'phobic anxiety'.

Yes, there is an association between burnout and anxiety. For example, researchers found that higher scores on the MBI measure were associated with anxiety symptoms.[4,5] However, Panagiota Koutsimani and colleagues undertook a comprehensive analysis of relevant studies and reported that burnout and anxiety were only moderately linked.[6] The conclusion? Though the two conditions commonly co-occur, they are not one and the same.

In clinical settings, patients with burnout are more likely to report worrying or generalised anxiety disorder symptoms and, sometimes, panic attacks and post-traumatic stress disorder symptoms. In our first study, burnout subjects reported: (i) an inability to relax, (ii) feeling constantly unsettled, (iii) feeling agitated, and (iv) finding it difficult to calm themselves. They also described feeling anxious when they were outside their 'comfort zone', worrying excessively about work when not there, and sometimes waking with a sense of dread.

We can conclude that burnout is *not* synonymous with anxiety but that those with burnout are likely to experience anxiety symptoms, either as a part of a burnout syndrome or as a consequence of its destabilising nature or impact.

Adjustment disorder?

The American DSM-5 classificatory manual of mental disorders states that an 'adjustment disorder' is characterised by emotional or behavioural symptoms in response to a stressor that causes marked distress or significant impairment in functioning.[7] Some researchers consider burnout as a type of adjustment disorder that results from a work-related stressor. Some further classify it as a DSM adjustment disorder with a specifier of 'depressed mood', the specifier denoting the presence of low mood, tearfulness and/or hopelessness. This effectively puts

DSM-defined burnout into the category of a 'reactive depression', an issue we consider shortly.

Most clinicians, however, would only consider the diagnosis of an adjustment disorder if it emerged shortly after the stressor commenced, whereas stressors leading to a burnout syndrome have generally been present for months, if not years. In addition, a defining feature of adjustment disorders is that they are *temporary*, either spontaneously resolving or settling quickly by neutralising, averting or addressing the stressor. This differs from the 'slow burn' trajectory of burnout.

Stress reaction?

Both of the major classificatory manuals of psychological and psychiatric conditions (DSM-5 and ICD-11) list a number of acute and chronic stress reactions. Clearly, 'stress' causes burnout and, as we have reviewed elsewhere,[8] the biological changes underpinning the two states are broadly comparable. Thus, we do view burnout as a stress reaction—but a nuanced one in that its precipitants have greater specificity to work or carer demands, as detailed in later chapters.

Depression?

The big-ticket item is whether burnout and depression are synonymous or different. This is important enough to deserve a separate chapter.

And if you're wondering, the ball costs five cents.

Notes

1 D. Kahneman, *Thinking, Fast and Slow*, Farrar, Strauss and Giroux, New York, 2011.
2 B.L. Hart, 'Biological basis of the behavior of sick animals', *Neuroscience & Biobehavioral Reviews*, 1988, vol. 12, no. 2, pp. 123–37.
3 S.S. Leone, S. Wessely, M.J. Huibers, J.A. Knottnerus & I. Kant, 'Two sides of the same coin? On the history and phenomenology of chronic fatigue and burnout', *Psychology and Health*, 2011, vol. 26, no. 4, pp. 449–64.
4 D.L. Turnipseed, 'Anxiety and burnout in the health care work environment', *Psychological Reports*, 1998, vol. 82, pp. 627–42.
5 Y. Ding, J. Qu, X. Yu & S. Wang, 'The mediating effects of burnout on the relationship between anxiety symptoms and occupational stress among community healthcare workers in China: A cross-sectional study', *PLoS One*, 2014, vol. 9, article e107130.

6 P. Koutsimani, M. Anthony & K. Georganta, 'The relationship between burnout, depression and anxiety: A systematic review and meta-analysis', *Frontiers in Psychology*, 2019, vol. 10, article 284.

7 American Psychiatric Association, *Diagnostic and Statistical Manual of Mental Disorders*, 5th edn, Arlington, VA, 2013.

8 G. Parker & G. Tavella, 'Is burnout simply a stress reaction?' *Australian and New Zealand Journal of Psychiatry* 2022, vol. 56, pp. 1065–7.

Chapter 6

Burnout versus depression

'It means just what I choose it to mean—neither more nor less'.
Humpty Dumpty in Lewis Carroll's *Through the Looking Glass*

To the big question now: is burnout the same (or much the same) as depression?

A debate about the difference or the equivalence of these two conditions has run for two millennia. As we saw in Chapter 1, Pope Gregory combined the concept of tristitia (viewed as sorrow, despair or despondency, and thus a depressive state) with acedia ('without care'), and effectively equated burnout with depression. Moving ahead a few centuries, when Herbert Freudenberger introduced the term 'burnout' into the modern era, he described a person suffering from burnout as one who 'looks, acts and seems depressed'.[1] While the debate is formally unresolved, we take a firm position that burnout is *not* depression, and now build our arguments for your consideration.

'Depression', whether as a normal mood state or a clinical condition, has a key defining feature: the individual experiences a *drop in self-esteem* (or self-worth) usually accompanied by feelings of self-criticism. The extent of the drop in self-esteem usually indicates the severity of the depressed mood.

A depressed mood is of course a normal experience. It generally follows a stressor that has dealt a blow to the individual's self-worth, such as failing a highly prized exam or being humiliated by a partner. Usually, a depressed mood will spontaneously lift after a brief period.

While there is no clear boundary between a 'normal' depressed mood and clinical depression, in diagnostic manuals these are the criteria generally used to differentiate clinical depression:

DOI: 10.4324/9781003333722-8

i it is more severe

ii it has a set of specific symptoms (e.g. inability to be cheered up or to obtain pleasure, appetite and sleep changes, even suicidal thoughts in some) in addition to a depressed mood

iii it has continued for at least two weeks

iv it is impairing or disabling (e.g. compromises work performance (*presenteeism*) or prevents the sufferer from going to work altogether (*absenteeism*)).

> Diagnosis of clinical depression can be made by checking whether the individual meets official classificatory criteria as listed in the DSM-5[2]—with a 'major depressive disorder' (or MDD) being its principal depressive class—or the ICD-11[3] manuals.

The burnout versus depression debate

While some studies argue that burnout is the same as depression,[4,5] others view burnout as different in being a psychological reaction to a *stressful* rather than a *demeaning* work environment (with the latter compromising the individual's self-worth and more commonly leading to depression). In the most recent MBI manual,[6] Christina Maslach's research team concurs with other studies that burnout is psychologically distinct from depression.[7,8]

Biological studies, too, provide evidence for the difference between burnout and depression. Sharon Toker and colleagues reported that depression was marked by hypercortisolism (i.e. a high level of the stress hormone cortisol), therefore demonstrating an excessive stress response.[9] Burnout, in contrast, was reported as associated with *hypo*-cortisolism, where the adrenal glands fail to produce enough stress hormones, resulting in a deficient stress response. However, in Chapter 7 we show that the cortisol story is not that simple.

Of the participants who took part in our first study, slightly more than 50% reported that they had experienced both burnout *and* depression at different times. They told us that in their experience, burnout and depression differ.[10] They describe the differences like this:

- **Differing attributions or causes**—44% judged that burnout and depression resulted from different causes, with burnout having a specific work-related cause and thus it can be 'fixed' once the extrinsic cause is removed.

  'I feel like myself when I'm away from work'. 'Things unrelated to work make me happy'. 'Depression is more global'. 'I believe that if only my work situation is fixed, I could enjoy things in life again'.

- **Level of functioning**—19% nominated a difference in performance levels. A key distinction was that, with burnout, they could continue to function, albeit with difficulty ('You just power on because you have to'), while, when depressed, functioning was limited or not possible at all.

- **Mood state**—19% offered differences in mood nuances between these conditions. Burnout is 'more like apathy' and feels 'like exhaustion without the depth of misery', while depression 'feels heavier and bleaker; tends towards self-destructive thinking; is emotionally extreme'.

  A perceptive quote captured the essence of burnout: 'I'm not sad, as such, I just feel exhausted and can't make myself care about things such as work, which I don't see as important anymore. My cup is empty'.

  And here is an insightful outline of the difference in emotional tone between burnout and depression:

  'In burnout there is less desperation. With burnout I feel tired all of the time and largely apathetic to things I would otherwise care a great deal about. But there is still something running in the background which compels me to keep going, to continue to run my life. Often, I will have a breakdown one night and cry for a few hours, but then I just pick up and keep going.

  Depression, however, is a black pit of desperation. It's the feeling that nothing I do matters or will ever matter. That I am an abject failure, and every minor mistake (like cooking the potatoes for too long) is simply confirmation of that. You feel beyond rescue with depression—no one can reach you within yourself.'

  Some in this group reported that burnout was more likely to be associated with anger and frustration, while when in a depressed state they were less likely 'to feel anything'.

- **Hopelessness versus helplessness**—approximately 18% suggested that depression is associated with greater feelings of *hopelessness* (feeling futile) than burnout, while burnout was dominated more by *helplessness* (an inability to find a solution to their problem). Thus, when compared, burnout and depression were said to be 'a grey dog versus a black dog'.

- **Anxiety**—18% considered that there were differences in anxiety levels. Burnout felt like a more 'active' and 'overwhelming' state ('everything in overdrive') and thus 'ratcheting up anxiety', while depression felt 'heavy... less active... as if everything is switched off'.

- **Exhaustion**—17% emphasised that exhaustion is the dominant feature in burnout, but less prominent in depression. 'Burnout is exhaustion without the misery'. 'Burnout doesn't feel as suffocating as depression—it's just a state of pure exhaustion'. 'With burnout I can still feel happiness and I'm not disinterested in life; I'm just so very, very tired'.

- **Lack of pleasure**—15% judged that while pleasure in life is compromised in both states, depression infiltrates all aspects of life ('like a grey blanket thrown over everything') while, during burnout, joy and happiness can still be experienced at times.

- **Self-esteem**—7% commented on dissimilar effects on self-esteem, with most reporting that it was depression that specifically drove self-blame and loathing, profound worthlessness or feeling 'inherently bad'.

- **Social impact**—4% noted differences in the social impact of burnout and depression. Most stated that they could still participate in some social activities while burnt out, whereas in depression they would effectively become a 'hermit'.

- **Self-harm/suicidality**—3% of the group reflected that burnout was not associated with suicidal thoughts but that depression is commonly associated with such ruminations.

A rider: The type of depression needs to be specified

Most studies assessing whether burnout differs from depression have failed to specify whether their depressed subjects have one or the other of the two principal types of depression—melancholic and non-melancholic depression. We contend that this is a substantial oversight. It has likely masked true similarities and differences between burnout and depression in previous—and current—research.

We now outline this distinction further.

Classes of depression: What are they and why is it important?

Since ancient times, clinical depression has been divided into two principal classes. One is a 'biological' type called *melancholic* depression, also known as 'endogenous' depression (i.e. coming from within). The other type, *reactive* or *non-melancholic* depression, occurs more in response to external depressing events (i.e. it has environmental causes).

Such a distinction has existed for centuries. As reported by Mark Altschule, St Paul divided tristitia (that ancient cardinal vice analogous with depression) into two kinds—one 'from God' and the other 'of the world'.[11] It was thought that the first type of depression was inexplicable and irrational: its onset was without reason as the individual's life situation and worldly *context* seemed satisfactory, and thus this depression must have been induced by God. The second depressive type was explicable and rational as it was *context-specific* and could be explained by the individual's depressing life events. In essence, St Paul was describing differences between melancholic/endogenous versus reactive depression.

In 1980, however, the American Psychiatric Association updated the manual for classifying psychiatric disorders (DSM-III) and effectively adopted a 'dimensional' model. This classifies clinical depression as essentially one entity that simply varies by severity. So the DSM-III and all editions of the DSM following (and we're now up to DSM-5) lump most types of depression (i.e. melancholic *and* non-melancholic) into a catch-all diagnostic category of 'major depression', while it also includes a set of minor or less severe depressive disorders.

DSM-5 defined major depression

DSM-defined major depression requires the individual to meet at least five symptom criteria, one of which must be either:

i   a depressed mood

ii   a loss of interest or pleasure for at least two weeks.

Other criteria include:

i   weight change

ii   insomnia or excessive sleep

iii   psychomotor retardation (slowed down) or agitation (highly restless)

iv   fatigue or loss of energy

v   feelings of worthlessness or inappropriate guilt

vi   impaired concentration or indecisiveness

vii   recurrent thoughts of death or suicidal thinking.

Most studies that seek to determine whether burnout and depression differ rely on DSM-defined criteria for 'major depression'. But the category 'major depression' is non-specific. It is as if you went to the doctor because you were seriously short of breath and received a diagnosis of 'major breathlessness'. That would not get you very far. You would wish to know whether your condition was, for instance, asthma, pneumonia or a lung clot. Thus 'major depression' is simply a generic category which, in fact, encompasses a range of quite differing depressive conditions (including melancholic and a set of non-melancholic depressive conditions), with each having varying symptom patterns (and different treatment responses). Thus, comparing burnout to 'major depression' disallows any consideration of the possibility that burnout could be equivalent to *one* of the two principal differing types of clinical depression, or differs from both. We now provide an aid to such a consideration.

What does 'melancholic' depression look like?

Melancholia has a genetic basis, with most sufferers reporting either close or distant family members who have suffered from depression.

Episodes may begin without any trigger, hence the classic descriptor of 'endogenous' (i.e. coming from within), or, if there are stressors, the depth and persistence of the depressive episode seems quite disproportionate to the severity of the stressor.

Detecting melancholic depression is not so hard, as people with melancholia show several distinctive symptoms and signs:

- Non-reactive mood—individuals can't be cheered up or feel pleasure in life, a symptom called 'anhedonia'.
- Energy loss—there is a marked lack of energy, it's hard to get up each morning; this is a physical symptom, not just a lack of motivation.
- Mood and energy levels tend to be worse in the morning and improve across the day, a symptom called 'diurnal variation'.
- Concentration is 'foggy' and it is difficult to remember details or to take in new information. Such cognitive slowing is usually associated with slowed speaking and walking (science-speak 'retardation') or physical 'agitation', with such changes captured by the descriptor 'psychomotor disturbance', a key feature of melancholia.
- Early morning waking (e.g. 3 a.m.), a symptom known as 'terminal insomnia', is a feature.
- Appetite disturbance is demonstrated by a distinctive loss of appetite and weight.
- Lost vitality is common during episodes and possibly best detected by a loss of light in the eyes.

A diagnosis of melancholic depression has treatment implications. Namely, people with melancholic depressive episodes respond well to antidepressant medication but poorly to 'talking' therapies (such as counselling). This reflects melancholia's more biological basis.

What does 'non-melancholic depression' look like?

Non-melancholic depression seems like a logical consequence of acute or chronic stressors (in contrast to the onset of melancholic depression, which can seemingly arise 'out of the blue') that diminish the individual's sense of self-worth. Stressors associated with the onset of non-melancholic depression may either act alone or be intensified by the individual's personality.

A non-melancholic depressive episode differs from melancholic depression in the following ways:

- Individuals are generally able to be cheered up and can derive some pleasure from normally pleasurable activities.
- Psychomotor disturbance (as defined previously) is absent.
- Mood tends to worsen or not vary across the day.
- Sleep is affected, but with the individual more likely to describe difficulty in getting off to sleep than to experience early morning waking.
- Appetite disturbance is more likely to lean towards appetite and weight gain rather than loss.

Personality 'styles' that make an individual more vulnerable to non-melancholic depression include characteristics such as anxious worrying, shyness, having a short fuse, being sensitive to judgement by others and carrying an intrinsic low sense of self-worth. Any of these predispose the individual to the impact of a stressor-inducing depression by making it easier for the individual's self-esteem or self-worth to be compromised.

There are treatment implications of a non-melancholic depression diagnosis as well. People with non-melancholic depression may find some benefit from antidepressant medication, but 'talking' therapies are often necessary to restore mood and generally more relevant than medication.

'Atypical depression'—last, but not least

A non-melancholic depression sub-type termed 'atypical depression' is worth knowing about as some researchers have aligned it with burnout. Individuals with atypical depression tend to be highly sensitive to judgements made by others—both rejection *and* praise. They quickly become depressed when they sense rejection and respond by sleeping more (hypersomnia) and craving/eating more food (hyperphagia). In earlier DSM manuals, one diagnostic criterion for atypical depression was that such patients could experience 'leaden paralysis', defined as 'feeling heavy, leaden feeling in arms or legs', suggestive of a manifestation or variant of exhaustion.

Burnout: Primarily a stress reaction

As noted in the last chapter, we position burnout as primarily a type of stress reaction (a 'stress fracture', if you like) rather than a depressive disorder. To advance the view that burnout and depression are not synonymous, we offer numerous differences in Table 6.1 (adapted from a research report that we have published elsewhere),[12] which contrasts burnout symptoms with both melancholic as well as non-melancholic depression (and not with 'major depression' as occurs in most scientific papers). So here we argue (by a review of features of the differing conditions) that burnout is not the same as depression, whatever its type.

Final reasons to position burnout and depression as distinct disorders

The table above assists clinical reasoning for an individual who wants to consider whether their condition is depression or burnout, and for health practitioners who seek to provide 'the' diagnosis and rule out other differential diagnoses (i.e. when differing disorders have similar symptoms). You might wish to tick the boxes that apply to you and then examine the pattern—the most likely diagnosis should become apparent by the varying tick numbers across the three categories.

Placing burnout side by side with *melancholic depression* illustrates that the disorders share only a few features: compromised energy levels, anhedonia and impairment in concentration and memory. Burnout and melancholic depression are not equivalent.

Burnout shares more features with *non-melancholic depression*: there is a psychosocial precipitant or cause (albeit varying in its impact on self-worth), certain personality styles such as perfectionism are over-represented, while energy levels and work performance are compromised. Overall, however, there are more differences than similarities. Burnout and non-melancholic depression are not equivalent.

Our study developing the Sydney Burnout Measure provided additional and fresh evidence that burnout is not equivalent to depression.[13] Here, depression did not emerge as a primary or independent construct in our analyses. Yes, low-level depressive constructs (i.e. feeling sad and empty, being self-critical, getting less

Table 6.1 Features assisting differentiation of the two principal depressive 'types' from burnout

Feature	Condition		
	Melancholic depression	*Non-melancholic depression*	*Burnout*
Family history of depression in first-degree and/or second-degree relatives	*Very strong (60%–90%).*	*Slight (20%–40%).*	*Unknown, but likely to be < 20%.*
Precipitant	May be an initial stressor but episodes tend to reoccur without clear causes and are both more severe and more persistent than warranted by the stressor. Any stressor is rarely work related.	Episodes always triggered by a stressor impacting directly on the individual's self-esteem, with depression severity reflecting severity of stressor and any vulnerable personality style.	Excessive formal work or informal (e.g. unremitting care for relatives) work demands that drain the capacity of the individual to keep on 'firing'.
Predisposing personality style	Not over-represented.	Multiple styles (e.g. anxious worrier, low intrinsic self-worth, introverted or avoidant, 'short fuse', perfectionistic, 'sensitivity to judgement') are over-represented.	A diligent, reliable, perfectionistic style is the most distinctive personality characteristic. Less common over-represented personality styles include having a 'Type A' personality, being sensitive to judgement by others, having low levels of hardiness and resilience, having an external locus of control and shyness.
Severity of depression	Severe, and individual likely to have no expectation of any relief.	Moderate to severe depression.	No depressive symptoms (if 'pure' state of burnout). Mild if present.
Primary symptom	Depression with profound hopelessness and minimal self-worth levels.	Depression with some level of hopelessness.	Exhaustion and a sense of helplessness (as against hopelessness).

Feature	Condition		
	Melancholic depression	*Non-melancholic depression*	*Burnout*
Family history of depression in first-degree and/or second-degree relatives	*Very strong (60%–90%).*	*Slight (20%–40%).*	*Unknown, but likely to be < 20%.*
Attribution	May nominate a mild or moderate stressor or suggest that episodes 'come out of the blue', consistent with melancholia (previously named 'endogenous depression').	Can identify an explanatory stressor, often interpersonally based and compromising self-worth.	Viewed as explainable by work overload.
Level of functioning	Severely compromised—generally unable to get to work (absenteeism), or if attending, work is severely compromised (presenteeism).	Mild to moderate impairment. Work may be useful in lifting the individual's mood.	Mild to severe impairment. May need to stop work or may continue to try to 'push through' at work.
Suicide risk	Moderate—and most will experience suicidal thoughts.	Slight—although a distinct percentage will contemplate suicide.	Rare to have suicidal thoughts.
Energy levels	Usually distinct lack of energy or 'anergia' (e.g. physically hard to get out of bed and may then just lie around; may not wash for days).	Minimally affected and, if so, more due to low motivation rather than to any physical lack of energy.	Compromised to varying degrees by exhaustion.
'Diurnal variation' (i.e. pattern change across the day)	Mood and energy generally worse in mornings, a minority worsening in evenings.	Either no variation or mood worsens as the day proceeds.	No clear variation over the day.
Cognitive functioning	'Foggy' thinking (i.e. hard to take in information and remember things) is extremely common.	May report poor concentration and, if so, generally due to lots of distracting thoughts and worrying.	Memory and concentration is commonly compromised, with individual 'scanning' rather than reading and reporting impaired registration and retention.

Feature	Condition		
	Melancholic depression	*Non-melancholic depression*	*Burnout*
Family history of depression in first-degree and/or second-degree relatives	*Very strong (60%–90%).*	*Slight (20%–40%).*	*Unknown, but likely to be < 20%.*
Sleep pattern	Generally wake early in the morning but a percentage report hypersomnia.	Either experience difficulty in getting to sleep or report patchy sleep.	Insomnia is common despite daytime exhaustion.
Mood reactivity	Unable to be cheered up, or only cheered up minimally or briefly by certain events.	Can generally be distinctly or completely cheered up.	Generally able to be cheered up by some distracting activity.
Anhedonia	Distinctive.	Slight to moderate.	Slight to moderate but more experienced as a broader lack of feeling tone and not just a loss of empathy.
Appetite and weight	Usually distinct decreases (although a small percentage will report food cravings or gain weight by eating and even craving 'junk food').	Minority will report changes (increases or decreases).	Minimal if any change.
Response to antidepressant medication	Distinctive, and a primary treatment.	Slight to moderate.	No benefit to be expected.
Response to counselling, psychotherapy or anxiety-reducing strategies	Minimal—with no impact on primary depressive state.	Slight to distinctive, response dependent on addressing the precipitant and/or the contributing personality style.	Slight to distinctive, being dependent on correcting work causal factors.
Cortisol status	Hypercortosolism.	Hypocortisolism.	Hypocortisolism.

pleasure from work and keeping to oneself) were present but their presence was better explained by viewing them as secondary to the primary burnout state.

However, and as just touched on, depression commonly accompanies a burnout syndrome. Despite our conclusion that burnout and depression are quite distinct, it is difficult to untangle them when they overlap (either over time or at any one time), as they can do. And here your newly honed clinical reasoning comes further into play.

Burnout can occur in those who already have a primary depressive condition

Here's a real, de-identified clinical example. A 30-year-old lawyer had suffered with melancholic depression for over a decade, and the many different treatments improved his depression only slightly, at best. Over the years there were times when he could not get to work but, as he was highly respected by his law firm, he was moved to a half-time employment contract. Even then, over the next few months he struggled to get to work. Once there, though, he could work assiduously, addressing very demanding tasks. But then, progressively, he developed burnout symptoms on top of his depressive disorder. At one stage he took a six-week overseas holiday. Asked about its benefits, he reported that his depression continued to 'grumble along' (preventing him from experiencing the very keen pleasure he could remember from such holidays in his pre-depression years) but that his burnout symptoms had improved distinctly.

Depression can be a consequence of a burnout syndrome and its contributing factors

Another example from our research is a senior public servant with a personality marked by very extreme perfectionistic tendencies who developed burnout, though she continued to work in her high-level position. She then applied for a promotion and was confident that she would be appointed—she met all the requirements and judged that other candidates fell far short. However, she was not offered the position. She described her self-worth as 'shattered'. She went on to develop a severe reactive depression, became actively suicidal and was admitted to a psychiatric hospital for three days. With counselling, her depression gradually settled but her burnout symptoms persisted.

Depressive symptoms often accompany a burnout syndrome

Most significantly, the majority of people with burnout will develop a set of psychological symptoms that are common after exposure to chronic stress. Such disturbances may include symptoms such as anxiety and sleep problems but also depressive symptoms.

Do you have burnout?

Hopefully this chapter and the preceding one allow you (whether a sufferer or an assessing health professional) to use a clinical reasoning approach to assist in determining whether the constellation of symptoms you are sorting through fit the pattern of a burnout syndrome or whether you judge it as a 'false positive' burnout state (perhaps due to a physical or other psychological condition that you have identified).

The most important differential diagnosis involves deciding whether burnout or depression is the diagnosis. The clinical implications of making the wrong diagnosis between these two conditions are distinctive, especially when deciding management strategies. It's important to be aware that most medical practitioners have limited training and clinical experience in differentiating burnout from depression, while we are not aware of any other detailed templates (such as we have provided) for differentiating the two conditions.

Remember that a high score on any burnout measure does not necessarily mean that a burnout syndrome is present. As those with significant depression will also generate high scores on most burnout measures, you, in your role as burnout detective (and possible victim), need first to consider whether burnout differs from depression (big tick) and then consider the points of distinction in order to apply a clinical reasoning approach. If burnout is indeed the diagnosis then its management requires a quite different approach from the strategies used to manage depression.

Notes

1 H.J. Freudenberger, 'Staff burn-out', *Journal of Social Issues*, 1974, vol. 30, no. 1, pp. 159–65.
2 American Psychiatric Association, *Diagnostic and Statistical Manual of Mental Disorders*, 5th edn, Arlington, VA, 2013.

3 World Health Organization, *International Classification of Diseases and Related Health Problems*, 11th revision, Geneva, 2018.

4 R. Bianchi, C. Boffy, C. Hingray, D. Truchot & E. Laurent, 'Comparative symptomatology of burnout and depression', *Journal of Health Psychology*, 2013, vol. 18, pp. 782–7.

5 K. Ahola, J. Hakanen, R. Perhoniemi & P. Mutanen, 'Relationship between burnout and depressive symptoms: A study using the person-centred approach', *Burnout Research*, 2014, vol. 1, pp. 29–37.

6 C. Maslach, S.E. Jackson, M.P. Leiter, W.B. Schaufeli & R.L. Schwab, *Maslach Burnout Inventory*, 4th edn, Mind Garden Inc., Menlo Park, CA, 2016.

7 P. Koutsimani, M. Anthony & K. Georganta, 'The relationship between burnout, depression and anxiety: A systematic review and meta-analysis', *Frontiers in Psychology*, 2019, vol. 10, article 284.

8 A.B. Bakker, W.B. Schaufeli, E. Demerouti, P.P.M. Janssen, R. Van Der Hulst & J. Brouwer, 'Using equity theory to examine the difference between burnout and depression', *Anxiety, Stress & Coping*, 2000, vol. 13, pp. 247–68.

9 S. Toker, S. Melamed, S. Berliner, D. Zeltser & I. Shapira, 'Burnout and risk of coronary heart disease: A prospective study of 8838 employees', *Psychosomatic Medicine*, 2012, vol. 74, pp. 840–7.

10 G. Tavella & G. Parker, 'Distinguishing burnout from depression: An exploratory qualitative study', *Psychiatry Research*, 2020, vol. 291, article 113212.

11 M.D. Altschule, 'The two kinds of depression according to St Paul', *British Journal of Psychiatry*, 1967, vol. 113, pp. 779–80.

12 The table was reprinted from *Journal of Affective Disorders*, vol. 281, Parker G. & Tavella, G., 'Distinguishing burnout from clinical depression: A theoretical differentiation template', pp. 168–73, Copyright 2021, with permission from Elsevier.

13 G. Tavella, D. Hadzi-Pavlovic & G. Parker, 'Burnout: redefining its key symptoms', *Psychiatry Research*, 2021, vol. 302, article 114023.

Chapter 7

The biology of burnout

> *'The brain is a wonderful organ. It starts working the moment you get up in the morning and does not stop until you get into the office'.*
> Attributed to Robert Frost

This chapter comes with a warning. Making sense of complex biological processes is tough and some of the details may make you feel uncomfortable, especially in relation to suggested changes in the brain attributed to burnout. So if you simply wish to know if you have burnout, and how best to rekindle your spirits, pass this chapter over. If, however, you are interested in 'looking under the bonnet' to see how the engine runs and what happens when an engine starts to strain, this chapter will be valuable to you.

The strain of burnout

What is happening in the brain when you burn out, lose your *joie de vivre* and just can't concentrate? There are physical markers of strain, measurable on lab tests and visible on brain scans. Thankfully, such changes can be reversed by differing therapeutic strategies, and we'll look at these later.

Because burnout is not reliably diagnosed, scientific studies of the physiological changes in burnout are compromised. Even if individuals with clear-cut burnout are studied, there may be no simple or consistent biological changes found. Differing biological factors can contribute to symptoms such as exhaustion, loss of empathy and impaired thinking. And there are different burnout patterns: a slow and progressive decline versus a 'crash and burn' pattern reflects variable biological factors in play. Physiological 'measurement' issues (such as the

DOI: 10.4324/9781003333722-9

time of day when measuring stress hormones) also build to confusing and contradictory findings. In addition, the varying physical effects argue for multiple biological disturbances, with some likely to be constant and others variable. For example, people with burnout report that it is more difficult for them to recover from a common cold. Why is that? Such features are difficult to capture. Perhaps it's like an orchestra: sometimes only the violins are in play, or the other strings or the woodwinds, and sometimes the whole ensemble. The consequences? Two systematic reviews exploring biological changes associated with burnout (particularly in relation to hormones and the immune system) could not identify any definitive biological markers of the syndrome.[1,2]

An account of acute collapse

Let's illustrate with a rare but striking onset pattern.

Justine Flynn is the co-founder of Thankyou Group, an Australian social enterprise that sells 'consumer products that exist 100% for helping end global poverty'.[3] She was interviewed by the first author for this book. Growing any business from scratch is a huge call. Starting up during the global financial crisis of 2008 and continuing to run a very successful social enterprise is seriously ambitious. It sounds like an excellent recipe for never not working. In 2017, Justine experienced huge pressures and noticed she was disproportionately 'sweating the small stuff'. Over the previous six months she had developed panic attacks and experienced constant infections and headaches, and she sometimes stumbled and fell. Her symptoms peaked when she collapsed and lost consciousness. She was taken to a hospital emergency department but discharged without a diagnosis after several medical tests. Subsequently, she noted more severe symptoms of exhaustion and memory loss, and, as infections continued, she consulted many doctors who generally just prescribed antibiotics and sent her on her way.

Eventually Justine consulted an 'integrative doctor' who, on testing, established that she had very high levels of cortisol, the body's primary stress hormone. She was told to take three months' leave from work. The timing was bad as she needed to travel to New Zealand to open a new office. After arriving in New Zealand, however, she suddenly 'flopped'. She was exhausted, dizzy, unable to read and just lay in bed feeling absolutely 'disabled'. She returned home and remained in bed for three months, although her capacity to sleep was severely affected. At the end of those three months she tried to walk to the beach but was unable to get beyond the front gate. She felt that she would pass out.

Thankfully, however, her symptoms began to abate two months later: 'Something clicked and I was out of it'. Justine then looked for strategies that would keep her well. She gradually engaged in Pilates, kayaking, exercise and caring again for her young son. In her interview with the first author, she noted the key stay-well strategies she had adopted: pacing herself (especially in managing the business), monitoring her breathing, prioritising rest and finding more time for her family and friends. She came across a book that resonated with her (*Present Over Perfect* by Shauna Niequist)[4] that advised ignoring the pressure to be perfect, and Justine subsequently modified her company's value set in response. 'Seeking excellence' was removed from Thankyou Group's mission statement as she judged it as promoting unhealthy perfectionism.

In 2019 Justine's company went through its most stressful year to date but she successfully 'rode through it', and those who watched the Australian SBS *Insight* program in which she featured would have been struck by her vitality.

What can we take away from Justine's story? Clearly, she had a severe burnout syndrome with all the central features: exhaustion, loss of capacity to feel, cognitive changes and compromised ability to work. But there were other distinctive symptoms, including inability to sleep, panic attacks, infections, headaches, lack of physical co-ordination and, eventually, physical collapse. Justine also detailed her personality style as strongly inclined to perfectionism and judged it as contributing to her breakdown, along with constant workload pressures. Importantly, and as for so many others whose stories we have set out in this book, she recovered completely.

And in terms of biological underpinnings? Justine was plagued with recurrent infections, suggesting compromised immune functioning, and also had very high cortisol levels. In the final personal story at the end of the book we provide an even more serious burnout scenario experienced by Grace. In contrast, Grace had very low cortisol levels when she collapsed and was taken to a hospital emergency department. So cortisol was implicated in both cases—but in opposite directions. Why?

The impacts of burnout on stress hormone levels and the body's immunity

To help explain the physical impacts of burnout, in this chapter we draw on a review of many scientific studies prepared by our research team member psychiatrist Adam Bayes.[5]

The autonomic nervous system

Burnout develops after exposure to prolonged 'chronic' stress. Responding to intense and immediate 'acute' stressors is a job for the autonomic nervous system (ANS) and the hypothalamic-pituitary-adrenal (HPA) axis (more about the HPA later). The ANS is the first to respond and does so within seconds. It activates the sympathetic-adrenal-medullary (SAM) axis, causing an increased heart rate and raised blood pressure, and the release of hormones such as adrenalin. This cascade galvanises so-called 'fight or flight' adaptive responses.

It is more difficult to reset body functions, however, after exposure to chronic stress. ANS changes have been examined in those with burnout by measuring heart rate variability (HRV). This evaluates the balance between sympathetic and parasympathetic nervous system activity. In studies of those with burnout, both decreased (most often) *and* increased HRV has been reported. Those with a burnout syndrome show persistent activation of their ANS.

Stress also disrupts the parasympathetic nervous system (PSNS). The PSNS regulates the body's basic functions, fostering the 'rest and digest' response that calms the body. It can usually suppress heart rate after *acute* stress and bring the body back to 'homeostasis', the steady internal state required for normal functioning. However, chronic stress overrides this 'brake'.

The pathway just outlined is the reasoning behind a theory called 'sustained activation'. Namely, prolonged exposure to a stressor and the continuous activation of the SAM axis prevent any return to homeostasis. It's like incessantly over-revving a car (and, as you know, if you then keep the brakes on, you'll be engaging in a different kind of burnout). An individual exposed to chronic stress begins to accumulate damage that can ultimately lead to burnout.

The hypothalamic–pituitary–adrenal axis

The HPA axis is a slower stress response system. It oversees an internal feedback loop in which three regions of the body—the hypothalamus, the pituitary gland and the adrenal glands—regulate the release of stress hormones. Cortisol (the primary stress hormone) and other hormones are released into the bloodstream. This build-up is self-limiting and after a certain concentration of such hormones is reached, and the 'threat' is over, the body returns to homeostasis.

Cortisol has diverse ways that help the body deal with a stressor. It increases blood sugar and energy levels and also suppresses the immune system. Cortisol levels vary across the day; they are low early in the morning but peak after waking, and then steadily decrease across the day. Clarifying whether high or low levels of cortisol are integral to burnout is blurred by studies that have measured cortisol at different times of the day and used differing sampling strategies (i.e. saliva, blood or urine) when such varying strategies are known to produce quite variable findings. Most studies, though, have concluded that burnout reflects a *hypo*cortisolemic state, where there is insufficient production of the stress hormones (although *hyper*cortisolemia, or excessive stress hormone production, has also been shown in a few studies).

We suspect, from clinical experience, that while HPA axis dysfunction is central to burnout, such disruption does not result invariably in either hypocortisolemia (i.e. low cortisol) or hypercortisolemia (i.e. high cortisol). Our working hypothesis is that early stages of burnout are marked by hypercortisolemia (as the individual faces stressors inducing burnout) and then by hypocortisolemia, or 'under-functioning' of the stress response after chronic activation.

The impacts of stress on the brain

> *'If the human brain were so simple that we could understand it, we would be so simple that we wouldn't'.*
>
> Emerson Pugh

Throughout childhood and adolescence, our brains are constantly changing and maturing as we learn new information and develop new skills. Even as adults, our brain continues to grow new cells (neurogenesis) and reorganise the connections between old ones (neuroplasticity). Unfortunately, exposure to prolonged stress reduces both neurogenesis and neuroplasticity (at least in studies using animals). This is partially ascribed to hyperactivity of the HPA axis.

Excess release of stress hormones impairs neurogenesis particularly in the hippocampus, a region of the brain responsible for memory and emotional regulation, as well as in the frontal part of the brain, responsible for behaviour control and decision-making. Once started, a self-destructive 'biological feedback loop' may grow, with HPA axis dysfunction increasing the release of stress hormones, which in turn impacts on those brain structures.

The above is known as the 'excito-toxicity' model and is thought to explain the mounting dysfunction seen in a burnout syndrome. But be reassured: such changes are potentially reversible, and we detail in Chapter 19 how certain strategies (e.g. exercise, meditation, mindfulness) allow restoration of these brain regions.

Structural changes in the brain

The brain cells of animals (usually mice and rats) that have been exposed to stress are, for obvious reasons, much easier to extract and examine under a microscope than the brains of (living) humans with burnout. So human brains are more commonly examined using brain imaging techniques to map *structural* changes—changes in shape and size—of different regions in the brain.

There have been a few studies using structural magnetic resonance imaging to record structural changes of the brain in those with burnout. Some (but not all) of these have shown that the volume of certain brain regions (the medial frontal cortex, amygdala, anterior cingulate cortex, dorsolateral prefrontal cortex, and the basal ganglia, to be precise) differ in those with burnout as compared to those without.

Functional changes in the brain

Brain imaging strategies can examine for *functional* changes: here, brains are scanned while subjects undertake tasks, and the regions of the brain that 'light up' while completing such tasks are identified.

There have been some studies of those with burnout assessing functional/connectivity changes in the brain. One chronically stressed group, imaged by positron emission tomography, displayed a functional disconnection between the amygdala—the 'emotion centre' of the brain—and the anterior cingulate cortex (ACC) and medial prefrontal cortex. The disruption of these paths from exposure to chronic stress was associated in this group with impaired emotional regulation and reduced ability to regulate responses to stressors. Another functional brain study, this time using functional magnetic resonance imaging, indicated that those with burnout were less able to suppress negative emotions due to reduced functional connectivity of the amygdala with the ACC, the dorsolateral prefrontal cortex and the motor cortex. This research suggests that burnout is associated with compromised connections within the emotion- and stress-regulatory networks in the brain, impairing sufferers' ability to regulate their emotional responses to stressors.

Non-specific brain changes

There are also non-specific brain changes found in those with burnout. An electroencephalogram records the continuous electrical activity of the brain. One such study demonstrated that patients with a burnout syndrome showed reduced 'P300 amplitude', indicating suboptimal electrical activity. Changes in electrical activity are also found in the brains of those with clinical depression and are associated with impaired thinking ability, evidenced particularly by memory and attention problems.

Lower levels of brain-derived neurotropic factor (BDNF)—a growth factor central to neurogenesis—have also been reported in those experiencing burnout. Similarly, lower BDNF levels have also been reported in cases of depression. Brain changes such as these found across diagnoses are thought to likely reflect a general 'stress-related' phenomenon rather than a change specific to burnout or to depression. And again, such changes are reversible with appropriate treatment.

External markers of burnout's physical impact

We now overview some external markers of burnout's physical impact.

Cognitive disturbances

Chronic stress impacts on hippocampal function (remember, the hippocampus regulates emotions and is also vital to the memory system), leading to deficits in visuospatial (i.e. visual mapping) and memory skills. Patients with burnout display deficits in non-verbal memory and in visual and auditory attention. These deficits are likely related to changes in brain structure and neuroplasticity. Several provisional studies indicate the reversibility of these changes.

Sleep disturbances

Further research studies point to the link between burnout and significant sleep disturbance. Those with burnout report non-restorative sleep (sleep without feeling rested), reduced sleep quality, feeling unrefreshed and sleepiness/fatigue during the day. Studies using polysomnography to monitor sleep parameters have found that those with burnout show greater sleep fragmentation, wake more frequently, experience less 'slow wave' (deep) sleep and have less rapid eye movement or dream state sleep.

Immune function and micro-inflammation

Higher burnout scores are linked with changes in the body's immune system, and more infections. The increased rate of infections associated with burnout is thought to be a consequence of sustained HPA axis suppression of the immune system.

Physical illnesses

Individuals with severe burnout are at higher risk of coronary heart disease and type 2 diabetes and a range of other conditions, because sufferers are more likely to have higher levels of cholesterol and triglycerides and lower cardiovascular fitness. These markers are suggestive of greater 'wear and tear' on the body (science-speak: 'allostatic load', AL for short).[6] The cumulative build-up of stress over a lifespan is measurable: blood pressure, glucose, insulin, body mass index and waist circumference all tell a tale. The good news? Stress management strategies can ameliorate or even reverse the physical marks of burnout.

And the implications of all this?

We noted at the start of this chapter that, even when clear-cut cases of burnout are studied, there may be no simple or consistent biological changes found, despite imaging and lab tests identifying markers of strain. However, we know that burnout develops after exposure to prolonged or chronic stress. This likely induces what is known as sustained activation and prevents the body from returning to homeostasis, the steady internal state required for normal functioning. A self-destructive biological feedback loop may then begin. Such increasing 'excito-toxicity' is thought to explain the mounting dysfunction seen in a burnout syndrome.

During the second and more distinct phase of burnout, adrenal fatigue may occur (a concept described by James Wilson and noted earlier in Chapter 1).[7] However, and as noted there, it is a controversial theory and its validity has been challenged and essentially rejected across the broader medical field.

Why is this important? Well, the downstream effects of all this biological perturbation include burnout's characteristic physical impacts: cognitive and sleep disturbances, compromised immune function and micro-inflammation, and increased susceptibility to physical illnesses.

Does burnout affect so many functions in all sufferers? Unlikely. At early stages and when not too severe, there may only be changes in the autonomic nervous system (only the brasses or the strings are in play). When severe (as illustrated by Justine's story) then all the multiple systems that we have overviewed may be out of tune (the conductor has lost control of the orchestra).

While the biological changes we detail in this chapter appear very graphic and are clearly concerning (who wants to hear that burnout could cause changes in their brain), we emphasise again that people can and do recover completely from burnout. In Chapter 19 we detail how some of the simplest de-stressing management approaches have the ability, when regularly practised, to correct both structural and functional brain changes.

Notes

1 M.B. Danhof-Pont, T. van Veen & F.G. Zitman, 'Biomarkers in burnout: A systematic review', *Journal of Psychosomatic Research*, 2011, vol. 70, no. 6, pp. 505–24.

2 I.H. Jonsdottir & A.S. Dahlman, 'Endocrine and immunological aspects of burnout: A narrative review', *European Journal of Endocrinology*, 2019, vol. 180, no. 3, pp. R147–R158.

3 SBS News and Current Affairs, 'Burnout', *Insight*, ep. 36, 29 October 2019, <www.sbs.com.au/ondemand/video/1623750211611/insight-burnout>, accessed November 2020.

4 S. Niequist, *Present Over Perfect*, HarperCollins, New York, 2016.

5 A. Bayes, G. Tavella & G. Parker, 'The biology of burnout: Causes and consequences', *The World Journal of Biological Psychiatry*, 2021, vol. 22, pp. 686–96.

6 B.S. McEwen & E. Stellar, 'Stress and the individual: Mechanisms leading to disease', *Archives of Internal Medicine*, 1993, vol. 153, no. 18, pp. 2093–101.

7 J. Wilson, *Adrenal Fatigue: The 21st century stress syndrome*, Smart Publications, Sparks, NV, 2002.

Part 2

Causes of burnout

The seed and the soil

Chapter 8

The workers' dilemma

'The reward for working hard is more work'.

Attributed to Haemin Sunim

It may be a truism, but the one clear and distinct cause of burnout is work, whether 'formal' or 'informal'. Covering 'white collar' through to 'blue collar' workers, formal work includes employment where there is a working agreement of some kind, with set pay and conditions. It also covers those in casual positions, sometimes dubbed 'the precariat' because of their precarious status. In contrast, informal work is a term that includes the unpaid domestic duties of carers, who often provide care for others with little or no respite—sometimes termed 'invisible' caring. As noted earlier, burnout has generally been considered only in those engaged in formal work, with the plight of those in informal working positions often neglected. We argue against such a limited domain and recognise that burnout is also likely to arise in informal work environments and that 'carer burnout' is common.

Either way, in terms of burnout's triggers, it's pretty much all about work, and in this and the following chapter we consider formal work ingredients that contribute to burnout, while considering triggers in the informal workplace in Chapter 11.

Why do you work?

'Well, we can't stand around here doing nothing, people will think we're workmen'.

Spike Milligan

DOI: 10.4324/9781003333722-11

Assuming that you are in paid/formal employment, here are three questions for you. Firstly, why do you work? Secondly, what are the advantages of work for you? Thirdly, does work give your life meaning?

The questions build to a work pyramid. At the base level, you may work simply (but of undeniable importance) to earn an income. At the next level up, your work may develop and use your strengths or even define your identity. At the apex of the pyramid, you may work to serve a cause you believe in, obtaining something even more from work: a sense of meaning.

In addition to these three distinct levels, across all work levels (except maybe for lighthouse keepers) there is a social context. We humans are social animals and work can provide 'workmates' who, if collegiate, offer a support network. At all levels, work can supply and enhance our skill set, enriching our sense of self-worth by adding a 'work identity' to our personal identity.

The American psychologist dubbed the father of 'positive psychology', Martin Seligman, detailed a similar hierarchy in relation to happiness and wellbeing.[1] Specifically, those leading a 'pleasant life' tend to view work as a 'job', the good life positions work as a 'career' (where one's character strengths are used) and the meaningful life views work as a 'calling' (here the individual uses their character strengths in service of some cause greater than themselves). As the hierarchy is ascended, wellbeing levels are advanced.

Wellbeing and its ingredients

Wellbeing is not simply happiness. Happiness is a transient state of pleasure, like a brief sugar hit that makes us hungry for more. Wellbeing is more about ongoing positive thoughts and behaviours that engage and fulfil us and make us content.

Those who rate high on wellbeing (so-called 'flourishers') assent to three key questions if asked. Firstly, if asked whether they are satisfied with life as a whole, they provide a big tick. Secondly, when asked whether they would wish to change things if they could live their life again, they tick the 'no' box. Thirdly, and a stand-out question, when asked whether 'most people can be trusted', they agree, and not because they are naïve. Their answer captures a personal quality: open-heartedness. Flourishers invest in relationships and find goals to enjoy.

Flourishers 'optimise': they can see positive meaning in ordinary events or even in adversity itself, and they find work fulfilling. But even flourishers can be stretched beyond their elastic limits.

Any individual's wellbeing is enhanced when their skill set matches the level of challenge, and the challenge is self-generated and valued. Wellbeing is compromised, however, if the challenge is too difficult and therefore frustrating (with multiple risks including burnout) or if it is too easy, as this leads to boredom.

Does money buy happiness?

'All I ask is the chance to prove that money can't make me happy'.
Spike Milligan

Well, Spike, and readers, you'll be sorry to know that neither wealth nor any other materialistic ingredient correlates with wellbeing levels. Those who have high levels of wellbeing are more focused on giving than receiving.

It was long held that wellbeing would be advanced as suffering eased and labour-saving devices became widely available. That prediction did not play out. In fact, in every western country, in a phenomenon known as the 'cruel paradox', wellbeing levels have remained stable or even decreased (especially for women) over recent decades.

The wellbeing/work paradox

Returning to Seligman's hierarchy, you might suppose that burnout rates would be highest in those who work simply because they have to, be less evident in those whose work furnishes them with a career, and lowest of all in those who are passionate about their work. We, however, argue that the inverse applies, as burnout rates appear lowest in those whose work is simply a job, higher in those who view their work as a career and highest in those whose work is at the level of a 'calling'.

Why is this? Because wellbeing is advanced by giving rather than receiving, members of the last group risk giving too much of themselves. As observed by Ulrich Kraft, burnout 'tends to hit the best employees, those with enthusiasm who accept responsibility readily and whose job is an important part of their identity'.[2] And those who view their work as a calling are more passionate about their work. Such passion links strongly with burnout, conveyed by the saying 'only those who caught fire can also burn out'.

As an invited commentator, former chairman of the Australian Human Resources Institute Peter Wilson, told us:

> We all like to be turned on with our favourite activities. Therein lies the dilemma when these sentiments apply to our work—to 'stay on fire' and do your best but to keep the flames within and around us under control. This reflects the complexity of managing burnout potential that every hardworking and committed worker experiences. Managing the fire and passion within ourselves, and also controlling the demon creatures working around us. These two forces magnify the risk of burnout when either force moves out of balance. If both occur at the same time, look out!

Gail Kelly, former CEO of Westpac Bank and author of the leadership book *Live Lead Learn*, also assisted us as an invited commentator on the topic:

> Workplaces should keep a watch out for their high-performance employees—the ones who are driven by achievement and routinely put their hands up for extra work, be it a challenging project, an urgent presentation, or a new business development assignment. These individuals see career achievement as a hugely defining factor in their lives (sometimes the defining factor) and, as a consequence, are prepared to sacrifice a lot for it. At some point, when juggling too many balls in the air and dropping a few too many of them, they may experience burnout—being absolutely exhausted and struggling to cope. Confidence is lost and pride is affected. I have encountered many senior executives finishing up their full-on, high-achievement careers and then confronting a well of sadness and despair. Their careers were their lives and everything else took a back seat. Now the work life is over, they debate, what is left? Who am I really, what is my life about? The desolation and sense of loss is palpable.

You may muse on aspects of this inverse pyramid as we consider work-induced burnout and several personal stories.

How does work cause burnout?

'When everything is coming your way, you're in the wrong lane'.

Anon

An obvious cause of burnout is work overload. As summarised by Christina Maslach and Michael Leiter, the workload may be 'too much, too complex, too urgent, or too awful'.[3] Consider these examples, fleshed out shortly:

- excessive work hours
- work tasks that are overly complex and relentless
- lack of downtime (with a strong contribution from open-plan workspaces that erode privacy and concentration)
- increasing technological demands (case in point: filling in electronic medical records is commonly nominated by young doctors as one of the key factors in their burnout)
- the '24/7/365' benchmark whereby many individuals are required to make themselves available to work at any time and all times.

In essence, all can lead to a state of permanent 'bleisure', where the boundary between business and leisure time is blurred.

Work factors linked to burnout

'I've used up all my sick days, so I'm calling in dead'.

Anon

Let's move to more specific work causes. Radha Sharma and Sir Cary Cooper[4] overviewed a set of organisation work factors that can trigger burnout, which are summarised in the box below:

Workplace factors linked to burnout

- Physical workplace environmental issues (e.g. noise, lighting, temperature).
- Workload (overload but with under-load also potentially stressful, risking burnout and 'rust out' respectively, especially the latter if the work is monotonous).

- Lengthy work hours and time pressure (consider the 'zero-hours contract' where the worker agrees to be available when and as required, with neither work hours nor time specified).
- Low role 'efficacy'—ensues if the employee feels insignificant in the work organisation. Poorly managed staff are unintegrated, unable to be proactive and creative, or advance their skill set. This stressor has even greater impact if the work is monotonous.
- Role conflict—between the individual and other staff or superiors, or in the work demands faced by the individual, or when the individual's expectations don't match those of the organisation.
- Role ambiguity—when there is a lack of clarity about the individual's responsibilities and work roles.
- Compromised career development—where the individual is insecure about their career, feeling at risk of redundancy or obsolescence, or that their career has become stagnant.
- A mismatch between the norms, goals and rules of the organisation and the values and objectives of the individual. This may be perceived immediately on joining the organisation or occur after organisational changes affect the work climate. Risk of burnout is further fanned if management is autocratic and unfair.
- Lack of control and autonomy for the employee in organising their own work activities, in relation to time and/or methods.
- Absence of or minimal rewards, or, worse, non-contingent punishment or injustice in the organisation's appraisal and reward system.
- Organisational changes (such as restructuring, downsizing, merging) that compromise the employee's beliefs about the mutual obligations they share with their organisation, compounded by the attendant risks of increased workload, job insecurity and compromised career plans.
- Lack of a social support system in the organisation (e.g. listening, appreciation, emotional support) can lead directly to burnout or advance its risk because there is no stress buffer.
- Lack of fairness and equity from the supervisor or organisation to gain or maintain 'power' over the employee. This may manifest as direct bullying by a supervisor or indirect bullying, such as 'gaslighting', in which psychological manipulation is used at a level that makes the employee doubt their own sanity.

How is the workplace currently driving high rates of burnout?

'Work' for the employed among us is rarely 'nine to five' nowadays, and the risk of burnout is predictably increased in those who apply themselves diligently to the new 24/7 norm. An ideal work–life balance comes at the risk of a cost–benefit imbalance. Increasingly plugged in and at the mercy of our emails, phones and other devices, linked to social media, and expected to be always within reach, we are assumed to be on top of all our schedules and timetables, and that we'll faithfully meet multiple deadlines. While George Orwell's book *1984* depicted political totalitarianism, the potential impact of employer totalitarianism is well laid out in Dave Eggers' Silicon Valley based parable *The Circle*.[5] Mae, the protagonist, is employed by the world's most powerful technology company and becomes progressively embroiled in a technological dystopia where the all-controlling company occupies and invades every aspect of employees' lives, all reinforced by homilies such as 'privacy is theft', 'sharing is caring' and 'secrets are lies'. Hyperbole? Sure. But there are sufficient truisms to induce some nods of recognition.

Such a creeping but distinct social change has been described by many commentators. In a 2018 article, director of education and training at the Tavistock and Portman NHS Foundation Trust Brian Rock described burnout as an increasingly insidious phenomenon: '…a drip, drip, drip… It's like a mission creep of sorts, where you find yourself working a bit later, taking calls on weekends, being less inclined to play with your children or feeling more isolated and irritable'.[6]

To repeat an observation by Pascal Chabot: 'Burnout is a disease of civilization. And civilization is bleeding the earth dry'.[7] Yes, we embraced technology as we thought it would liberate us from labour, but as Chabot noted, while machines were invented to augment our performance, we are now at risk of emulating them—to our detriment: 'The automatons are not as autonomous as advertised. They need us. Those computers that were supposed to do our calculations for us instead demand our attention: for ten hours a day, we are glued to our screens'. He judged that management systems subjugate, control, coerce and undermine solidarity, and humans have become a replaceable resource:

'When we expect workers to manifest unquestioning perfectionism, our unconscious motivation is often the desire to make people resemble machines—reliable, polyvalent, and soulless'.

Radha Sharma and Sir Cary Cooper[8] also noted the impact of globalisation in the workforce: '…increasing competition and technological advancements… major transformation in strategy, structure, systems, and styles for enhancing quality, efficiency, and productivity'. They referenced US data quantifying that 33% of Americans experience job burnout due to workplace stress, with those in helping professions (e.g. doctors, nurses, counsellors, police) showing a particularly high rate. Time pressure and meeting deadlines are perceived as the greatest stressors. Major contributors to burnout come from 'running' to meet milestones and deadlines, because of the fear attached to falling behind—and then being left behind.

Absence of limits mandates a personal firewall

Such arguments are persuasive. But are we ignoring previous times? What was the possibility of burnout prior to the twenty-first century? What was the impact of the Industrial Revolution that started in Britain in the latter half of the eighteenth century before spreading internationally? Have we forgotten those 'dark satanic mills' that chained workers to dangerous, dirty, boring and repetitive work at minimal wages and with the ever-present risks of job loss putting their families at peril? Did many of those factory workers experience burnout? We can only suppose so. Our academic predecessors back then weren't knocking on dilapidated doors and handing out the MBI or other questionnaires. Perhaps burnout is only now seen as a 'modern illness' because work oppression has moved up the social ladder to become over-represented in the middle and professional classes as a consequence of the current technology revolution. Nonetheless, our generations (Boomers, Xs, Ys and Zs) may need to create a personal firewall to reduce technology-furthered burnout risks.

Should we not seek a new 'Jerusalem' (apologies to William Blake)?

> Along with deleting those dark, satanic emails
> Bring me my iPhone for hurling
> Bring me no longer schedules for 24/7 responding

Bring me through this charred firewall
Return me my empathy
And then I will cease from mental flight and fight.
Nor shall I sleep across the day
Till we have built a new mental curriculum
In this blackened and burnt-out land.

A personal perspective

As ever, personal accounts enhance our perspective on such issues. As you will remember we earlier noted how Arianna Huffington (co-founder and editor-in-chief of the *Huffington Post*) described her own rapid onset of a burnout syndrome after working 18 hours per day, seven days a week.[9] It led to her sudden collapse to the floor of her home office as a consequence of exhaustion and lack of sleep. Her 'wake-up call' encouraged her to redefine success, typically understood to be the 'American dream'—weighting money and power—as it was neither enough nor sustainable.

To foreground the real priorities in life, Huffington asks us to consider funeral eulogies as revealing how we are remembered. Eulogies, she suggests, rarely record that an individual increased the market share of their company, ate lunch at their desk each day to maintain high productivity or handled every email in their inbox each night. The eulogy recaps our life differently. It more reviews what we gave, and what we meant to family and friends. So, Huffington queries, why do we spend so much time focusing on things that will ultimately be seen as too unimportant to remember?

Does the present predict the future?

Major changes in the workplace over the last 20 years have resulted in increased stress. Deregulation, privatisation, restructuring and down-sizing have, overall, dialled up the pace and pressure of work, and the growth in casual and temporary work as well as 'contracting out' have caused increased job insecurity. This has created a climate where people feel constantly under threat at work. The push for higher productivity and cost cutting most often results in inadequate staffing and resources, high workloads, and a pervasive culture of long hours. The mantras 'harder faster' and 'smarter not harder' so often just mean more hours at your desk.

Paradoxically, the increasingly available option to work from home for at least some of the time means that you are never 'not at work'. Outside a formal workplace setting there is a lack of shields and structures to mitigate whatever the work projects demand. In this case there are, broadly, two flight paths. Highly reliable and perfectionistic people may become isolated from their colleagues and work longer hours, while the 'no worries, she'll be right' group will pace themselves (catch up on social media, take naps on demand) and be at decreased risk of burnout, as always. Those who combine working from home with the additional demands of childcare or other home responsibilities put themselves at increased risk of burnout.

And overall? Rates of burnout are set to increase.

If you feel you may have developed burnout from your work, please go to Appendix B and identify which workplace factors might be relevant to you. These are the triggers that corrective strategies will need to address.

Notes

1 M. Seligman, *Authentic Happiness: Using the new positive psychology to realise your potential for lasting fulfillment*, Free Press, New York, 2002.
2 U. Kraft, 'Burned out', *Scientific American Mind*, June/July 2006, <www.scientifi camerican.com/article/burned-out/>, accessed July 2020.
3 C. Maslach & M.P. Leiter, 'Early predictors of job burnout and engagement', *Journal of Applied Psychology*, 2008, vol. 93, no. 3, pp. 498–512.
4 R.R. Sharma & C. Cooper, *Executive Burnout: Eastern and western concepts, models, and approaches for mitigation*, Emerald Group Publishing, Bingley, UK, 2017.
5 D. Eggers, *The Circle*, Knopf, New York, 2013.
6 M. Sarner, 'How burnout became a sinister and insidious epidemic', *The Guardian Weekly*, 18 March 2018, <www.theguardian.com/society/2018/feb/21/how-burnout-became-a-sinister-and-insidious-epidemic> accessed September 2022.
7 P. Chabot, *Global Burnout*, Bloomsbury Academic, New York, 2019, pp. 2, 3, 34.
8 R.R. Sharma & C. Cooper, *Executive Burnout: Eastern and western concepts, models, and approaches for mitigation*, Emerald Group Publishing, Bingley, UK, 2017, p. 1.
9 A. Huffington, *Thrive*, W.H. Allen, London, 2015.

Chapter 9

The toxic workplace

'The beatings will continue until morale improves'.

Anon

In the previous chapter we considered factors causing burnout in workplaces. Such factors reflect contemporary work patterns and demands and the increasing 24/7 norm. The emphasis was on the 'form' of work. In this chapter we consider the office culture. Some workers are exposed daily to a toxic work culture. This may be down to a manager or supervisor who is a bully and harasser, other staff (individually or in concert) who intentionally sabotage your work success, or just a 'sick' organisation. Whatever the exact cause, a toxic workplace increases the risk of burnout dramatically.

Let's set the scene. Here are descriptions from three study participants who attributed their burnout to a toxic workplace. The first two give a helicopter view, and the third details how effectively badgering and intimidating elements can be woven together to create a grievous mix:

> The office jungle was best described to me by an older friend who'd spent a number of years as a senior adviser to a politician: 'You need to know who's who in the zoo'. Surviving (particularly when you're a bit like me and not quite so interested in normal social cues about what you do and don't say to your boss) is a bit like filming a series of Survivor on the Pakistani border with ten tourists as the unwitting participants. It's only a matter of time before someone steps on an unexploded mine.

Note the word 'surviving'—we'll return to it shortly. When the boss or manager is malignant, the scene is rarely static. The pressure, the

DOI: 10.4324/9781003333722-12

harassing and the bullying generally progress step-by-step—or blow-by-blow. A second story, from a personal assistant (PA):

It started with a new CEO who did not value PAs at all, thought we were obsolete and told us so. Played the favourites and was a bully and intimidated all those who disagreed with him. Suddenly the firm I had loved working at had a big culture change. Money and innovation were the buzzwords instead of team and balance, and everything was to be 'electronic'. But the resources weren't there for that to happen. Change was implemented without consultation and the technology provided didn't make things more efficient, it just meant we had two systems operating instead of one. And with the rise of email correspondence, clients expected responses immediately: it seemed all we did was respond to 'urgent' emails but never got any actual work done. And the work was still there to do. It just built up and up until I had no idea what was on my desk.

Then another PA left and they decided not to replace her. So I went from working for three people to five with none of the other task 'extras' that had been tagged onto my job over the years being taken off. Then things got really bad. Our office manager and HR manager both retired and were replaced with one person with no HR experience. Our 'go to' people had left and, because I am okay with technology, I became the 'go to' person when people didn't know how to do something. Another assistant left and I inherited the PA work for the management team, including the CEO, so I was then working for eight people. Staff started leaving in droves and as one of my 'extras' was Word training, I had to train any new staff about this package.

I asked to work with management to address my job overload. I drew up a list of what my job was supposed to be compared to what it was. I also listed all the work I'd been delegated from people who had left and not been replaced. Management's response was: (a) I should have done my notes in Excel not Word (I kid you not), and (b) 'you have the skills to do this work, we need you to continue'. End of story. That night I went home and thought about closing the car shed door and leaving the car running.

A brief note before the third story. We humans (as animals) have options when we come across another human animal. Basically, we can kill them, try to coerce/control them or co-operate with them. To promote a healthy workplace, the optimal qualities for a manager are predictably the last. A competent manager, as well as being firm and fair, should be caring and co-operative, able to advance collaboration within the workplace, and supportive enough to bring out or magnify their employees' strengths. Toxic managers are the antithesis of this—uncaring, usually controlling and sometimes setting out to 'destroy' a selected employee or multiple staff members. Their skill set is, rather, a 'kill set': pathological, playing favourites, belittling, isolating and objectifying their victims. For the employee who stays in the game it becomes one of survival, sometimes with fatal consequences.[1] An aside, what drives such managers? Thought for the day, as observed by Eric Hoffer: 'Passionate hatred can give meaning and purpose to an empty life'.

As a psychiatrist, the first author hears variants of this next burnout story half a dozen times each year.

> I am a staff specialist at a major teaching hospital in Victoria, where I have worked for more than 25 years. I consider myself to be a conscientious and moral person who likes to do things properly and to a high standard.
>
> For the majority of my working career I have greatly enjoyed work, particularly the intellectual interest of medicine, communicating and interacting with patients, the satisfaction of doing procedures well and keeping up-to-date with medical education and advances in procedures.
>
> Over the last few years my work environment has changed for the worse with the appointment of a new director. My workplace has become a toxic environment. The director has a poor understanding of the running of the department, plays favourites, does not have the best interests of the department at heart, tells mistruths and has created an environment where she can avoid clinical work while dumping the work on others in the department, including on call, weekends and public holidays. There is no longer equity and impartiality in the department.

The commonly used techniques by the director are divide and conquer and punish those who do not toe her line, while rewarding those who are subservient and don't question her directorship. Leave, pay, obstruction, poor governance, undermining of non-favoured staff and promotion of favoured staff are the tools of her trade. Leave in all its forms (annual, long service, conference leave) has been weaponised. Leave is easily granted by the director to those who support her whereas those who do not agree with this (corrupt) governance find their leave withheld or not approved.

When the issue is formally raised with administration or professional bodies, the director backs down and gives various disingenuous excuses, but by that stage the victim has gone through weeks or months of torment and it is usually too late to book a holiday or conference. This pattern is repeated time and time again, year after year. Similarly, medical certificates and statutory declarations are requested from some staff (those who have questioned her policies) but not from those who are unquestioning or subservient. Proxies, which include medical administration, are often used by the director to implement her punishment. Innovations and improvements to the department are opposed without valid reason.

Staff meetings are frequently held by the director with insufficient notice, with key stakeholders absent, with the director writing up the minutes reflecting her biased and distorted view of the meetings. Several long-standing experienced sub-department heads who were non-compliant were replaced by much more junior staff who owe their position, and therefore loyalty, to the director. There is no natural justice in the department. Favoured staff have privileged treatment—turning up for work late and leaving early, working from home or having non-documented days off, whereas no credit is given to dedicated staff who put in extra hours.

Numerous representations to administration by many senior staff to rectify the situation have fallen on deaf ears. The pattern of poor behaviour by the director has taken a serious toll on senior staff—recent resignations of long-term, highly experienced staff, multiple senior staff on extended sick leave and long service leave.

I used to love going to work. With the current work scenario, I no longer gain any satisfaction from my workplace, in fact, I dread going to work. Similarly, many other senior staff have described their extreme apprehension in returning to work from leave. On my last return to work, I slept poorly, waking in the early hours of the night and not being able to get back to sleep, ruminating about the current episode of harassment or other ongoing problems in the department. I felt constantly on edge and stressed due to work. I used to be trusting, idealistic, calm and even-tempered. Over the last few years, I have become suspicious of people's motives and untrusting and irritable when at work. I am particularly cynical and untrusting of administration due to their numerous failings over recent years.

Over the last few years, negative work issues have insinuated themselves into most aspects of my life, occupying much of my thoughts. This has significantly negatively affected my family and personal relationships. My partner, although very patient, at times has her limits in hearing me describe my difficulties at work. Other senior colleagues have disclosed very similar feelings and similar impacts on their family life. I have become despondent and disillusioned due to the work environment for some years now, seeing a once well-functioning department slowly go downhill and becoming a dysfunctional department.

However, having taken a recent break from work or previously when on holidays, I find my sleep pattern rapidly improves as do my stress levels and mood. When away from work I soon return to my premorbid state. Now with the opportunity to look at things in perspective and in a logical manner, I unfortunately see no future in my department, where I have spent most of my career. After years of trying to remedy the situation, the only viable option I see, to preserve my health and happiness, is to leave.

This vignette powerfully captures the artfulness, imagination and strategic brilliance of a divide-and-rule manager. And we can appreciate the doctor's quandary. He loves medicine, he is conscientious and reliable, he has worked for the one hospital for an extended period and has shown his loyalty; it has been his career. But he has become another one of the director's victims. In this toxic adversarial work environment there is no prospect of a just outcome. And where lies the pathology? Is it the doctor or the director who is 'sick'? The doctor is certainly designated as sick—burnt out, stressed, demoralised and requiring periods off work to recuperate. What about the director?

If it's a game, and clearly it is at one level, then who are the winners? Not the doctor, not his family, not most of his medical colleagues and not the patients. The hospital itself also loses, now deprived of a dedicated, conscientious and caring specialist, forced to divorce himself from such a toxic environment. Perhaps the director is the winner, but at what price? (Yes, you are probably right. She'll be promoted.)

So what should the doctor do? He could leave, of course, but this is not an easy option for someone who is conscientious and loyal, and who would feel that he is 'deserting the ship'. Should he instead continue to work under the conditions that have been in operation for some time, and be morally and spiritually crushed as well as burnt out? Take industrial or legal action? The last seems logical but the first author's experience observing such scenarios over the decades is that the process is inexorably slow and rarely resolved in any way satisfactory to the worker. And during time on sick or other leave, personal demoralisation creeps into the worker's bones and they develop a sense of being an invalid and no longer a 'worker'. Even worse if they need to take up an invalid pension for financial reasons: this may give them a new identity as someone who is impaired, and a title like that can be hard to shake off. In such burnout scenarios, repair and recovery is extremely difficult, especially when the victim carries the continuing sting of unfairness and lack of redress.

In our experience, the 'cut your losses and leave' option is usually the best in these sorts of circumstances for burnout symptoms to be relieved, but persuading reliable workers that this is their best option is rarely easy.

Note

1 S. Butcher, 'Workers fined $115,000 over bullying of cafe waitress', *The Age*, 8 February 2010, <www.theage.com.au/national/workers-fined-115000-over-bullying-of-cafe-waitress-20100208-nlrj.html>, accessed July 2020.

Chapter 10

Occupations at high risk

'We all live under the same sky, but we do not all have the same horizon'.

Konrad Adenauer

Burnout is consistently shown to be more likely in those working in 'people professions', where the worker is involved in regular and usually demanding interactions with other people. The extent of interaction is probably not the primary factor—it's more likely that burnout arises from the demands tied to such interactions.

As regards to professions most at risk, various 'hit parade' lists have been published in the last few decades, and they show impressive consistency. Health care workers (i.e. doctors, nurses, social workers, dentists) and veterinarians are top of the pops. Then come teachers, lawyers, police officers and senior managers. The clergy are rarely listed but should be—nor are full-time carers, who, as we will discuss in more detail in the next chapter, also risk experiencing severe burnout.

Such high-risk occupations are marked by demands that, for the most part, are extremely emotionally taxing. The worker not only carries vast responsibility but must also be exceptionally caring. And they are usually required to undertake an excessive amount of 'shadow work'—added responsibilities that although not core duties are often monumental. Let's overview some occupations and their nuanced job demands leading to a risk of burnout.

Doctors

Many will have read London doctor Adam Kay's account in his book, *This Is Going to Hurt* (subsequently a seven-part television series), with

DOI: 10.4324/9781003333722-13

his final paralysing book anecdote of the mother whose baby died during a caesarean delivery despite the medical team doing all that could be done.[1] He notes how hospital staff afterwards were very kind to him, reassuring him that it was not his fault. But, as he observed, 'doctors can't acknowledge how devastating those moments really are'. He ruminated about the 'might haves' and returned to work the next day 'in the same skin, but I was a different doctor—I couldn't risk anything bad ever happening again'. He described how he went six months without laughter. He changed his job within the hospital but 'after a few months, I hung up my stethoscope. I was done'. He left the National Health Service.

Family physician Dike Drummond described how burnout hit him just after his 40th birthday, when 'everything came to a sudden and mysterious halt'.[2] He described mind-numbing fatigue enveloping him as he stepped into his surgery; his joy and interest in his work had drained away overnight. Food tasted like sawdust while colour vanished; everything was black and white. He took a one-month sabbatical but, only hours after his return, 'I knew I could not continue. I put in my notice and walked away from my practice... My days as a full-time clinician were at an end'.

Burnout is not a new phenomenon in doctors. Sir William Osler (1849–1919), often called the father of modern medicine and one of the founders of the Johns Hopkins Hospital in the US, had episodes of burnout that caused him to experience 'periods of tiredness, lack of enthusiasm, cynicism and diminished sense of personal achievement and satisfaction', and which ultimately led him to leave and take up a position at Oxford in the UK.[3]

Lisa Rotenstein and colleagues identified 182 studies published between 1991 and 2018 estimating rates of burnout in physicians.[4] The number of doctors sampled exceeded 100,000 and they quantified an overall rate of burnout of 67%. As the majority (86%) of the studies used the MBI and applied quite varying cut-off scores, there is the risk of an over-estimate, though Thomas Reith in 2018 reported similarly high rates in trainee physicians in the US (overall 69%, but 79% in surgical residents).[5]

As noted in Chapter 2, Tait Shanafelt reported that 'Numerous global studies involving nearly every medical and surgical specialty indicate that approximately 1 of every 3 physicians is experiencing burnout at any one given time'.[6] More recently, a 2020 Medscape report of a voluntary online survey of more than 15,000 US physicians quantified a somewhat higher prevalence of burnout at 42%,[7] a rate that is alarmingly close to half the workforce. The physicians nominated the main causes as overwhelming workloads, long hours and lack of support. Rates were highest in 'Generation X' respondents—those at a mid-career stage and presumably also juggling multiple roles outside of work—and also higher in women, deemed to be because women 'take on more work at work', bear more of the load in collaborative work and tend to take on more of the work at home than men. Two-thirds of physicians surveyed judged that they would handle the pressure by themselves as the overload was either not completely devastating or they were, ironically, too busy to seek external help.

Factors implicated in physician burnout

- High levels of responsibility.
- Uncertainty over outcome.
- Schedules constantly disrupted by emergencies.
- Completing time-consuming electronic medical records.
- Being 'on call' after routine work hours.
- The ever-present threat of legal action or malpractice suits, whether about acts of commission or of omission—and, interestingly, often due to concerns by the doctor about what they might have said to a patient.
- The need to be a superhero and not show any weakness.
- The emotionally draining impacts of dealing with incurable or dying patients.

Nurses

One of our study participants—a 42-year-old nurse—listed the symptoms of burnout she had experienced:

- continual feeling of fatigue despite regular sleep
- feeling overwhelmed when asked questions or given requests at work

- disorganised workspace but unsure where to start with organising
- lack of pride in work completed.

Thomas Reith, in his review mentioned earlier, cited studies from the US quantifying a burnout rate of 43% in hospital nurses and 37% in nurses working in nursing homes.[8] Many of the factors considered for doctors also apply to nurses, particularly as the roles expected of a nurse have moved from carrying bedpans and spreading comfort and optimism to patients to tasks that demand high technical skills. Research also reveals that a key factor in nursing staff burnout—and a somewhat surprising one—is conflict with patients.

Veterinarians

Veterinarians experience high rates of burnout and have a high incidence of suicide, twice as high as for physicians and dentists.[9] Reasons include the worries of running a business, pet owners who expect miracles, vets' own unrealistic self-expectations and the burden of euthanising animals.

Teachers

A 42-year-old male teacher and study participant observed:

> I have taught 518 students this year, which is far too many. When coupled with the nature of bureaucracy within the education system, I am nearly dead on my feet. I do tend to view my job through a moral lens and feel down if I am not getting my students where they need to be.
>
> I have started to become irritated quite easily, despite being a relatively placid person. I wake up at night ruminating about what I have to do at work each day and process as many possible scenarios as possible. My need to get out and socialise is quite diminished.

The data on teacher burnout tend to be anecdotal, but high rates (50 to 90%) are quantified in western countries. Teaching is inclined to attract those with selfless intentions. Burnout factors include the work volume (too much and not enough time for its management, so that it eats into home hours), inadequate resources, tedium, poor student behaviour, lack of support from parents and other teachers, and ineffective or antagonistic administration. Because of such stressors, more than 15% of teachers in the US leave the profession each year. The turnover varies markedly across the country, reflecting local stressors that rise from deficits in funding and support and from student disadvantage, and it is markedly higher in more disadvantaged areas.

Lawyers

A 30-year-old female study participant noted:

> I'm a family lawyer. I work only on legal aid cases, so high levels of conflict, and all families difficult, with various issues (drugs, domestic violence). Poor management, little resourcing to do the job I need to do well, responsibility for training and supervision of younger staff without appropriate plans and guidance as to how to do this. I despair about my ability to do my job, I'm tearful, lack empathy for clients and feel that anything that goes wrong at work is my fault.

In an overview, Kate Mangan suggested that burnout was distinctly over-represented in lawyers: job demands often exceed resources, the work is difficult, with long hours mandated (motto: 'You can sleep when you're dead') and with matters often being confrontational.[10] There is further pressure in the rush to obtain 'billable hours'. The necessary perfectionism demanded of a successful lawyer contributes to the problem as a law career demands great attention to detail and carries large penalties for mistakes.

Police officers

A 41-year-old police officer and study participant observed:

> I'm tired, grumpy, forgetful, get angry easily, feeling like I'm 'treading water' in life and not getting anywhere at work, self-employed husband and the associated paperwork, three kids (nine, eight, seven years), disorganised house, financial stresses!

Stress soon takes its toll on law enforcement officers. We can't begin to imagine the emotional impact of attending a road accident and witnessing maimed and dying people (especially children), visiting parents at 2 a.m. with the news of their adolescent child's drug overdose or death in a car accident, going on duty daily to a city area where there is a high chance of being assaulted or worse. Studies indicate that police officers have one particular stress protection—a personality attribute of 'hardiness'. Factors leading to burnout in this profession can include those shared with other occupations, such as indifferent or hostile supervisors, excessive demands and few rewards. But some factors are relatively specific to the policing profession: the demand to provide help in multiple diverse ways, front-line mediation of conflict, scant resources and back-up in times of extreme pressure and, not uncommonly, the risk of bullying and a lack of support from peers.

Managers

A 45-year-old female IT manager who participated in our study gave this summary of the causes of her burnout:

- Demanding work tasks with a lack of value attached to them.
- Doing lots of reporting and justifying work to more senior managers without any idea of what they are looking for or why.
- Lack of balance in work/life—seems the more you work, the more you work!
- Lack of acceptance in the corporate world that life is not all about work.

The usual factors such as an excessive workload, time pressures and long hours are at play here. Managers, by and large, seek out such a career as they enjoy decision-making, the potential autonomy and the opportunity for career advancement. However, management also comes with the need to juggle numerous tasks and challenges (often with unclear expectations and all at once), high accountability, fuzzy goals, dealing with a dysfunctional team or organisation, little support from those 'up the chain', monotonous work and lack of recognition for their efforts.

Human resources expert Peter Wilson added:

> IT workers are the new recruits to burnout. Whilst the global digital world has offered exciting new work, the inherent unreliability of technological connections and the incompatibility of product capabilities from the major providers (e.g. Microsoft, Apple) make for a stressful work environment. When you combine that with the need for bulletproof cyber protection, the incessant pressures make burnout a much higher probability for the IT worker.

The clergy

A 64-year-old clergyman who was a study participant offered the following outline of his burnout symptoms:

> Loss of initiative, drive, ambition, passion (work or personal); some memory issues; attitude of 'what does it matter'; emotional flatness—almost no highs or lows; procrastination (letting things slide); some withdrawing from interaction with other people; avoidance of conflict even when needed to resolve issues; lack of desire for administrative responsibilities (when formerly that was a core part of my work); fatigue; increased feeling of incompetence in work; time lapses—recently I sat down for a few minutes and two or three hours later didn't recall the interval.

In western societies, more clergy students end up leaving training seminaries early than graduating. Up to 90% of ministers do not stay long enough to reach retirement age. A pastoral role, it is argued, entails satisfying more service components than other professions while carrying the expectation that such a person will be the 'master' of all and be 'all things to all people'. Burnout factors shared with other professions include excessive workloads and poor resources. More career-specific stressors include the need for clergy to be always on call, the repetitive nature of much of their work, the absence of tangible results and unclear measures of achievement. Other destabilising factors are the lack of standards for defining effective pastoral work, ambiguity in the job description, the expectation that they will always be a solid 'rock', continued exposure to tragedies, little time for family life, conflict with church members (more common than might be expected) and the 'fish bowl' effect, with the clergy and their family under constant scrutiny.

An overview of professionals

Peter Wilson said further:

> Such findings confirm what I have learned from workplace studies over the last two decades: they have some common features and, in most cases, very high-order professional standards need to be maintained to hold your place within the professions of law, medicine and public health. Further, the work itself of such professionals can profoundly affect another person's life, livelihood or both. The cost from one single mistake of judgement can be very high, and sometimes fatal. While teachers don't have the same demanding annual professional development requirements, their stewardship as trustees over the education of young children and adolescents can impose very high stress levels. For those employed in the public sector, they have to cope with a 'less is more' philosophy on the modern approach to use of public funds and an often unyielding bureaucracy of form filling driven by an accident that occurred somewhere in the dim distant past. At least lawyers can walk away from work if it is not economic.

Implications for managers

We earlier noted how recent changes in the workplace have increased stress and the risk of burnout. Those in the 'people professions' are at greater risk, and we have detailed shared factors and some nuances that are relatively specific to particular professions.

At present, in Britain, the Americas and most of Europe there is no occupational safety and health standard that requires an employer to have a workplace 'employee burnout' policy for dealing with workers affected in this way. There is, however, a duty for workplaces to protect employees from workplace hazards, and studies clearly establish that employee burnout has the potential to impact many facets of work performance and safety. Because of these potential risks, it's important for workplaces to take appropriate precautions, if for no other reason than to reduce potential liability, and have policies in place now.

Notes

1 A. Kay, *This Is Going to Hurt: Secret diaries of a junior doctor*, Picador, London, 2017, pp. 257, 258.
2 D. Drummond, *Stop Physician Burnout: What to do when working harder isn't working*, Heritage Press, Collinsville, MS, 2014, pp. 10–11.
3 J.J. Kopel, 'Sir William Osler: A forerunner of mindfulness in medical practice', *Baylor University Medical Center Proceedings*, 2019, vol. 32, pp. 456–8.
4 L.S. Rotenstein, M. Torre, R.C. Ramos, C. Guille, S. Sen, R.C. Rosales & D.A. Mata, 'Prevalence of burnout among physicians: A systematic review', *Journal of the American Medical Association*, 2018, vol. 320, no. 11, pp. 1131–50.
5 T.P. Reith, 'Burnout in United States healthcare professionals: A narrative review', *Cureus*, 2018, vol. 10, no. 12, article e3681.
6 T.D. Shanafelt, 'Enhancing meaning in work: A prescription for preventing physician burnout and promoting patient-centered care', *Journal of the American Medical Association*, 2009, vol. 302, no. 12, pp. 1338–40.
7 L. Kane, 'Medscape national physician burnout & suicide report 2020: The generational divide', *Medscape*, 15 January 2020, <www.medscape.com/slideshow/2020-lifestyle-burnout-6012460>, accessed November 2020.
8 T.P. Reith, 'Burnout in United States healthcare professionals: A narrative review', *Cureus*, 2018, vol. 10, no. 12, article e3681.
9 B.L. Lovell & R.T. Lee, 'Burnout and health promotion in veterinary medicine', *Canadian Veterinary Journal*, 2013, vol. 54, no. 8, pp. 790–1.
10 K. Mangan, 'How to recognize and prevent lawyer burnout', *Lawyerist*, 1 August 2019, <https://lawyerist.com/blog/recognize-prevent-lawyer-burnout>, accessed July 2020.

Chapter 11

Forgotten caregivers

> 'They say what doesn't kill you makes you stronger. At this point I should be able to lift the Opera House'.
>
> Sydney studies research participant

This chapter is a tribute to a largely invisible cohort: caregivers. Burnout is not confined to the workplace; it also occurs outside of formal work environments. Many respondents to our first questionnaire were in this neglected and overlooked category. Some were single mothers holding down insecure casual jobs while managing disabled or demanding children. Others provided around-the-clock care to a partner or parent suffering from dementia. Many carers were 'sandwiched' between the needs of a young brood and elderly parents. Divorces, abusive partners and serious health conditions were additional centre-stage stressors. It's likely in such family-based burnout scenarios that some factors listed in the previous chapters are relevant. There are also unique factors that come into play in this group experiencing 'carer burnout'.

The universal carer

> 'Many women return from work to home, ready to start their "second shift"'.
>
> Anon

As recently as the 1960s, it was not unusual to find older women who had been required (almost invariably by their fathers) to leave school at an early age to look after their family. Generally, it was the only or the oldest girl in a family who was charged with this non-negotiable role.

DOI: 10.4324/9781003333722-14

From their mid-teens they became a 'dutiful daughter' to their parents and mother to their siblings. Surprisingly, these women were often accepting of such a dedicated and generally thankless caring role taken on at such a young age. Now, however, times have changed, and our expectations of dutiful daughters are rather that they will establish a career, then find a partner, and next produce children—and *then* they will add the conventional 'dutiful daughter' caregiver role to their job description after ticking off the rest of the list, by looking after their ageing parents. The burden of care at home (highlighted by the recent pandemic) has always fallen disproportionately on women, as has formal job loss or reduced hours in times of change.

In answer to the question 'What's the principal cause of you feeling burnt out?', one of our study participants (a 54-year-old government manager) offered this summation:

> The demands of work: long hours, quick and unrealistic turn-arounds, lack of skilled staff. I rely on the stability of my work—I have responsibility of all financial risk. Also, living with three teenagers and having a carer role for an elderly grandmother (part-time) plus carer role (full-time) of a now-adult child with physical disability and limited education.

Delivering care into a perceived void

> *'The best way to describe the unpaid carer is like the mortar in the wall. It's there, but it's hidden'.*
>
> Peter Charleton[1]

'Caregiver burnout' is often described in relation to a family member looking after an elderly relative with a medical or psychiatric condition who needs and demands care across much of the day, seven days a week, and where the relative is seemingly unaware of their carer's contribution. The caregiver may be dogged by the sense that their task is endless and/or unlikely to bring any distinct benefit to the person they are caring for (and worsened if their initial expectations were unrealistic). Their care seems poured into a void, making them feel powerless and ineffective. On top of this, they often also need to resign from their formal workplace to undertake this care.

In addition, when looking after a parent, 'role confusion' is added to the mix. There is a psychological impact in changed roles: the child now acts as the parent's parent. Additionally, the carer's feelings of isolation and being undervalued are heightened when other family members fail to provide support (mysteriously becoming fully engaged in other activities) and augmented by a general lack of helpful resources and an inability to secure any 'time out'.

In such circumstances, burnout in the caregiver generally shows the classic pattern: exhaustion, decreased empathy (sometimes seeding resentment and the potential for abuse of the person in their care), concentration problems, social withdrawal, anxiety, irritability, depression, sleep disturbance, lack of energy and feelings of helplessness. In this context the damage caused by burnout is often also accompanied by guilt: the carer feels that they are not as supportive and as empathetic as they are generally and 'should be'.

The depleted parent

Caregiver burnout can also occur when parenting a fractious infant or a child who allows no respite (perhaps sleeping minimally plus having frequent tantrums), or in the course of raising an intellectually impaired child with challenging behaviours, or looking after a profoundly physically ill or disabled child requiring constant nursing care by the parent.

A single mother in her mid-40s with an intellectually disabled child observed:

> I often feel overwhelmed by all my tasks and want to do none. I cry at the drop of a hat and feel anxious constantly. I react to noises and movement like I never used to. I am often short of breath when stressed. Some days small challenges make me want to SCREAM.

The few studies undertaken support the proposition of 'parental burnout' in these circumstances. Annika Lindahl Norberg reported that mothers of children who had survived a brain tumour scored higher on a burnout measure than mothers of children with no history of chronic or serious disease.[2] Isabelle Roskam and colleagues adapted the MBI

(Maslach Burnout Inventory) to develop a Parental Burnout Inventory or PBI, with their applied research confirming two of the MBI scales—exhaustion and reduced personal accomplishment—but with the MBI 'depersonalisation' scale being replaced with an 'emotional distancing' scale.[3]

Guilt bred from perceived daily failings (where the carer judges their often astounding attention to their charge as falling short) may drive the carer to invest even more time in caregiving tasks, so completing a 'vicious circle' where they are convinced that their efforts are endless and ineffective.

When caring for others is herd work and a cow of a job

In 2019, Australia's SBS TV's discussion program *Insight* ran an episode about burnout, with invited audience members detailing its impact on them and outlining its particular causes.[4] The first description came from Stephen Hawken, who, together with his wife, Cheryl, had experienced burnout in recent years. The two own and work a dairy farm; Stephen is a sixth-generation farmer and has farmed for over 30 years. As the costs of running the farm are high and the income from milk low, Stephen and Cheryl are the only workforce. Stephen estimated that he works a minimum of ten hours a day—and many days 16 hours—seven days a week, including Christmas Day, and without any holidays, while Cheryl works 80 hours a week. As Cheryl observed, 'every day is a Monday' for them: the workload of caring for the dairy herd is endless.

Stephen started working on the farm as an adolescent and is passionate about farming, viewing it as his 'life'. He is hardworking, regimented and methodical. He detailed his burnout symptoms in an interview with the first author. Currently he feels exhausted, like 'a rocket booster out of fuel', and runs on autopilot for much of the time. He can sleep anywhere, taking micro-naps when not working (even in the dentist's chair). His passion for farming has gradually become compromised. Currently he feels he is losing focus and is less methodical than usual. Irritable and asocial (he just needs to sit down and blank out 'after running all day'), he feels guilt about involving Cheryl in such relentless work.

Their story extends the paradigm of burnout past its nexus with formal work and demonstrates the reality that caring for animals unable to care for themselves can also be a cause of burnout.

Those for whom work is a 'calling'

As noted in Chapter 8, the literature on wellbeing views it as hierarchical and a triad. 'Work' is categorised as either a job, a career or a calling. Each, respectively, leads to a 'pleasant', 'good' or 'meaningful' life. The model posits that the further an individual ascends the hierarchy, the higher their level of wellbeing.

> *'Burnout is not a condition caused by laziness. Those affected are conscientious, passionate, devoted to their work. In fact, that is part of their problem'.*
>
> Pascal Chabot[5]

Consider the above observation by Chabot. We build on this and present again a paradox: that the prevalence of burnout is more likely to *increase* as the hierarchy is ascended. Thus, those for whom work is their calling or passion tend to be constantly 'giving' and may be unable to stop (even when the cows come home). The positive feelings associated with giving, dubbed 'helper's high', may lock them in even further. But there is a cost. Burnout can reflect the dark side of self-sacrifice.

Petrea King's story

Petrea is the CEO of the Quest for Life Foundation, the organisation she founded more than 30 years ago to provide resilience programs and support for people affected by terminal illnesses and other complex or traumatic situations. Petrea is the author of nine books and many meditation programs and is a regular guest on radio. She has worked with people living with life's greatest challenges for over 35 years, with her world revolving around those with life-threatening illnesses, depression, tragedies, violence, trauma and abuse, and imminent death. Yet, after three decades at the front line, she was unaware that she herself had reached the edge of her capacity to cope:

It didn't occur to me that I was beyond exhausted until I arrived at a holiday apartment in Queensland. Some weeks before, Paula (a patient with leukaemia) had pressed into my hand a set of keys to her holiday home in Mooloolaba, saying, 'For goodness sake, take a holiday!' Was it so obvious to people that I needed one? I had been increasingly feeling under pressure from the demands of so many people with life-threatening illnesses. I was frustrated and irritated with myself. I felt unable to keep hearing their stories of anguish and suffering. I felt trapped.

I'd always been a 'wake up/get up' kind of person who set high personal standards. I was no longer leaping out of bed to embrace the day. It was a slow drag to get my reluctant feet on the floor, especially after a night of unpleasant dreaming. In a frequent recurring dream, I would be struggling to not fall asleep in front of a patient. There were times, occasionally, when nearly falling asleep during a consultation was a reality. I reacted by blaming myself for the lack of compassion I sometimes felt and worked longer hours on more days to meet their pleas for help. I was a 'yes' person—to everyone but myself. I was oblivious to my needs because other people's needs outweighed my own. Outside of my work, I was increasingly impatient with conversations about trivial matters.

There were several times when visiting my children, who lived over an hour away, that I couldn't recall any details of the journey.

I began to loathe the phone and its endless messages from people wanting something from me. These calls had to be returned after my day of seeing patients and so consumed my evenings. I dreaded making the calls then berated myself mercilessly if I wasn't able to accommodate everyone's needs. I felt irritated and judgemental with some of my less-likeable patients.

The enthusiasm I felt when I started my practice as a naturopath began to be overshadowed by a growing dread—there would always be an endless line to the horizon and beyond of people who were suffering.

The first evening in this beautiful apartment, bounded by the sparkling Pacific Ocean before me, and the Mooloolah River behind, I had turned on the television to a program about prisoners with AIDS. An overwhelming wave of despair and grief engulfed me and I collapsed, sobbing, in a fetal position on the floor. My only thought was, 'Who's going to hold them?' I sobbed on and off, mostly on, for two solid weeks. I fell asleep on the floor from the sheer exhaustion of weeping. I couldn't bear the company of people or to look them in the eye, and so I remained in the solitude of the apartment. My appetite disappeared. An over-whelming dread consumed me as I contemplated the life I was living—a life which now had me trapped.

As my 'holiday' came to an end, the prospect of hearing more stories from people facing their mortality through cancer, AIDS or some other illness seemed insurmountable. Stories of grief, of loss, of anguish, violence, abandonment, rejection, fear, anxiety, abuse, panic and, sometimes, abject cruelty. I knew this work was my vocation but was unsure how to thrive among so much emotional distress.

Looking back, three decades before, in September 1983, I had been diagnosed with acute myeloid leukaemia and was told that I wouldn't see Christmas—just three months away. My children were aged four and seven. In the month before, my brother had taken his life—he had told me when we were children that he knew he had to kill himself by the age of 30. Though younger than him, I had always felt responsible for him and now I had failed to stop his plan, which had remained a secret between us. He took his life in Kathmandu. There was no funeral, no memorial, no packing up of his possessions. He had none. It was difficult to take in the reality of his death. A visit to my parents' home by Federal Police had conveyed the message of his death—and that was that. We were all left reeling.

During this time also, my husband had disappeared without a word from the tiny cabin we had in the US, where we had moved to study for our yoga and meditation teaching qualifications. I was left grief-stricken about my brother, without funds but with two small children, who were distressed and confused by their father's dis-appearance. He had returned to Australia. Within weeks of his departure, I received the leukaemia diagnosis—which at least explained the extensive bruising over my body and the complete exhaustion I felt. I had put my exhaustion down to the guilt and grief I felt about my brother's suicide. I felt I'd failed him and my family.

My initial reaction to the prognosis was relief. Life was too hard. There had been a long history of other traumas in my life stretching back to childhood. I was a great 'coper' who never cried or let on to anyone that I needed anything. Maybe I could do a 'good death' as I felt ill-equipped to do a 'good life'. However, the agonising thought of leaving my children quickly displaced my initial ambivalence about living. If I was to die, I yearned to find peace before that day dawned.

During my illness, I took refuge in the cave where St Francis retreated to from the busyness of Assisi centuries ago. I found a good deal of peace in that cave through many hours of meditation, reflecting on my life and the weeping of long-suppressed tears. Everyone in my family was expected to 'cope', never to show or even allow the expression of any emotions other than the long, stony cold silences or angry outbursts from my father or brother, which I had found terrifying. The Eremo delle Carceri monastery became my sanctuary. In this tiny cave I could no longer suppress my tears, and, for the first time in my life, I wept—and wept.

It is a much longer story (recounted in my memoir *Up Until Now*) but when I returned to Australia some months later, after blood tests, my doctors told me I was in remission! But then, after observing that such a remission was 'unexpected', they added that it wouldn't last.

So I returned to live with my parents. My husband had insisted that, before I died, I sign over all my assets to him, including custody of our children. I was in debt to my generous parents and unsure how to recreate a life worth living, especially as my remission seemed temporary. For three months I lived in limbo, in the transit lounge of life, waiting to die. But I possessed a gritty determination to not be defeated by life. That tenacious determination had stood me in great stead as a child and teenager. Aged 15, I was told I would never walk again after enduring a dozen surgeries to reconstruct my legs, which would constantly dislocate after I had experienced a growth spurt. After the final surgery— where they had rotated my femurs outwards to straighten my legs—my broken legs had lain inert in traction for nine months as the bones refused to heal. My legs had become skinny white 'sticks' attached to my body. No matter how much willpower I exerted, I couldn't move either of them. It took every ounce of my drive and determination to walk again.

Now, however, the great uncertainty about how long I might live was difficult. Though I felt at peace with the idea of death, my preference was definitely to live. But how? The only assets I had were qualifications as a naturopath, herbalist, massage therapist, and yoga and meditation teacher—plus an insatiable curiosity about life, and a gritty determination to not be defeated by it. A great mentor[6] had encouraged me to go into practice as a naturopath. I wasn't sure that this was my path or how I could start my life again when my health was so uncertain, but given that I was at a loss for what to do, I gratefully accepted the suggestion. Within the first two weeks in my practice a woman with breast cancer and a man with AIDS came to see me. Both had been told they wouldn't 'see Christmas', just as I had been told 15 months previously. I felt I'd met my tribe: people who lived at the edge of life, the edge of despair, the edge of mortality, helplessness, hopelessness and powerlessness. Within a few months I was inundated with patients living with a life-threatening illness. My life became consumed with people who were facing their mortality and the occasional care of my children when their father allowed me to see them.

I often asked my patients, 'What is it that stands in the way of you being at peace?' Sometimes their answer was about distressing physical symptoms—nausea, lack of appetite, pain, night sweats or insomnia. I was able to use my knowledge as a naturopath to ease or allay such symptoms from illness or the side effects of their treatments. Then, as people's physical symptoms subsided, the conversations about peace or, more often, its absence would become our focus. Stories of anguish, fear, loss, grief, broken relationships, shattered dreams, anxiety, shame, trauma, violence and child abuse filled my days. There were many stories of great love, inspiration and joy too. I began to teach meditation and mindfulness and created support and meditation groups to provide a safe and confidential environment in which people could utter the unutterable.

As soon as I could afford to, I moved into my own small apartment where I could see patients at home. People so appreciated being in a homely environment in contrast with the clinical environment of the hospital where they were being treated. Occasionally, a patient who was suicidal or very unwell would move into my home for my care.

At this time, meals in hospitals were being left outside AIDS patients' doors, as there was so much fear about close contact. I couldn't bear the thought of people being so sick—as I had recently been—and being viewed as untouchable. So I set up a voluntary massage program for them at St Vincent's Hospital. Before long, I was training other therapists to massage people who were at the edge of life and death. I started a weekly support group at the Albion Street Clinic for people with HIV/AIDS. This enabled those participating to resolve a host of past issues about identity, family, shame, the hostile judgement and violence they had endured, and to discuss their fears, anger, frustrations, suicidal thoughts and anguish.

I started hosting residential retreats for up to 50 people with life-threatening illnesses. These were intense weekends of healing, camaraderie, shared insights and rituals to acknowledge the many people we had loved in our support and meditation groups who were now lost to us. Horse riding was a feature of these retreats and, frail though many of them were, it was heartwarming to see them return with a satisfied look of freedom and mastery. Their smiles and often the colour in their cheeks were testament to their enjoyment and the benefits of being in fresh air and nature.

Sometimes I moved in with a family if a child or a young parent was dying. We have a good deal of assistance in being born but little help when taking our leave. A journalist described me as a 'midwife for the dying'. Nowadays, this role is called a 'death doula', but in the mid-80s, having someone experienced in being with families living through the dying and death of a loved one was a new and much needed service. We never know what other people's suffering feels like. We can only know our own. Because I had so recently embraced my own inner torment, I was unafraid to bear witness to other people's suffering. When I wasn't with my patients, I pursued further knowledge to assist them.

As my reputation grew, more and more people wanted to see me. I could not say no as my heart ached for people going through the tumult that was so familiar to me. By this stage, 200 people with life-threatening illnesses were attending support and meditation groups or counselling with me every week in my home. My diary was fully booked six weeks ahead, yet people kept calling saying, 'But I've only got four weeks to live'. My response? 'I'll see you on Sunday'.

So, at the time I was given the keys to the Mooloolaba holiday apartment, my days were consumed with seeing patients and conducting multiple support and meditation groups. My first appointment of the day was at 7.30 a.m. and, between conducting groups and consultations, I rarely finished before 7 p.m. I seldom ate or even drank water during the day. I saw patients every day of the week. On Sundays I spent time with my children, and also visited people in their home, hospital or hospice if they were too sick to visit me.

One of my patients was a nine-year-old girl called Christie. This beautiful child lit up my consultation room every time she and her mother visited me. Christie had a rhabdomyosarcoma of the heart that would end her life some months later. One day, Christie brought me a picture she had drawn of Garfield, the cat. In the bubble of his thoughts were three hearts. She told me she had drawn me two pictures, but the wind had blown the other one away. When I asked about the other picture, Christie said that it was identical to the one she had given me, except the hearts were all shattered down the middle. I cautiously ventured that maybe the wind was telling her she didn't need to have broken hearts. She simply replied, 'No, Petrea, you don't understand. Sometimes hearts have to break before they heal'. Christie said she would send me a replacement picture, which she did. These two drawings still hang in my office, and her words became the title of my book, *Sometimes Hearts Have to Break*.

In the beautiful Mooloolaba apartment, overlooking the sea, Christie's words gave me both permission and courage to weep for all the stories of human suffering I heard each day. Curled up on the floor, I came undone. I slowly gained some release, and in the calm that followed I knew my life had to change. It was on the drive home from this cathartic time that I asked myself some tough questions—and made some resolutions.

Why do I need to be needed I asked myself. It was ridiculous and unhealthy for my diary to be so booked up without a moment for myself. My old habit of putting someone else's needs ahead of my own had replicated without control. This time I had made people who were dying more important than meeting my own basic needs for rest, regular eating, exercise, friendships and socialising; the only people I saw socially lived with a life-threatening illness. I had been driven by 'survivor guilt': I was meant to die and didn't, or hadn't yet. Once I understood the compulsion behind my workload, I considered what would need to change so I could work from a healthy foundation.

My days had been spent listening intently to other people's stories. I would need to find someone who would listen to me as keenly as I tried to listen to everyone else. In the weeks before I left for my holiday, my daughter had come to live with me, much to our shared delight. From now on I would drive her to school at 7.30 a.m. instead of seeing my first patient. This gave us some precious time together and, as she now attended my old school near Balmoral Beach in Sydney, I would walk the entire length of the Esplanade after I had dropped her off. I could meditate there, have a fresh juice and a short black coffee and still be in my office by 9 a.m. for my first patient. Now that she was living with me, we introduced regular mealtimes together. I found a wonderful psychiatrist and saw him every week for nine years. He knew most of my practice was pro bono, as people who are sick are often financially challenged, and he never charged me. He helped me to understand how past issues had impacted on present circumstances. For instance, group participants often wanted to discuss suicide and euthanasia: I needed to be aware that I might unconsciously be trying to 'rescue' my brother over and over again.

Implementing the essentials of self-care and appropriate supervision reinforced the foundations of my life: they were essentials, not luxuries, and they were non-negotiable. The things that replenish me have continued to evolve from that time. Now I relish solitude, a loving relationship, my garden, orchard and veggies, and living a full and satisfying life that I find meaningful. I am filled with gratitude and humbled by the many teachers who have enabled me to grow and flourish.

On my return from Queensland, a voicemail from the Department of Corrective Services awaited me. Would I be interested in working with the prisoners with AIDS in Long Bay jail?

Now that sounded interesting!

Petrea's story is illuminating on so many levels. She has been an ultimate carer, not only across time (for years working seven long days a week) but across territory that is little traversed or commonly avoided by health professionals and carers. People facing the most difficult tragedies that life deals out need therapists with unlimited reserves. Although therapists understand that they must recharge themselves regularly in order to have enough left to give to others, this knowledge is sometimes lost when they are immersed in a sea of needs.

In her opening paragraphs, Petrea graphs her rapid slide into burnout and how aspects of self-preservation were foreign to her nature. Her backstory details an overload of traumatic events, with these shaping her extraordinary resilience. As for many others who develop burnout, she self-describes high 'personal standards', 'diligence' and 'healthy perfectionism' (as we consider later in Chapter 13). Petrea's resurgence after burnout is due to wise introspection, the assistance of a supportive therapist and recalibrating aspects of her life. Many of the strategies that she has used (and other advocates of such strategies) will be covered in later chapters.

A final observation. Mother Teresa of Calcutta embodied the archetypal giver and carer. She taught in India for many years before experiencing her 'call within a call'. From then on she focused on the poorest—the blind, aged and disabled—and the reviled—those with leprosy. Her humanitarian work was recognised when she was awarded the Nobel Peace Prize in 1979.

Her commitment to those in need went beyond imagination. While she never stopped working herself, she was aware of compassion fatigue and burnout (as conceived of in her time) as she required her employers to ensure that each of her nuns had one year off work every four years.

And did Mother Teresa herself deplete her vast store of compassion? In 2007, six years after her death, some of her private correspondence was released (against her declared wishes to have them destroyed); the Vatican ordered they be preserved and they were collected in a book with excerpts reported by the media. For example, *Time* magazine quoted from one of her undated letters:: 'Where is my Faith—even deep down right in there nothing but emptiness and darkness—My God—how painful is this unknown pain—I have no Faith'.[7] This deeply personal quote mirrors the torment of the ancient monastics we spoke of in Chapter 1, conveying the essence of acedia. Mother Teresa is the epitome of the person whose work is a calling and who, despite experiencing the consequences of burnout (including doubting their own faith), endure and work until they expire.

Taken together, this chapter and the preceding ones portray the effects on individuals when relentless demands, chosen or unchosen, are inescapable. Physiology takes command and they wither physically and mentally, even when fortified by a vocation.

It is clear that caregiving can ignite and flame searing pressures that result in burnout. So, the threat of burnout is not confined solely to intolerable formal workplace demands. As illustrated, those who provide care may also buckle under the strain. In the next chapter we look at predisposing factors that influence individual vulnerability to burnout, regardless of the setting.

Notes

1 J. Macaulay, 'The "hidden" role of unpaid carers in lockdown', *BBC News*, 30 April 2020, <www.bbc.com/news/uk-scotland-52480568>, accessed August 2020.

2 A. Lindahl Norberg, 'Burnout in mothers and fathers of children surviving brain tumour', *Journal of Clinical Psychology in Medical Settings*, 2007, vol. 14, pp. 130–7.

3 I. Roskam, M.E. Raes & M. Mikolajczak, 'Exhausted parents: Development and preliminary validation of the parental burnout inventory', *Frontiers in Psychology*, 2017, vol. 8, p. 163, doi:10.3389/fpsyg.2017.00163.

4 SBS News and Current Affairs, 'Burnout', *Insight*, ep. 36, 29 October 2019, <www.sbs.com.au/ondemand/video/1623750211611/insight-burnout>, accessed November 2020.

5 P. Chabot, *Global Burnout*, Bloomsbury Academic, New York, 2019, p. 5.

6 Marcus Blackmore, AM, naturopath, philanthropist and former executive director of the public company that markets 'Blackmores' vitamin and herbal products.

7 'Mother Teresa's Crisis of Faith', *Time*, 9 March 2007.

Chapter 12

Predisposing factors

'Issues innate don't always dictate fate'.

Anon

While it is generally put that burnout is all about work—whether formal, as in contracted and paid, or informal, such as caregiving—we earlier noted that burnout evokes a seed and soil analogy and is best modelled as a 'diathesis–stress' condition. Work is a *stressor* or precipitating cause and is generally the key or only factor considered by those assessing the causes of burnout. Now, however, we consider an additional set of *diatheses* or predisposing factors that increase an individual's risk and vulnerability. Many influences have been investigated and, rather than provide specific references to a vast number of studies, we summarise findings.

Gender

Some studies have reported equal rates of burnout in men and women, but the majority suggest that women are at greater risk. This could be an 'artefact' of research, reflecting the fact that women are more likely than men to disclose personal feelings and psychological problems, while men are more likely to deny them. Several senior businessmen told the first author that their career would be at risk if they admitted to any such state—they must appear resistant to everything, including kryptonite, and everyone.

Some real factors also operate. Firstly, as a generalisation, women tend to be more 'giving', and thus at greater risk of depleted energy stores, be they physical, emotional or spiritual. Secondly, and especially in recent decades, women are expected to have three roles—wife,

DOI: 10.4324/9781003333722-15

mother and worker (none of them bit parts!)—and thus they have a more extensive and demanding 'job description' than men. In essence, a 'second shift' operates every day for many women, the first their formal work life and the second their role as homemaker, with domestic labour still falling largely on women. The duties that cause or contribute disproportionately to burnout in women don't seem to come from commonly shared household chores such as stacking the dishwasher. They instead arise more from a mountain of family manager responsibilities. Most women, for example, 'own' tasks such as remembering shopping needs, taking charge of the majority of home upkeep jobs, being home for service calls, and meeting the multiple needs of the children. Add on the pressures of relentless aspiration—homemade and nutritious food, smart clothes, sculpted bodies—as well as activities, adventures and skills for the children to make them more 'well-rounded' and, phew, where's that blue and red outfit with the big 'S' on it? Thirdly, and as argued by Pascal Chabot, in the workforce, some women feel 'indebted' when hired for a job, 'perhaps because their hiring is perceived as a token concession to gender equality', and thus they feel under greater pressure to perform.[1]

Age

Several studies have shown a high risk of burnout in young (mid-30s and earlier) employees. Such age vulnerability may be because older workers are more experienced at dealing with work stressors, and/or because younger workers are less established in their careers and thus work tirelessly towards career progression. However, Generation X (those born between 1965 and 1979) are also prone to burnout. Now in their 40s and 50s, they are at an age when, as well as their work obligations (where they may be mid-career and concerned about their next career stages), they are often responsible for multiple parenting duties.

Marital status

As also applies to rates of depression, rates of burnout are lower in employees with partners than in those who are single. Interpretation: a committed partner offers a supportive buffer against stress.

Education level

Burnout rates are greatest in those with higher education levels. This association is most simply explained by the fact that such individuals are more likely to be employed in the most demanding and stressful jobs that require high-level qualification attainment.

At-risk personality traits or styles

The demographic variables just discussed aren't the only culprits that predispose to burnout. Individual differences in personality styles can put someone at risk. The following vignette captures the interaction between work and personality as experienced by one of our subjects, a 40-year-old school counsellor:

> I feel constantly overwhelmed to the point where I can't think, process information and work efficiently, like my brain has gone into a post-'fight/flight' state and has blown a fuse. Feeling a constant state of stress at work. Feeling that all my work is reactive and ineffective, not productive, as I don't have time to plan or conceptualise my cases, I am always just responding to new crises and putting paperwork on hold as it builds up. Feeling unhappy with my lack of skills development, just in a rut or regressing skills-wise.
>
> Depersonalisation, losing empathy for the children, no longer seeing them as individuals but as cases to be managed or dealt with. Not having the energy to do anything but work during the week. Struggling to get out of bed and go to work, no motivation to exercise, feel like whingeing all the time. Feel very reactive and startled by the constant noise at work. Mind goes blank often—forget what I'm doing in the middle of writing a sentence and can't figure out basic things like the date.
>
> Stressful job with unreasonable demands, public health system referring everything back to school level, so lack of support from external agencies in case management. I feel responsible for the welfare of over 100 children, work at three different schools. Lack of understanding from colleagues about the requirements of my job, lack of structured supervision and advocacy from employers.

Lack of external validation or closure with nature of job. Emotional labour from dealing with suicidal adolescents every day combined with huge amounts of paperwork. Lack of work breaks or opportunities to have lunch and leave office. Working in an environment where my role is very different from all my colleagues and I must maintain confidentiality when talking to them. Perfectionist personality, low self-evaluation, get stressed easily.

In relation to our argument for the relevance of personality, her last sentence is actually the bottom line—the soil for the seed.

In a recently published resource on burnout, Sharma and Cooper listed a number of predisposing personality styles or characteristics that put people at risk of developing the syndrome, including the following.[2]

Neuroticism

'Neuroticism' is used to describe a personality style where the individual's ongoing emotional state is defined by negative reactions and feelings. Neurotic traits make an individual particularly sensitive to environmental stress. People with neuroticism are more emotional, sensitive, anxious and prone to worry than others. A high level of neuroticism predisposes the individual to burnout as the individual is more stressed by work triggers, with symptoms likely to be accompanied by distinct anxiety and related features. Individuals with high levels of neuroticism are inclined to internalise their anxiety, resulting in excessive worrying, or externalise it via irritability, being 'crabby' and having a short fuse.

A study participant observed that, as part of her burnout symptoms: 'My stomach feels like a bag of cats. Fighting'.

Locus of control

People with an *internal* locus of control believe they are able to influence events, and are therefore adept at problem-solving: they have their hand on the tiller and control the boat. People with an *external* locus judge that events occur without any capacity on their part to influence them: their 'boat' goes where the wind and the waves take it. Having an external locus of control promotes the belief that fate and destiny dictate outcome. An external locus renders the individual at greater risk of exploitation or bullying in the workplace, and less likely to seek to address or rectify work stressors.

Type A personality

A 'Type A' person is defined as competitive, achievement orientated, keen to seek control, preoccupied with work and deadlines (commonly a workaholic and having the mantra of 'let's get it done'), unable to delegate and—of key importance—has (and radiates) a sense of time urgency. Faced with demanding or impossible tasks, Type A individuals drive themselves even harder, and in work environments they are more likely to experience high levels of work stress, quite often self-generated. Type A workers are therefore at high risk of burnout. Their burnout syndrome is dominated by exhaustion but they almost invariably seek to continue meeting all targets and deadlines, whether part of their job or self-imposed. They are exemplary hamsters, running endlessly within the wheel. If taken out of the wheel (for instance, if carted off to hospital after a heart attack), they are back at work the next day (after demanding an early discharge from hospital).

Self-efficacy

A low sense of 'self-efficacy'—where the individual lacks a sense of personal control and competence—can tip the scales to burnout. Self-efficacy is a 'state' response (a reaction to a particular circumstance) rather than a stable personality trait, and so more specifically tied to work nuances. Self-efficacy levels influence behavioural responses to work stress: low levels elicit passivity and helplessness, thereby increasing the likelihood of burnout. Similar to those with an external locus of control, individuals with low self-efficacy are more likely to be exploited and bullied at work.

Emotional intelligence

'Emotional intelligence' is the ability to recognise one's own feelings and read the emotions of others. A low level of emotional intelligence has been held to feed maladjustment in the workplace and thus heighten the risk of burnout.

Three key personality styles often overlooked

Sharma and Cooper's list neglects to include personality styles of 'sensitivity to judgement by others', 'introversion' (or shyness) and 'perfectionism', each of which, we believe, are common risk factors for burnout, although these authors later briefly note that 'perfectionism' (along with several other personality patterns) may 'increase the person's susceptibility to stress and even lead to burnout' (p. 19).

Sensitivity to judgement by others ('hyper everything')

A personality style of being hypersensitive to judgement by others is relatively common in the general community. Such individuals have an unstable self-esteem or sense of self-worth. Instead of being 'thick-skinned', their skin is more like a semi-permeable membrane open to the arrows of social judgement. Thus, their self-esteem skyrockets if they are praised and crashes if they perceive actual or imagined criticism. When stressed by criticism they commonly respond by sleeping excessively (hypersomnia), developing food cravings and binge eating (hyperphagia). Such hypersensitivity increases their risk of burnout if their manager or workmates are judgemental or critical of them.

Introversion

Introversion, sharing features with shyness, is at the opposite pole to extroversion. Extroverts are gregarious, enthusiastic and self-confident, which advances their sense of personal and professional competence. Introverts are introspective, reserved, diffident and often meek. Several studies note that extroverts are less likely—and shy/introverted people more likely—to develop burnout. The assumption is that introverted people might be given excessive workloads and not speak up, and for similar reasons, they are at higher risk of bullying in their workplace.

Perfectionism

We regard perfectionism (or a high degree of dutifulness) as the key personality style of relevance to burnout. This judgement is supported by findings from our first study and is also evident in the self-reports of so many contributing to this book.

As perfectionism is so distinctive, we will consider its nature and 'stand-out' contribution in the next chapter.

Implications

Exposed to similar external circumstances, some people develop burnout and others do not which suggests that differential susceptibility plays a part, emerging particularly from personality factors.

Recommendations for treating burnout usually focus on de-stressing strategies. If, however, certain personality styles predispose to burnout—and to its maintenance—then attention to such traits becomes central to any successful management approach.

Notes

1   P. Chabot, *Global Burnout*, Bloomsbury Academic, New York, 2019, pp. 60–1.
2   R.R. Sharma & C. Cooper, *Executive Burnout: Eastern and western concepts, models and approaches for mitigation*, Emerald Group Publishing, Bingley, UK, 2017, p. 252.

Chapter 13

Perfectionism

'Done is better than perfect'.

Sheryl Sandberg

We now focus on what we view as the key personality style that amplifies the risk of burnout: perfectionism. At its most functional, 'healthy' perfectionism is expressed in the individual's inclination to be diligent or dutiful. A diligent employee is one who goes about his or her work carefully and expends considerable effort. The term 'diligence' itself is reassuring: a nice sibilant and affirming word, without any negative or critical connotation—unlike the words 'perfectionism' and 'workaholism' (perfectionist, for example, invites the synonym 'anal retentive'). Diligence is a trait that strengthens as personality constituents mature. It (and perfectionism) carry an imputation about character: that such individuals are moral people, always seeking to do a good job and not let the side down.

Diligence, the sunny side of perfectionism

'What we hope ever to do with ease we may first learn to do with diligence'.

Samuel Johnson

Those who are diligent (i.e. are dutiful or who have 'healthy' perfectionism) aim to succeed. They therefore work to predict future stressors and plan effectively to minimise any potential obstacles to success.

The workplace loves people with such characteristics. They are reliable, conscientious, hardworking, focused on achieving set goals and always trying to do their best—what's not to love? But slide further

DOI: 10.4324/9781003333722-16

along the spectrum and things get darker: strong perfectionistic traits can gradually gum up natural capacity. At the extreme, perfectionism may paralyse an individual as they become mired in detail, hypercautious and rigid, possessed with an irrational fear of failure and perceived 'exposure'. As you will have observed already from stories within these pages, those who burn out are highly likely to have such characteristics, and it is only when they have modulated such traits that they report a settling or resolution of their burnout.

Perfectionism is rarely recognised in the burnout research literature as a predisposing risk factor. Most studies generally focus on other traits, as overviewed in Chapter 12, or consider only the external work factors at play. Pascal Chabot is an exception, observing that a key contributing factor to burnout is 'unsustainable perfectionism', with workers expected to 'manifest unquestioning perfectionism', and that burnout occurs when 'perfectionism runs out of steam'.[1] In our first study (overviewed in Chapter 4), our quantitative analysis identified a 'work-focused' factor in those with burnout. The items that contributed to this factor included the individual viewing work as important and essential, being driven to meet work responsibilities and finding work enjoyable—on the surface, benign and admirable characteristics... until relentless pressure builds up, either from managers, colleagues or clients at work, and/or from within the worker themselves.

Perfectionism's downside

Our study participants described their perfectionism in several ways, starting with a 35-year-old administrative assistant:

> I'm constantly competing against the clock to have as much as possible done without wasting a minute. Constantly feeling I need to keep developing myself to be employed/progress. The ability to retain information and multitask is decreasing. Not able to switch off (it's my personality), decreasing ability to laugh at silly things, negative towards others not performing. Single parent for many years as partner works abroad and trying to maintain a high standard at work, home, socially and educationally, whilst also trying to give time to ageing parents. Anxiety, making small tasks

complex, forgetfulness but still having the desire to excel with what
I'm doing. Constantly juggling tasks without finishing them 100%.

A 50-year-old manager in the public service observed:

Reduced capacity to work under stress. Developed extreme tiredness for an extended period after working under stress. Depressed
mood on and off. Reduced mental capacity and memory on and
off. Causes? The interaction of my own personality (perfectionism,
etc.) with doing a higher-level job that had high importance to me
from a self-worth perspective.

A 22-year-old hospitality worker stated:

I think it's because I try too hard to do everything perfectly, and
sometimes it's not possible. If I try to do something less than perfectly to just get it done, I feel sick and anxious. I feel like I'm not
capable of doing what I signed up for.

A 35-year-old office worker added a perceptive observation:

Perfectionism can be useful at times, but it should not be an
obsession. British writer Jay Griffiths has a perspective on perfectionism that I find useful. She believes something that is perfect is
in fact dead because it has ceased to develop and grow. To leave
something 'un-perfect' is therefore to ensure that it can progress,
that it can throw off shoots and inspire further creation.

A 27-year-old accountant also provided insight and wisdom:

One trap I've constantly fallen into in the past is that sticky pot
called perfectionism: 'I am fatally flawed therefore I must appear
to be perfect'. Nothing struck terror into my heart more than
thinking that someone might find out there is something wrong
with me! Thus no task was too arduous, no workload too great.
And as these tasks were accomplished, colleagues would nod
approvingly and pile more on my plate. A critical mass would
occur, one at which anyone would crack, and I'd come tumbling

down. The moral of this particular story is simple: strive to be the best you can be but realise that, like everyone else, you have limitations. You don't have to be superhuman. On reflection I've often found that the times when I nearly 'lost it' at work were times when most people would have been suffering great stress. I now find it useful to take a step to one side and analyse the situation: 'Is this a situation that most people would find stressful? What steps can I take to minimise my stress and get the job done?' This rational path takes the self-flagellation factor out of play and allows me to move forward rather than getting stuck in a loop.

Defining and detailing perfectionism

'I don't like the word "perfectionist"... I prefer "particularist"'.
Whit Stillman

Perfectionistic people have high standards, are self-disciplined and yoke themselves tightly to self-control and commitment to ensure productivity and achievement. They may manifest their perfectionism at home only, work only or across both domains. They are usually ideal employees as they work hard, commit themselves fully to the things they undertake and push themselves to be the best. Richard Winter added other characteristics to the perfectionist profile—high standards, punctuality and precision, valuing control, cleanliness and tidiness, and showing moral integrity.[2] As a colleague observed, 'Don't treat perfectionists, employ them!'

In their book *Too Perfect*, Allan Mallinger and Jeannette DeWyze detailed personality nuances that are evident when perfectionism is pronounced.[3] These include wanting things to be 'just so', the need to know and follow rules, a preoccupation with making the right choice and perceiving expectations more acutely than others. Perfectionistic people have an all-too-acceptable addiction to work; their 'workaholism' may be of the sort where they are always working or thinking about work and also feeling 'driven' in their spare time. Or perhaps they are a 'thinkaholic', where their 'all or nothing' thinking weighs heavily on a mind already bogged down with painful worrying and ruminations. In addition, perfectionistic people tend to be overly detailed in their conversation. They are also driven to meet professional and personal needs by using every minute at their disposal productively. Leisure can make perfectionistic people feel guilty or undisciplined as they constantly 'hear' stated and unstated obligations as if 'shouted through a megaphone'.

Other elements of perfectionism

'Perfectionism is internalized oppression'.

Gloria Steinem

Fear

Fear can be a feature of severe perfectionism. The individual may be fearful that others will see their flaws: they have a need to be right about everything and often show a critical (and self-critical) attitude, so that others see them as 'picky'. There is a burden in leisure activities—it can take on the overtones of an obligation, and the individual may be guarded against intimacy in an unstructured situation. Such caution generally reflects a fear of being 'found out', and a fear of trusting others in case of being let down. As observed by Michael Law: 'At its root, perfectionism isn't really about a deep love of being meticulous. It's about fear. Fear of making a mistake. Fear of disappointing others. Fear of failure. Fear of success'.[4]

An existential dilemma for most of us is how to reduce risk and vulnerability, to avoid mistakes, to feel safe and secure and to ensure that our self-perceived fallibilities are not shamefully exposed. Perfectionistic people, as a subset, are ultra-wary, have difficulty trusting and value self-reliance and independence, and so are distrustful of spontaneity. The immutability of this personality style is intrinsic to its makeup. It is also reflected in the individual's distaste for surrendering control or wholeheartedly relying on another person.

Strong perfectionistic tendencies are underpinned by a set of cognitive 'schemas' (unconscious mental representations that underlie beliefs) such as: 'I have to be the best'; 'Others are careless and unreliable'; 'It's a disaster when things go wrong'; 'I can only rely on myself to do things well'. It requires skill and subtlety to alter these schemas that underlie a perfectionistic person's world view. If a perfectionistic individual believes that worthwhile people do not lower their standards, then they will resist others' efforts to convince them that perfect performance is not necessary, and that they should ease up on themselves. Thus, perfectionistic beliefs can become a self-perpetuating trap.

Pro... cras... tin... ation

When stressed, perfectionistic individuals tend to brood over past behaviours and future decisions, their self-criticism increases, they suffer from injured pride and they become indecisive (which can lead to behavioural paralysis). Procrastination is the perfectionist's signature. He or she will hesitate and then become 'locked'—in fear of making errors. They are hypervigilant and cautious, seeking flawless end results. They strive for total control of their feelings too (loss of control is a prominent concern) and position themselves to allow no space for criticism. Those with this personality style tend to 'externalise' their sense of self-worth. They pour themselves into work and judge themselves by the quality of their work rather than by who they are as a person, rendering themselves vulnerable to stress and burnout. Very prone to self-criticism—and even more vulnerable to criticism from others—they experience any negative judgement of their work or other areas where they have invested their self-worth as shattering. An event of this kind can set off a destructive downwards spiral, marked by rumination and anxiety.

Externalised self-esteem in a perfectionistic person may reflect a childhood where one or both parents provided love or care that was conditional on the child's performance (such parents often seek to live vicariously through the lives of their children). In consequence, the child views their parents as critical and hard to please, and that they have never been loved for themselves, so they never feel secure or good enough. On the other hand, many perfectionistic people appear to have had no exposure to such conditional parenting. In this group—whose perfectionism emerges early in their life—it is likely that genetic factors are more relevant.

Black or white, not grey, please!

Perfectionistic people have a low—or no—tolerance for ambiguity. Options must be binary (go left or go right), a characteristic known as 'all or nothing' or 'black or white' thinking. When there *are* multiple options, perfectionism causes the individual to waver between them. A 'stable/unstable' model is in operation when they consider their binary options. As soon as they favour one option, the other one becomes more attractive. The instability lies in the constant oscillations; the stability is in the lack of any forward progress. The end result? Often there is no decision, no resolution and no change in the multi-status quo—thus, a 'stable/unstable situation'. In practice, composing what is meant to be a short email ends up exhausting the time available, while minutes of a meeting take hours to compose.

OMG, the sky is falling!

Perfectionistic people are prone to catastrophising if they judge they have failed to any degree. A perceived screw-up is framed as a disaster, with themselves as incompetent failures. 'Shame'—as against 'guilt'—is their concern. Brené Brown defined shame as 'the fear of disconnection—the fear of being perceived as flawed and unworthy of acceptance or belonging'.[5] Richard Winter observes that the 'problem with perfectionism begins when we move beyond the legitimate pursuit of excellence to live under the tyranny of believing that perfection is possible and failures are unacceptable'.[6] This may be the cue for shame to come on stage.

Perfectionism may lead the individual to adopt rigid and controlling behaviours. If thwarted in reaching a goal, they may find it difficult to either walk away from the situation or adjust to it—they have to achieve their original target. They must be in control; fully trusting others is too hard. This makes it difficult for them to either delegate tasks or to seek help. Thus, perfectionistic people lack the 'bamboo' flexibility required to deal with challenging circumstances. This creates a further vulnerability to stress and burnout.

In Chapter 10 we listed a set of occupations that generate high rates of burnout. All have intrinsic stressful demands, but they also demand diligence and a level of perfectionism from the worker. Some occupations, especially medicine and the law, attract inherently perfectionistic people. Thank goodness: if you are not perfectionistic at the start of a health care career, you must adopt this mindset so as to be able to practise safely, diligently and responsibly—otherwise your patients can die and/or you will be evaluated for fitness to practise by a medical board. In law, also, insouciance can lead to serious (and expensive) consequences. We see examples of imperfect practitioners headlined daily in newsfeeds.

In stark contrast, and not surprisingly, we observe that those who rate as low on diligence and perfectionism, who are easygoing and operate with a mantra of 'no worries', are unlikely to develop a burn-out syndrome. The first author was informally provided with a keen observation on burnout: 'I've never come across a sociopath with burnout'. Fast brain response: 'Huh?' Slow brain response: 'That's one of the most insightful observations I've heard about burnout'. Consider the defining features of 'sociopaths' or 'psychopaths', who operate to a Gordon Gekko 'greed is good' code.[7] They have no moral compass, they are indifferent to the feelings of others who they manipulate and exploit (without empathy), and they are consistently irresponsible, blaming others for things that go wrong. When two sociopaths meet, it's an 'I' for an 'I'! We previously noted that burnout is increased in 'givers'. Well, sociopaths are 'takers' and, thus, fireproof.

As noted early in this chapter, there is, of course, 'healthy perfec-tionism'. This is most clearly evidenced by diligence, dutifulness, con-scientiousness, perseverance and being achievement-focused, and not necessarily with significant levels of perfectionism. These character-istics serve people well, keeping them a step ahead of others in a competitive world and allowing them the appreciation of a job well done. But perfectionism lies along a spectrum. This chapter has detailed its more severe components. As the degree of perfectionism increases, so does the risk of burning out. Later in the book we focus on perfectionism at the higher end of the spectrum in order to present effective modifying strategies.

It is poignant, but the sad thing about burnout is that it is more likely to afflict good people.

Notes

1 P. Chabot, *Global Burnout*, Bloomsbury Academic, New York, 2019, pp. 4, 31, 34.
2 R. Winter, *Perfecting Ourselves to Death: Bridges to wholeness and hope*, IVP Books, Illinois, 2005.
3 A.E. Mallinger & J. DeWyze, *Too Perfect: When being in control gets out of con-trol*, Random House Publishing, New York, 1992, p. 91.

4 M. Law, informal talk to students, College of Education and Human Development, Georgia State University, USA.
5 B. Brown, *I Thought It Was Just Me (But It Isn't)*, Avery, New York, 2008, p. 36.
6 R. Winter, *Perfecting Ourselves to Death: Bridges to wholeness and hope*, IVP Books, Illinois, 2005.
7 O. Stone, producer, *Wall Street*, Twentieth Century Fox, California, 1987.

Part 3

Overcoming burnout and rekindling the flame

Chapter 14

Resolving burnout

An introduction

'The harder the fall, the higher the bounce back'.

Anon

Ask most experts about how to alleviate or resolve burnout and those with a background in organisational psychology will quite reasonably offer a set of work factors to address. Ask therapists, on the other hand, and they will generally recommend de-stressing strategies. We believe both strategies are needed, plus identifying and addressing any personality contribution. Burnout is generally a consequence of both predisposing and precipitating factors, so any focus on only one domain risks missing the 'big picture' (and the target). Further, any approach that is 'one size fits all' isn't fit for purpose. Best practice management requires a pluralistic model, addressing specific nuances of these three contributing domains—work, stress and personality style—so in the next chapters we consider strategies for handling work and stress challenges as well as a key predisposing factor—perfectionism.

Burning out or burnt out?

A further consideration is whether the affected individual is 'burning out' or has actually 'burnt out'.

Remember Hooke's law of elasticity from your school physics class? This states that the amount a spring will stretch is proportional to the force applied to it, and when you remove the force the spring will return to its original state. But this only holds true within the specific elastic limits of that spring—if it is stretched beyond those limits it won't bounce back. This analogy applied to burnout would predict that if burnout is caused *entirely* by some work stressor, then—if the

DOI: 10.4324/9781003333722-18

stressor is removed—most individuals would spring back, as they have retained their 'elasticity'. However, if the work stressor is both severe and prolonged, and if personality factors have locked the individual into this disabling cycle, then intrinsic elasticity may be lost and that individual will not bounce back so easily, or at all. This may apply even if the stressor is 'neutralised' by a correcting strategy or removed altogether.

The prospect of bounce back

Thankfully, the accounts from our study participants, and from those who entrusted their stories to us, suggest that a complete loss of elasticity is rare. The vast majority of people who judge that they are 'burnt out' are actually still in a burning out phase. They have retained some capacity to bounce back and are able to recover.

For those who are truly burnt out, we believe an additional component is needed for their recovery. As mentioned earlier, a candle that has been extinguished requires differing strategies for re-ignition to one that is barely flickering. Thus we suggest that those rare individuals who are completely burnt out need a more emphatic reset. Such life transformations are possible: see Dr Jayson Greenberg's recount at the start of this book, and the final personal story by Grace.

A motivational issue also comes into play. Many who are burning out may lack motivation to change or judge that they cannot modify their lifestyle. Dedicated carers, for example, intrinsically kind and supportive people, may feel locked into caring for a family member (and are perhaps more dutiful by necessity than perfectionistic by nature). And many professionals are hostage to their talents and/or workplace. For example, a doctor with a reputation for excellence and a very high success rate in 'curing' or assisting patients who is always 'on call', and has few if any outside interests or hobbies, may grind away at a punishing schedule, sucked in by its centripetal force. He or she can become too dazed by immediate demands to believe in or deal with the deterioration of his or her own physical and mental health and relationships. Work in cases such as this is both a calling and a passion, and the self-identities of such professionals are almost entirely composed of their professional reputation, enhanced by the heartfelt thanks from patients whose lives they have restored or saved. As the ancient Greek physician Hippocrates wisely observed, 'Everything in excess is opposed by nature'.

So perhaps burnout has a role in self-preservation: the intrinsic exhaustion prevents driven people from working themselves to death. The symptoms send a wake-up call, a signal quite appropriate for the exhausted and a descriptor often used by those who emerge on the other side of a burnout syndrome with a new perspective or a new career. We rarely alter things to any significant extent when life is proceeding swimmingly or even when we are in a rut. But we are likely to transform when a complete crisis occurs as it signals the need for change, and the opportunity for growth. 'Burnout' is not just a state but a signal—the need for renewal.

And so we now cover the key components that are essential for resolving burnout: addressing work issues, adopting de-stressing strategies and addressing any perfectionism traits.

Chapter 15

For managers

'Healthy employees, healthy bottom lines'.

Arianna Huffington[1]

This chapter offers recommendations for organisation heads, workplace managers and human resource staff. Research confirms the huge cost that burnout represents to an organisation, both via worker 'absenteeism' (extended periods off work) and 'presenteeism' (turning up for work but unable to 'fire up'), both of which severely compromise the performance, quality and output of a workplace. And unfortunately, burnout appears to hit some of the best: reliable and diligent staff—even the CEO—who may initially develop a physical illness that they can't shake off, followed by performance issues, and who finally leave saying that they are burnt out or, more commonly, leave without any clear explanation.

So, if preventing burnout is the ideal, then spotting potential burnout is a skill to be cultivated. We know that deft assistance to staff with burnout symptoms can return individuals to full productive functioning. We now consider both prevention and support strategies.

Prevention of burnout: Occupational health and safety, work conditions and culture

Occupational health and safety

Governments (at least in most western countries) have a responsibility to ensure that people are not killed, maimed or made sick by their work. Employers are consequently obliged to operate to legislative requirements. Organisations are required to provide a healthy and safe

DOI: 10.4324/9781003333722-19

workplace where risk is eliminated or minimised. All employers are also obliged to minimise their employees' exposure to work-related factors that can increase the risk of stress.

In operation, this duty of care may be handled by management or by an organisation's occupational health and safety division. In best practice, a proactive management will plan for and prevent health and safety issues. Such plans should be designed collaboratively between management and their staff, integrating both parties' insights. Exemplary employers initiate honest consultations with workers or their representatives, seek to identify health and safety risks and how best to provide safety training and supervision, monitor work conditions, and address hazards.

While identifying a physical safety issue, such as a trip or fire hazard, is relatively simple, identifying and preventing psychological stressors is more complicated. This is often grey territory. Programs for prevention of repetitive strain injuries are now common, but a focus on preventing an equivalent 'repetitive stress injury' that could result in burnout is still lacking. That said, there has been some promising recognition of the latter in recent years, with one exemplar being the American Medical Association's STEPS Forward program, which offers strategies for doctors to reduce or address their own burnout.

'I have so much paperwork… my paperwork has paperwork'.
Gabrielle Zevin

There is a caveat to the seemingly sensible strategy of having risk-minimisation programs. An increasingly litigious society spurs employers to determine all possible risks to limit their legal exposure to some negative event. Witness the birth of standard operating procedure (SOP) manuals and mandatory training courses. Policy can become disconnected from productivity as staff toil away in their engine room creating 'directives' and 'dictates' which then threaten to overrun the organisation. For instance, one health organisation in Australia has 85 mandatory policy training courses for its staff, most to be completed on a yearly basis. A mere six (e.g. fire training) seem worthy of mandatory attendance and possibly another half dozen worth completing less frequently. Here we ask a semi-serious question: do SOPs and policy training actually contribute to staff burnout? We suggest those in charge review all SOPs, mandatory training and other programs for their workplace to determine which ones are actually necessary and effective, then jettison the flotsam.

Optimising work conditions

Apart from having the right to work in a safe and healthy workplace, workers are also entitled to seek and receive an acceptable level of remuneration (which may come in the form of appreciation or other benefits if one is an unpaid worker or carer) as well as reasonable working conditions, such as feasible hours, a decent work area, the prerogative to take time off without criticism (e.g. for a sick child or a medical appointment), the space to mix with co-workers and adequate break times. Workers need the necessary resources to meet work expectations, and ongoing training to maintain or advance their competency. Add-ons such as 'protected time' (opportunities to meet with colleagues to discuss work), team-building strategies and investment in lifestyle programs during work hours identify an employer who is offering superior work conditions.

There are now many companies that provide employees with in-house and online health and wellbeing programs, a worthwhile investment as these act as 'fireguards', reducing the risk of highly valued employees resigning, taking time off or performing poorly due to stress. The cost of losing highly trained employees is immense. For example, Rajeev Kurapati reported that a physician experiencing burnout was more than twice as likely than their peers to leave the organisation and that the cost of a replacement physician ranged from a quarter of a million to one million dollars (US).[2] Though most health and wellbeing programs focus on stress reduction (and some on depression), their provision also acts to prevent or reduce the risk and consequences of burnout.

Workplace culture

While burnout is largely a consequence of environmental factors and structural workplace conditions (particularly excessive hours combined with 'shadow work'—added on responsibilities), the overall culture of a workplace can operate to influence the development of burnout at a more insidious level. Optimally, an individual's work output is recognised by the employer. There is an implicit 'social contract' at work: in exchange for labour, the worker (even the company's CEO) expects not only monetary remuneration and reasonable working conditions but also that their contribution will be noticed and acknowledged. This is a central ingredient for a healthy workplace. In contrast, lack of recognition or appreciation from managers, combative social interactions with colleagues and other isolating practices are all factors that can breed a negative workplace culture. A negative culture in an organisation may operate independently or link with the corporation's working conditions.

Burnout rates are lower in organisations that have effective and supportive leadership, are flexible, foster training and staff development, have constructive conflict resolution procedures, evidence justice (procedurally and interpersonally) and try to ensure that staff have meaningful work. Other ingredients of a 'healthy' workplace include it being intrinsically stable, having impartial and non-discriminatory rules and procedures, providing training and upskilling for staff, weighting trust above blame and censuring, ensuring that employees feel that their work is valued, and adopting values rather than simply proclaiming them.

One invited commentator Gail Kelly (former CEO of Australia's Westpac bank) observed:

In articulating the purpose of the firm, the best workplaces make it clear that the business is about much more than maximising profits and looking after shareholders—and they achieve that through clarity of purpose, providing meaning for employees as they set about their daily work, understanding the 'why' of what they do and not only the 'what'. Evidencing 'the way things get done around here' shows employees that they matter, and that their health and safety are priorities, as does establishing an environment where people can thrive and prosper. Work flexibility must be perceived as real, with such factors increasing the quotient of trust between employer and employee. The workplace should make it clear in words and actions that 'living a whole life' is critical for the long-term success of both the employee and the business—that being happy and productive at work starts with healthy, happy relationships at home.

Rob Goffee and Gareth Jones listed six recommendations in their *Harvard Business Review* article on how to create the 'best workplace on earth'.[3] These follow below, with some supplementation by us:

- *Let people be themselves*—famous American investor Warren Buffett said: 'I found in running businesses that the best results come from letting high-grade people work unencumbered'. Individuals bring differing perspectives and core assumptions that enrich the organisation. Tap each worker's knowledge and talents to increase the impact of their collective contribution. In essence, work to the adage that the whole is greater than the sum of the parts: 'None of us is as smart as all of us' (Ken Blanchard).
- *Unleash the flow of information*—allow management to receive clear, candid and timely information. This proposition argues that staff should be encouraged to tell the truth, whether 'good' or 'bad'. Such freedom keeps the manager in touch with what's really going on. Hypocrisy is readily spotted and is acidic.
- *Magnify peoples' strengths*—it's less about how much value to extract from workers and more about how much value to instil in them and how this might best be achieved. And, if you are a really adroit leader, you will operate to Lao Tzu's maxim: 'When the best leader's work is done the people will say, "We did it ourselves"'.
- *Stand for more than shareholder value*—people like to be part of something bigger than themselves, and work may advance that aspiration. If there is shared meaning rather than empty mission statements, the individual can feel proud to work for the organisation.
- *Show how the daily work makes sense*—people seek meaning from their daily activities and the workplace can help to provide it.
- *Make rules that people can believe in*—organisations need structure and rules, but the rules must be viewed by employees as both legitimate and necessary.

Goffee and Jones' list may be from a journal perused by those who sit at the apex of the corporate world, but such principles are relevant across all healthy and productive workplaces because they're about trust and inclusion. The emphasis is on culture, not physical environment, with attention to interpersonal factors as the main 'cultural' ingredient. As noted, any effort that a worker or a caregiver expends is a form of social exchange. There is an implicit 'contract' in each social exchange that carries the expectation of a reciprocal response such as recognition or gratitude.

Care versus control and enabling self-actualisation

Such interpersonal aspects are worth examining further. Research has long established that two dimensions underlie all principal inter-personal relationships (e.g. parent–child, husband–wife, teacher–pupil). The dimensions are care versus indifference, and control/overprotection versus encouragement of independence/autonomy. The model extends well to manager–employee relationships. Optimal management *cares* but does not *over-control*.

And we note another construct: actualisation. The term 'self-actualisation' was introduced to describe humans' capacity to achieve self-fulfilment (once lower-order needs like shelter have been met) by being free to 'actualise'—find, pursue and use their higher-order capabilities. This construct was prominent in California in the 1960s and it can sound a little pretentious, but it's a worthy aspirational target for managers. In essence, the manager should seek to identify qualities and strengths in employees unrecognised by themselves and advance each individual's 'actualisation'.

When it comes to bullying, great respect is commanded by that able leader who excels at 'spot-the-bully'. We are all aware of the stories of impressive figures who do a quiet circuit of the organisation and take its pulse. They instil civic values by example and seem to know the name of each employee. Of course, sometimes bullying and harassment echo a dog whistle from the top echelons, or a toxic environment may have grown in the shadow of a hostile takeover of the firm. Distortions aside, a healthy workplace depends on people in the management hierarchy recognising and dealing with such aggressors, be they managers or fellow workers.

Bullies won't interact in such ways with the boss, obviously, quite the opposite. To their seniors, bullies will appear dutiful and deferential, perhaps flattering and ingratiating. If you receive a complaint about them, they will have a reassuring answer and may perhaps co-opt you, so be aware of the possibility. Scanning for possible toxic 'hot spots' (e.g. multiple team members complaining or taking excessive sick leave) never goes astray, and if a worrying incident emerges it is wise to investigate that incident in detail. If confirmed, incisive action emphasises that such behaviour either from managers or those further down the hierarchy is unacceptable.

Supporting an employee who is burning out

The 'boiling frog' story is just a myth, but it's a helpful metaphor. It goes like this. If a frog is placed in boiling water, it will thrash around in distress until it dies. If, however, it is placed in water at a comfortable temperature, which is then gradually heated to boiling, the frog will show no distress right up to its death. The lesson? We tend to react minimally or not at all to threats that creep up on us (climate change tolls a bell here) and we only react distinctly to acute events.

So if burnout develops by increments in your employee, the individual may not be aware of the phenomenon for some time and will be unlikely to interpret their growing raft of symptoms as a 'wake-up call'. Likewise, a manager is unlikely to notice anything obvious at first.

When burnout's onset is more rapid and distinctive, an employee displays more distinct signs. They may appear exhausted much of the time, and to have lost their previous *joie de vivre*; they may become more irritable and short-tempered and keep to themselves in an uncharacteristic way (possibly turning down work-based social events). An employee thus affected, though initially feeling threatened, will quite often welcome a 'conversation' with a sympathetic manager. Not an 'RUOK?' enquiry, as this question can elicit a monosyllabic 'yes' (particularly by males), getting us nowhere. Instead, approaching downwind, it's possible to conduct a sympathetic conversation in a private area at a time when both people are unlikely to be interrupted. A clinical observation: it's important to have mapped out beforehand the likely directions and pathways that the conversation can take, and that you are sure of the outcome you want and the resources available. Be prepared for denial and defensiveness, and they will need reassurance about process: that this is a private conversation with their confidentiality respected.

If the employee does report symptoms of burnout, fortunately it's not for the manager to confirm or even pursue the possibility of such a diagnosis. A practical approach could instead canvass how the employee feels they might be best helped. They may report specific work stressors and, if so, the discussion can then centre around how such issues might best be addressed by you as their manager and/or by your organisation's Employee Assistance Program—if one such exists. They may seek time off—and meeting their request will be worthwhile, but be aware that they will nearly always underestimate the recovery period actually needed.

A conversation of this sort probably finishes best with a clear statement indicating that support is ongoing and that you would like to see them again—along the lines of: 'Can we meet in x weeks to review things?' or 'How should we move ahead to ensure that your needs are best met?' This sign-off carries two reassurances: it damps down the employee's rumination that their performance problems are putting their job at risk, and it is a meta-communication that you are concerned about them. Compassionate enquiry is not violating their boundary—it more suggests respect for the aphorism, 'When in doubt, be human'.

Notes

1 A. Huffington, *Thrive*, W.H. Allen, London, 2015, p. 34.
2 R. Kurapati, *Burnout in Healthcare: A guide to addressing the epidemic*, Sajjana Publishing, Middletown, DE, 2019.
3 R. Goffee & G. Jones, 'Creating the best workplace on earth', *Harvard Business Review*, May 2013, <https://hbr.org/2013/05/creating-the-best-workplace-on-earth>, accessed August 2020.

Chapter 16

For workers and caregivers

'You can't do a good job if your job is all you do'.

Anon

We now consider how workers themselves might *identify* and *manage* workplace nuances that have brought on their burnout symptoms. To begin with, we will focus on those whose demanding work is considered 'informal', that is, those whose main occupation is caring for others in a setting where there is no 'pay' and no oversight of working conditions. Some of these people (mostly women) have a 'formal' job as well, with these formal jobs the focus of the second part of this chapter.

The informal workplace: Managing burnout as a carer

'Taking care of yourself doesn't mean me first, it means me too'.

L.R. Knost

Identifying stressors

In the universe of informal work, your workplace is generally a home, *your* home, and you risk burnout in the face of the excessive physical and psychological demands placed on you as you are giving care to a family member/s. This may be a child with severe physical and/or intellectual limitations, or a parent with dementia, or both. Try to step back for a moment (you deserve a ten-minute break) and identify the drivers. Most should be readily identifiable. You work far beyond the formalised 40-hour work week, yes? Next, and this is more

DOI: 10.4324/9781003333722-20

complicated, identify how you might be furthering this pile-up. Perhaps you set no limits on your physical caring—reflecting love for the person you are caring for, there being an absence of choice, or even feelings of guilt. Identify which factors are in play, then consider how each could be neutralised, disempowered, reduced or taken out of the game.

Managing stressors

There are two priorities in the plan to safeguard your health: reduce your workload and ensure adequate 'time out'. Discussions with your partner or other family members may generate options. Social or community workers are generally the professionals best at providing focused advice and being aware of relevant support services. They may be attached to a hospital or your local community service. Your local council should have support services, both professionally provided and volunteer helpers, that can lighten some of your load. There will be a response from some exhausted carers that this is 'mission impossible' but consider the reason for that response. Is it that there's no money to pay for part-time help? Try to think 'sideways' then. An example: if you have a spare room, could you give a university student free board in return for their spending some hours a day assisting you or otherwise sharing the load? If that is not a strategy that appeals, consider why and don't believe everything you think! Is it because of guilt? If so, challenge its validity. For each doubt you have about reducing a particular call on your time, there *will* be an option.

The moral here is though you are totally, admirably and *dutifully* committed to caring for your family member/s, you *must* have time out for independent activities (some of which we discuss in the next chapter) or you will start to run on empty. And running on empty helps no one, including those you have the responsibility of caring for. As the air steward says, put on your own oxygen mask before helping others.

Need proof? Recall Petrea King's story in Chapter 11: as a carer for the sick and dying who worked around the clock, she eventually had to learn to put herself first if she was to continue to care for others. Author and motivational speaker Jim Rohn advises, 'Take care of your body. It's the only place you have to live'.

The formal workplace: Managing burnout as an employee

'It's not the load that breaks you down, it's the way you carry it'.

Anon

Identifying stressors

So what can you do if you are an employee faced with excessive workplace demands that are sparking burnout? Firstly, go to Appendix B and identify each of the triggers that apply to you. Rate the degree to which any such 'woeful workplace' factors operate (individually or compounded). Are they low, moderate or high?

The severity of our stressors is hard to judge objectively when we are under pressure. To assist, let's get you to step back and see how severely stressed this study participant is:

> The distraction of an open-plan office and the loss of such terri-
> tory that was mine that came with hot-desking made me feel like a
> 'human resource'... with not much emphasis on the 'human'.
> Additionally, we had techlash—the repeated failure of a new IT
> system. The pain (and cost!) of installation was exacerbated by the
> hype and poor delivery and tinkering needed to shackle it onto the
> organisation's systems. This culminated in a 'no can do' attitude
> that spread through my workplace.

This is likely a low-severity scenario. Yes, the employee felt dehumanised (and had developed a burnout syndrome) but the last sentence indicates that there was a 'we're all in this together' mentality (albeit passive aggressive in part) rather than this individual feeling separated out from the work tribe. It's also a situation that is readily addressed if management and staff work on correction strategies.

Low-level factors generally reflect working conditions. These include excessive workload levels, time pressures, lengthy work hours, a lack of autonomy for the worker and minimal rewards.

Now what is your judgement of this personal story?

> Primarily, the nature of my work is 'burst' work with a residual
> level of anxiety/adrenalin. Anything could, and does, go wrong at

any moment with huge consequences to my team and the business for every moment a fault is in progress. Lately, unreasonably high workload levels have been placed on my shifts, leaving me physically and mentally exhausted during and after shifts. Couple this with company decisions to further reduce staff numbers (cutting costs) while the remaining staff are being expected to react quicker, more accurately and to absorb more of other people's work than ever before. Additionally, this extra burden is compounded by the awareness that no one else in my family is bringing in an income, so I can't back down from the work responsibilities to recover.

Our call here is that this participant describes a moderately severe scenario. The work stress *is* high. The risk of error is ever present and error is perceived as a 'calamity'. Add in the major financial stressors faced by this woman—she is the sole breadwinner. Some factors appear correctable, others, less likely. The work pressures are high but (as in the previous example) not personalised. The worker may have no option other than to hang on to this job and employ some of the de-stressing strategies that we cover in Chapters 17 and 19.

High-level stress scenarios are ones where workplace stressors are distinctly severe but where, in addition, the worker feels that they have been selected out for special attention, harassment and/or bullying. When this focus is at a 'toxic' level, the individual will feel punished or persecuted—victimised—and may adopt a victim stance or mindset. The employer, manager or even fellow workers then generally respond with greater harshness and bullying. This can take the form of 'gaslighting' the employee, where they come to feel full of self-doubt—including doubting their own sanity in the face of such an unpleasant 'reality'. If the worker seeks support from others (including human resources), the oppressor/s may become even more antagonistic and persecutory. The worker may then be so nullified as to decide to suffer in silence. This is one of the least helpful of possible responses.

Such toxic scenarios can play out in a stable organisation but are more common and generally more vicious when an organisation is restructuring or downsizing. The first author remembers a patient whose employer was ordered to reduce the workforce by half. The patient's work performance provided no clear argument for his termination, but the supervisor clearly detected his shyness and pounced on that perceived vulnerability. For six weeks the employee had his supervisor sit behind him and yell every time he made a spelling or grammatical typing mistake when preparing emails, while progressively and prominently compiling a list of the employee's mistakes for 'formal processing'. The patient's burnout symptoms started shortly after this victimisation and only started to settle after he was 'cut' from his job of ten years' standing.

Managing stressors

Let's assume that there are environmental workplace factors such as excessive or inappropriate workplace demands in relation to your skill set (selected from Appendix B) and that you have a supportive manager. The strategy here is straightforward. There may be advantages in first discussing the issues with trusted work colleagues, particularly if they have handled similar problems and can offer informed guidance. Your primary course of action, however, is to initiate a discussion with your manager. Hopefully he or she can wave a corrective wand over the evils (e.g. arranging a change in work role, more flexible hours or a reduction in work overload). The same strategies hold even if the primary stressor is outside of work:

> My employer was amazing. When I told my CEO that my partner was ill and there were immediate things I had to deal with, the response was, 'What can we do here at work to support you through this?' This blew me away. It was understood that I would need time from work to care for my partner, and this was dealt with in a most constructive way. It was all about my employer being part of a solution to help me do what I needed to do. I worked together with her in coming up with a temporary work plan that made sure I could care for my partner and look after myself. She helped me to reach a balance of maintaining some connection with work whilst still enabling the flexibility I needed to get through this stressful period. I thought that this approach was so insightful, and it helped me greatly—definitely a hallelujah moment. This is what it should be like: out in the open, constructive, supportive and respectful.

Yes indeed. If, however, the issues are less straightforward and there is a risk that your concerns might be misconstrued as 'slacking' or just general bellyaching, it's worth preparing. Before approaching your line manager, think ahead and map out the outcomes that you seek. Is it clarification of your roles and responsibilities, more training or support for your work overload, fewer hours, flexible working arrangements, more regular work meetings, a different reporting line, or all of these? You would be wise to take details of your position description, your recent duties and emails or whatever refers to the current stressors to the meeting. Be prepared to offer solutions and be willing to negotiate. Put the issues to the manager in black and white, staying specific and factual rather than going *off-piste* in the discussion and consequently feeling angry if things go belly up. Record the meeting afterwards, not during the interaction, as such notes will be invaluable to refer back to at a later stage if needed—a devious employer could deny any knowledge of the encounter and the next agreed steps. An email trail is worth considering, as long as you stick to the facts.

If your work hours and commitments are exhausting then time out will be restorative. If you have severe burnout, however, time out may only allow your symptoms to improve temporarily. Symptoms will redouble on return to work if the stress drivers have not been addressed and, predictably, intensified in your absence, or if you have not implemented any de-stressing strategies (considered in Chapters 17 and 19). Further, those with burnout—whether they take time out or not—need a 'turning point'. Burnout is a wake-up call. Things need to change and change actions must be initiated.

Now let's consider how to address some of the more nebulous work stressors that can precipitate burnout. The list would include absence of rewards or recognition, concerns about company values, and threats coming over the horizon, such as downsizing. If shared by co-workers, such issues are best tackled at staff meetings—subject to management being attentive or at least prepared to listen—or by you and your colleagues speaking to management. If your disquiets are not shared, you could request a meeting with your line manager. You may detail such environmental factors as issues you would like to raise for subsequent attention rather than expecting any immediate resolution. Indeed, your manager may also be hamstrung by seniors and need time to reflect on solutions. Your objectives in a meeting of this sort are to try to determine whether such problems are potentially correctable, who might have the authority to address them and whether your manager is likely or not to assist. You could then finish the meeting by thanking them for their time and asking when the next meeting will be scheduled to advance progress. Softly, softly.

Now let's take it up a notch. What should you do if your burnout is driven by factors that are unlikely to be redressed by the manager, for instance, if he/she has a personal style of being non-responsive or acts on behalf of a harsh management board? Then you may need to obtain external advice from your union or other relevant adviser prior to the meeting. At the meeting it is best to express your concerns objectively—that certain environmental factors require addressing. Refrain from declaring that such factors are making *you* overly stressed as the manager may view the situation as due to *your* limitations and therefore not requiring redress, or worse, start or continue to harass you. If your manager is non-responsive or antagonistic, it's not a good idea to throw petrol on the flames by threatening or even heralding your next steps. Consider the way forward after the meeting and when you have had time to cool off and obtain further advice. This might include calling on your Employee Assistance Program (EAP), involving the HR department or some other equivalent support service.

Burnout is now recognised as an occupational disease in at least nine European countries, and compensation for a burnout syndrome has been awarded in Denmark, France, Latvia, Portugal and Sweden.[1] Occupational health and safety standards governing work-related burnout are at different stages of development, but are mostly confined to Europe and the UK. More widely recognised is the accepted duty for workplaces to protect employees from workplace hazards, and burnout is clearly a potential hazard.

If your firm provides independent EAP assistance (and thus ensures confidentiality) then their counsel could have considerable merit—their collective wisdom, the capacity to individualise the advice they give to you and their 'neutrality'. If, however, the EAP is run by your company then keep in mind that they (as for the HR department) may exercise unconscious bias and, in a dispute, could tend to favour the employer.

And now let's crank it up a further notch. Imagine you have a manager who is coercive, controlling and a latent bully—and who has

contributed to your work-induced burnout symptoms. (Ironically, he/
she probably has a framed wall hanging proclaiming *People are our
most important asset.*) You are sure that he/she will not respond
proactively and is more likely to victimise you. What are your options
here? These are some common responses we suggest should be
avoided.

Option 1: *Passive coping.* As described by a study participant, 'I
avoid conflict and office politics. I learned from the Cheshire Cat in
Alice in Wonderland:... I imperceptibly absent myself, fade out, leaving
only my smile behind'. Passive coping is not a good option, because
being marginalised, not 'heard' or otherwise ignored frustrates and
disempowers us. As humans, we seek and need to solve problems.
Reflect on the maxim attributed to Lao Tzu: 'If you do not change
direction, you may end up where you are heading'.

Option 2: *Thinking, no action.* This runs along these tracks: 'I'll wait
it out: things will get better when my luck changes'; 'I don't have a
problem: they're to blame'; 'I can run my own life'; 'I favour stoic
acceptance'. Again, a passive coping strategy and not a good option
when action is needed.

Option 3: *Action and potential overreaction.* Here we note the
recommendations made by one of our study participants: 'I read up on
some steps to take to regain my sanity while I considered the situation.
I got things clear in my head, wrote down the perpetrator's patterns
and he and his toadies' actions. That shored me up a bit and I started
believing in myself again. I checked my impressions against the observations of a friend at work (being careful not to drag them into it).
Then I started a written record of situations as they happened. It was
obsessive but sort of enjoyable. There was one particularly blatant
undermining of my work in front of some sympathetic workmates.
Bingo! I later told the bully that I was accumulating a pile of info with
a view to taking action about both overt and covert bullying by him and
his cronies. I didn't fall into the trap of arguing "chapter and verse" with
him, just stalked out in what I hoped was a dignified fashion!'

Here, action was taken. Our study participant was assertive, signalling that she cannot be readily walked over. Good! But the problem in
declaring that anti-bullying action would be taken is that she is now a
self-declared target. Perhaps the manager smiles as the worker leaves
the room, rings his friend in the HR department and warns them that

one of his 'high-maintenance whiners' is creating all sorts of problems in the office and he'd appreciate it if she could be hung out to dry. Manager puts phone down firmly and contemplates a range of subtle revenge strategies. The game may play out over weeks or months but, despite the hurt and unfairness of the process, the employee leaves, ideally finding another job with a decent work environment where her burnout symptoms slowly improve.

And finally, let's go up yet another notch. You know your burnout syndrome is totally due to a toxic work culture as when on holiday you find that most symptoms ease. You take sick leave and are pleased that your symptoms settle, but you like your job and/or you feel ambivalent about leaving, and so you return to work. All the symptoms then come flooding back. At this stage, your superiors may also have amped up the bullying blowtorch (possibly in response to you taking leave in the first place), perhaps by increasing your workload, being quite unresponsive to any of your needs and/or commencing to victimise you to force your resignation. But you are determined to stay and obtain justice.

Next round: the pressure increases and you need time off again—on sick leave. Your employer then demands a letter or report from your managing doctor as to the nature of the sick leave and is probably informed that you are 'stressed' or that you have 'work-induced stress'. You have contacted your work's EAP and HR departments, but each is non-committal and unhelpful. You are both burnt out and angry that management is clearly out to get you. You could retire but you don't want the bastards to win. Game on and, sometimes literally, to the death.

You are now operating to Ginsberg's theorem:

1   You can't win.
2   You can't break even.
3   You can't quit the game.

So, in response, you take longer leave. Your employers (or your income protection company) will then seek regular reports from your managing health professionals, looking for avenues for your exploitation or dismissal.

For example, they may seek a fitness for duty report (FDR) or equivalent document. In this game-play the adroitly drawn up FDR will lay out your duties and then management will ask your health practitioner if you are fit and competent to perform such duties. Your health professional knows you are capable of these duties, but not in the current environment. And here's the rub: if the professional answers 'yes', the employers will demand a return to work; if the professional answers 'no', management may seek to retire you on the grounds that you are not 'fit and competent'. Here the health professional simply needs to state that you are intrinsically completely fit (that is, you have no inherent limitations) on condition that the work stressors (perhaps throwing in 'toxic' for extra grunt) are redressed.

If you are judged as 'not fit' by the assessing health professional, the FDR is also likely to ask (i) whether there should be any restrictions attached to your duties, and (ii) when you will be 'fit' to return on a full-time basis. Here the health professional should argue that there is no need for any work restrictions but that return to full-time work is still dependent on the employer correcting the workplace factors (use 'toxic' again as it is a useful adjective as long as the evidence is clear). The FDR may also seek information on any medication being taken by you that could impact on your work capacity. This is a minor trap. A 'yes' to medication could be seized on by the employer. Or, a variant, the FDR may ask if any medication is being taken at all, and if so, for details to be provided. If you *are* taking medication, the employer may then claim that the possible side-effects of such medication compromise your 'fitness' to work. And, if you are a member of a profession such as law or medicine, then the FDR may seemingly caringly ask if your professional licensing body should be notified. Again, your health practitioner should protect you by indicating that any impairment is not intrinsic to you and what you bring to your job but is a reflection of the workplace environment.

In this Ginsberg game, however, you are not likely to recover or win. No psychological stress-reduction strategies will have much or any benefit for you while you remain in this setting. Your gloom and anger towards the perpetrators will further drain you and perpetuate the burnout. If you take legal action (for instance, initiate a workers' compensation claim) there will be a lengthy and enervating process, lasting at least many months and often years. All confidential files held by your health practitioners will be subpoenaed. Lawyers for your employing organisation will search through the records for any undeclared pre-existing condition that can be used to absolve their responsibility or culpability. Even if you win it risks being a Pyrrhic victory and, on return to work, you are highly likely to be marginalised or victimised and put in the 'naughty corner' without anything to do.

On the other hand, if you resign and use your income protection insurance (if you were lucky enough to have taken out such a policy), the insurance company will pursue you and your health professionals on a regular basis, draining your remaining spirits (and by this point, you may indeed be draining spirits yourself). Worse, if you were to take up a disability pension there would be the meta-communication (to you and to the world) that you are not only 'disabled' but permanently so. You would then be not just jobless, but your personal identity would be compromised. So there are times when it's best to 'let the bastards win' (on a technicality) and for you to get out of the game smarting but smartly, snatching at least some victory from the jaws of defeat. In other words, resigning may be the best option, but do so deftly of your own accord and set sights on a new job, rather than signalling to those around you that you are permanently down for the count.

To tell or not to tell?

So after considering the scenarios presented in the last few paragraphs, should you declare to an employer or manager that you are starting to (or have) burnout? It depends, of course.

Scenario A: Imagine that you are a brilliant creative advertising guru and that your employing company has been enriched by your high-quality work. Here you should inform your company openly and directly. They will almost certainly immediately offer you considerable time off to recuperate. Why? You value-add to the company at a very high level, and your loss would be their loss.

Scenario B: You are a junior doctor who has developed distinct burnout symptoms due to months of excessive hours on duty. In this case, declaring is generally the best action, and it is best to notify medical administration. Their staff will be well aware of the high rate of burnout in junior doctors and that a near-dead resident or registrar risks higher error rates and compromised patient safety, care and satisfaction. This option is generally better than telling your current rotation consultant as this steely immortal may hold an 'in my day we worked 100 hours a week and thought nothing of it' mentality.

Scenario C: Your organisation is downsizing and your manager is putting increasing pressure on staff to determine who will seek redundancy or simply resign. You may well seek sick leave but do not state on any such application form that you have burnout as this is likely to identify you to management as warranting further pressure.

In essence, your decision about declaring burnout can be judged by the following rule of thumb. Put on 'employer spectacles' and you will see that organisations work to a cost–benefit model. The employers of the visionary advertising genius need their man in good shape, ready to run back on the field and score even more goals for the team. By disclosing his burnout, adman has alerted his manager to the fact that he needs to recharge or he will no longer be able to produce his golden eggs. Management will be supportive and generous ('Take as much time off as you need'). The employer of the junior doctor will also be supportive—an impaired doctor is a safety risk, replacing interns is a pain and expensive and the junior doctor will probably not need much time off or much tweaking of duties to make it a win–win situation. However, the manager of the downsizing firm will likely judge that the employee reporting burnout is an easy weak link to target, and might veer as soon as possible to that age-old responsibility absolver, 'Sorry, but we're going to have to let you go'.

So assume the manager/employer's viewpoint and adopt a cost–benefit analysis. What are you worth to them? To tell or not to tell then becomes an equation that is easier to solve.

These are your workplace options

Firstly, **reduce the pressure trigger points**. For those who give care to family members that places excessive demands on you then 'time out' and 'share the load' strategies are fundamental. Identify the pinch points that are potentially correctible, list solutions, then pick the best options and apply them rapidly, as extended decision-making fuels burnout and hesitation may actually lead to choosing the less successful option. In formal employment positions with a co-operative manager or employer, dialling down pressure trigger points is often readily achieved.

Secondly, if such strategies (and trialling de-stressing strategies overviewed in Chapter 17) do not work—and particularly if your workplace is toxic—then consider whether you need to **change your workplace**. This strategy worked for Dr Jayson Greenberg, as described earlier, and only by so doing was he able to achieve 'wellness'. If you have held your position for some time, if you feel guilty about leaving, if you are perfectionistic, if you view the work scenario in 'win/lose' terms, or if you are angry about the way you have been impacted by toxic environmental factors, you may wish to stay in the ring and 'win'. But winning against the forces of darkness is rare and always comes at a price. As Finnish writer Erno Paasilinna wrote: 'It is also a victory to know when to retreat'. In so retreating you also have the opportunity to retreat into yourself where you are more likely to find a stillness and sanctuary that is itself therapeutic.

While in this chapter we have focused on coping strategies for handling the physical work domain, in Chapters 17 and 19 we focus on personal stress-reducing strategies. For most people experiencing burnout, both domains need to be addressed and corrective strategies actioned.

Note

1 A. Lastovkova, M. Carder, H.M. Rasmussen et al., 'Burnout syndrome as an occupational disease in the European Union: An exploratory study', *Industrial Health*, 2018, vol. 56, no. 2, pp. 160–5, doi: 10.2486/indhealth.2017–0132.

Chapter 17

De-stressing

'It's not always the first key in the bunch that opens the lock'.

Anon

In the two previous chapters the focus was on lessening or eradicating work stressors. We acknowledge, however, that work factors cannot always be readily corrected (e.g. when you are so financially dependent on a job that leaving the position would increase rather than decrease stress). Where the causes of burnout cannot be escaped, it is useful for burnout sufferers to have strategies up their sleeve to help ease the stressful impact of such triggers. So here and in Chapter 19 we focus on one priority issue: how to de-stress when you are experiencing burnout.

For most medical and psychological conditions, treatment recommendations are supported by scientific evidence. Practitioners like to state that they provide 'evidence-based' treatment—the term has cachet and is reassuring. So this chapter will overview the evidence base for candidate de-stressing strategies: are the proofs of their efficacy solid, only presumed or distinctly 'flaky'?

Before doing so, we need to consider what counts as 'evidence'. Scientific evidence in relation to treatment and control of any condition is predictably graded. We first overview and illustrate the commonly accepted levels of scientific evidence (from low to high) used when an intervention is evaluated. Then we report how current burnout resolution strategies rank.

Observational studies

Grade of evidence: very low

DOI: 10.4324/9781003333722-21

Here the 'evidence' may simply be someone's observation and/or hypothesis about a particular treatment. The observation may or may not be valid. Was bloodletting with leeches a valid treatment? After all, it started 3000 years ago in Egypt, spread around the world and was used to treat many conditions. No, not valid, but it was only discredited in the late nineteenth century (though interestingly, lab-bred leeches are still used to finesse some surgical and medical procedures). How could such a treatment last so long as a mainstream strategy? Well, presumably some people who had the treatment recovered from their condition. This recovery occurred either naturally, by spontaneous remission or via a placebo effect. However, therapists and patients of the time employed flawed reasoning around this outcome, known as the *post hoc ergo propter hoc* fallacy. In essence, this is Latin for 'it has been conclusively proved that the beating of tom-toms restores the sun after an eclipse'. Just kidding. It really means that correlation is not the same as causation. We humans tend to judge that when two events occur together, one must have caused the other. Thus, the co-occurrence of bloodletting and recovery would have led the patients and practitioners to view bloodletting as an effective treatment.

Qualitative studies

Grade of evidence: low

The next level of scientific evidence involves observations again, but here they are actually evaluated—though non-numerically—to determine their validity. Consider the huge difference in the rate of handwashing pre- versus post-COVID-19 and how that process came to achieve its high take-up. We owe a lot to Ignaz Semmelweis, the mid-nineteenth century Hungarian doctor who wondered why so many women were dying from puerperal fever in his hospital's obstetric wards. His initial hypothesis was based on his observation that when a woman died, a priest would walk through the ward with his assistant ringing a bell, and that this event terrified the women and caused more to die (an excellent example of *post hoc ergo propter hoc*). So the priest's routine was changed and the bell excluded—but there was no change in mortality rates. His next hypothesis was also based on observation. The doctors and the medical students were not only delivering babies but also undertaking autopsies on cadavers. Semmelweis conjectured that they might be picking up infective material from the dead bodies (although the existence of 'germs' was not known in those days). In consequence, he arranged for the doctors and medical students to clean their hands and instruments with chlorine—and the death rate from childbirth fever dropped dramatically. Simple qualitative and observational 'evidence', but of the highest order in terms of benefit. Since then, soap and water have gone hand in hand.

Quantitative studies

Grade of evidence: moderate

A higher level of evidence comes from quantitative studies where numerical data are analysed. A useful example is the story of scurvy, a horrible disease that killed 50% of sailors on long trips and was mismanaged with the generic and favoured treatments of the day (e.g. bloodletting) or idiosyncratic treatments dreamed up by various whackos (e.g. an 'elixir' of diluted sulphuric acid, or turf applied to the mouth to counter bad air). These were, predictably, ineffective. Then in the mid-eighteenth century, James Lind, a pioneer in naval medicine, conducted an experiment on 12 sailors suffering from the disease. He divided the group into pairs and trialled six different treatments (cider, salt water, the 'elixir', a paste of herbs and spices, vinegar, and two oranges and a lemon daily). The two that received the citrus fruits (rich in vitamin C) recovered by the end of that week. However, his remedy took nearly 50 years to be formally adopted by the Royal Navy (and vitamin C was not formally identified as the therapeutic agent until 1928). So Lind discovered a valid and effective treatment by quantifying the respective effectiveness of differing interventions, though the underlying biological mechanisms remained unknown for nearly two centuries.

Randomised controlled trials

Grade of evidence: high

The next level of scientific evidence comes from randomised controlled trials (RCTs). Here, a hypothesised treatment for a specific condition is compared against a placebo (an inert drug) to determine if the treatment is effective, or compared against another established (or standard) treatment to determine if the test treatment is superior. Although informative, any one RCT showing the superiority of a particular treatment is not enough to be conclusive proof, and so it is common for several RCTs to be undertaken to determine the benefits of a particular treatment.

Meta-analyses

Grade of evidence: highest

The next level of evidence emerges from meta-analytic studies, which (recognising that individual studies may achieve a positive finding simply by chance or chicanery) involve aggregating and analysing all the available and relevant individual RCT data sets for a particular treatment. Such a 'study of studies' can determine if, overall, a treatment is effective, and/or quantify the comparative effectiveness of differing treatments.

And studies of treatments for burnout?

So in relation to burnout, how sophisticated is the evidence base? Basically, most of the treatment data are anecdotal and qualitative and there are very few acceptable RCTs. As a result, meta-analyses are rare, and those undertaken fail to provide a clear 'evidence base' for treatments and interventions in this area.

Kirsi Ahola and colleagues reported a meta-analytic study in 2017.[1] Their search of all studies of interventions for alleviating burnout identified 4430 potential studies but, of those, only 14 (not even 1% of the studies identified) met basic scientific study criteria, with those 14 studies examining the impact of 18 treatments. A meta-analysis was undertaken on just four studies, which examined a range of interventions. The most common intervention was cognitive behaviour therapy or CBT, a 'talking' treatment designed to change individuals' unhelpful ways of thinking and/or behaving that is commonly used to treat other psychological conditions such as anxiety. The course of CBT was generally provided with variable add-on treatment components. The comparison group comprised untreated subjects with burnout. Ultimately, Ahola's meta-analysis failed to find significant differences across the two groups and the authors concluded that 'it is impossible to draw guidelines regarding how to treat burnout'. This negative finding could well have reflected CBT being targeted at burnout symptoms rather than at any predisposing personality style. In Chapter 18 we suggest that CBT may make a key contribution to addressing the latter.

Such findings are, at first pass, dispiriting, but this is not unusual. Negative meta-analytic findings are not confined to burnout territory. Numerous standard surgical procedures that are widely 'accepted' in the medical profession as effective treatments have also failed to show superiority over 'sham' interventions in meta-analyses. Similarly, several meta-analyses have reported that antidepressant drugs are not superior to placebos (a somewhat concerning finding considering the commonplace prescription of antidepressants in western countries and their judged benefits by so many patients). There are many reasons for such disconnects between the RCT meta-analytic findings and 'real-world' observed effectiveness of an intervention, but we won't pursue those here (other than note the CBT nuance) and will instead consider why a scientific evidence base is lacking in relation to burnout.

Why scientific treatment studies do not inform us how to deal with burnout

Meta-analyses and RCTs work best when the condition under investigation is clearly defined and, ideally, categorical (like a heart attack— you either have one or you don't) rather than dimensional (like 'stress', which ranges in severity), as well as when the treatment under evaluation is provided in a standardised way. Herein lies burnout's problems, specifically:

1   Burnout is variably defined (and study participants may actually have had primary depression, exhaustion, anxiety or even physical states instead, a problem put under the microscope in Part 1 of this book).
2   Burnout as it is currently defined ranges in severity and is therefore dimensional rather than categorical. The underlying biological changes in burnout are likely to vary with differing levels of severity and the degree to which certain symptoms (such as cognitive changes or loss of empathy) are dominant or not. Thus, any

one treatment may only be effective (if effective at all) at only a certain level of severity or only for certain symptoms.

3   Treatments are often evaluated without consideration of their 'target'. For some sufferers, improvement is dependent on neutralising or weakening the 'driver' (e.g. addressing workplace stressors). For others, improvement will only occur if the focus is on reducing stress symptoms, while for others, modulating personality may be the key priority. If, say, a focus on the third factor is central to improvement but only the second is prioritised, then accurate judgement of treatment effectiveness is compromised.

4   Most burnout sufferers will benefit from a pluralistic treatment plan (i.e. addressing all three target domains as per the previous point). Pluralistic models are very rarely evaluated in the scientific studies as designing such studies is necessarily complex.

5   The *post hoc ergo propter hoc* fallacy may operate.

One size does not fit all

Our key position is this: *When dealing with burnout, differing solutions will have differing benefits for differing people in differing circumstances.*

The existence of three differing contributing factors (as considered earlier) argues against any 'one size fits all' treatment that is just waiting to be identified. Instead, a pluralistic and customised approach is invariably required to resolve burnout, and this is one of the main messages of this book. As the personal accounts show, no individual claimed that a single strategy solved their problems. Many tried mixes of de-stressing strategies, often having to trial an array of regimens before finding the ones that matched their needs. Others needed to change their career—and others their life course.

In light of the lack of formal scientific evidence identifying the benefits of differing interventions, let's examine the observations of the many participants who contributed to our two burnout studies.

Study 1 findings

Our first study involved 1019 participants with burnout. We asked them, if they wished, to nominate strategies that they had found helpful to bring their debilitating symptoms under control. In Table 17.1

Table 17.1 Most common strategies employed by study participants in managing their burnout

Strategy	Percentage nominating
Reaching out for support	23.7%
Exercising	14.3%
Taking a brief or lengthy break from work	13.0%
Meditating	9.8%
Improving sleep or rest	9.6%
Practising mindfulness	6.5%
Reducing hours or working less	5.6%
Going for walks	5.2%
Participating in new activities outside of work	5.2%
Taking medication	4.3%

we list the most common strategies reported (and percentages nominating each).

Study 2 findings

In our second study we sought firmer data about the best strategies for resolving burnout by providing a list of representative strategies. We asked the 622 participants to tick those that they had trialled and, of those trialled, the degree to which each was judged as effective. The returned data are shown in Table 17.2 along with the ranked 'helpfulness' ratings.

Considering participants' reports from both studies, the most useful strategies appear to have been:

- talking to someone and seeking support (from a family member, friend or health professional)
- walking or other exercise
- mindfulness and meditation
- improving sleep
- leaving work completely or taking time off work.

Unexpected findings

There were some unexpected findings from the second study. One-third of the participants (207 people) had trialled an antidepressant drug

Table 17.2 Strategies employed by study participants in managing burnout and their judged helpfulness

Strategy	Percentage who attempted each strategy	Percentage who found the strategy helpful
Increasing exercise (other than walking)	44%	82%
Going for walks	60%	81%
Quitting my job	24%	79%
Consulting a mental health professional	54%	78%
Taking some time off work	44%	77%
Talking to a family member or friend	59%	75%
Meditating	35%	73%
Taking an antidepressant medication	36%	72%
Going on a relaxing holiday	21%	71%
Talking to a colleague	40%	71%
Taking up new hobbies/activities	28%	69%
Improving sleep and/or resting more	47%	69%
Consulting a general practitioner	50%	69%
Practising mindfulness	46%	67%
Taking medication other than an antidepressant	15%	62%
Going on an action-packed holiday	8%	55%
Talking to my boss/manager	26%	46%
Using a web-based self-help tool	25%	45%
Using drugs or alcohol to cope	34%	37%
Talking to human resources at work	9%	30%

and, of that group, more than two-thirds had found it helpful. Now, while there have been hundreds of controlled trials of antidepressant drugs for depression and anxiety, we are unaware of any significant trials involving those with a burnout syndrome. If antidepressant medications *are* beneficial, we would wager that the pharmaceutical companies would be testing, advertising and promoting them widely for this syndrome, particularly when burnout provides a large 'market'. But such promotion has not occurred, and our clinical observation suggests that very few people with a true burnout syndrome find antidepressants beneficial.

So why did antidepressants receive such support in our study? Could it have been that many of our participants actually had a primary depressive condition? To test this possibility, we compared those with and those without depressive symptoms (the two groups were similar in number) and found that equal percentages in each group reported antidepressants as helpful. So probably throw out that explanation. Second possibility: certain antidepressants, especially the selective serotonin reuptake inhibitors (SSRIs), are effective as much for their anti-worrying properties as they are for lifting depression (and are therefore often prescribed to those with anxiety disorders). So, those who worry and ruminate excessively during their burnout state might receive de-stressor benefits from an appropriate antidepressant. In such instances, while it may not solve the problems causing the burnout, it can reduce the intensity of any associated psychological distress. This accords with reports of many people who take an SSRI for anxiety or depression and state that their problems are still there, but that they feel that they're swimming with them now rather than sinking. And thirdly, antidepressants can improve sleep and may have been beneficial to our exhausted burnout sample for this reason.

Note two strategies that didn't rate highly for resolving burnout. Discussions with employers or human resources staff received a 'low helpfulness' rating (a somewhat surprising finding, but recall our 'to tell or not to tell' quandary in Chapter 16 as a potential explanation for this), as did coping by increasing drug and alcohol intake (not so surprising).

We judge that our participants inform us more than anything we can identify in the scientific literature about the most helpful strategies to resolve burnout and 'de-stressing' in general. Scientific findings are desultory, and there is no 'evidence-based' best treatment. Causes of burnout (and therefore targets for treatment) include many and differing work stressors and, commonly, a personality contribution.

Implications

There is no 'one size fits all' panacea. De-stressing strategies need to address the specifics of the stressor and, more broadly, 'chime' with an individual's preferences, pace, patience and personality.

Participants' most favoured approaches were to: seek help and support; increase exercise, meditation and mindfulness; and take time off work (briefly or completely). Some changed jobs and some left the workforce altogether.

In Chapter 19 we detail the specifics of some de-stressing strategies highlighted here (especially exercise, mindfulness and meditation) and consider how they can assist in enhancing overall wellbeing.

Note

1 K. Ahola, S. Toppinen-Tanner & J. Seppänen, 'Interventions to alleviate burnout symptoms and to support return to work among employees with burnout: Systematic review and meta-analysis', *Burnout Research*, 2017, vol. 4, pp. 1–11.

Chapter 18

Managing perfectionism

'Good enough is good enough'.

Therapist Directive

In the previous few chapters the focus was on lessening or eradicating external work stressors contributing to burnout and employing de-stressing and wellbeing strategies. However, as detailed in Chapters 12 and 13, burnout is not only caused by external 'seed' precipitating factors but also contributed to by internal 'soil' factors that predispose someone to burnout. Predisposing or *diathesis* factors that are especially influential are certain personality styles, most notably perfectionism.

As noted in Chapter 13, there is, of course, 'healthy perfectionism', most clearly demonstrated in those who are dutiful, conscientious, persevering and achievement-focused. Such traits serve people well. They keep a step ahead of others in a competitive world, and they (and their employers) can appreciate jobs well done. But perfectionism lies along a spectrum where, perhaps combined with being excessively dutiful, the individual is simply too meticulous, and we have previously detailed its more distinctive and severe manifestations.

Our research has shown that perfectionism is a (probably 'the') key predisposing risk factor to developing burnout. If you have burnout and are perfectionistic, you need to consider how to tweak and modulate that personality driver. As the degree of perfectionism influences the level of risk to burnout (and compromises its ultimate resolution), we focus more on perfectionism at the extreme end of the spectrum and note some strategies for your consideration.

DOI: 10.4324/9781003333722-22

Fourteen building blocks in the perfectionist's castle

Allan Mallinger and Jeannette DeWyze offer those with perfectionistic tendencies some suggestions for making changes.[1] These are summarised here and occasionally augmented with the views of others and our own counsel:

1 Don't accept the perfectionist's credo, that little voice in your head that tells you if you make a mistake or display a fault, you'll drop off the social register. In fact, being right all the time is more off-putting, so admit to mistakes or flaws. As Richard Winter puts it, have the courage to fail.[2] Or, from Robert Schuller, 'Better to do something imperfectly than to do nothing flawlessly'.

2 Confront your inner 'saboteurs'. Expose yourself to situations you fear. Challenge that all must be perfect. Just do as well as possible *within the given time*. Make 'good enough is good enough' your mantra.

3 Focus on *completing* tasks rather than ensuring they will be perfect before you even start them. As put by Jennifer Ritchie Payette: 'If you want things to be perfect, you walk away with nothing. Just jump in and get started'. Mallinger and DeWyze suggest to 'aim for average'; average means your output will increase and its quality is unlikely to suffer, while cluttering details will fall away and leave a clearer outline. They also advise tackling a project in brief, structured periods where time is better under control. However, Winter acknowledges that aiming for average is a 'nightmare for most perfectionists'.[3] He instead suggests identifying specific goals, for example being less concerned about the right outfit each day, and then setting practical strategies to achieve them, for instance, limiting the time spent on getting ready in the morning.

4 Streamline your life and de-clutter: get rid of excess belongings. Even in conversation, check a tendency to provide too much information.

5 Block any leaning towards fault finding—both in yourself and others—by distraction strategies.

6 Overcome indecisiveness. As Winston Churchill is said to have observed, 'The maxim "Nothing but perfection" can be spelled "Paralysis"'. Be aware of the tendency to oscillate between binary

choices for fear of making the wrong choice. Doing so creates that 'stable/unstable' situation we spoke about in Chapter 13— 'unstable' in that choices go backwards and forwards, but 'stable' in that there is no forward progress. Avoiding commitment maintains the status quo. Instead, look for the third, fourth and fifth choices that will most likely be at your disposal. In other words, avoid black-or-white thinking and consider (fifty) shades of grey.

7 Adopt a less fatalistic and a more common-sense approach to making decisions. For example, buying a car: if you need a car but can't get on with it because it might be a lemon or because there might be a better deal on the horizon, you may get bogged down and remain carless. Instead, identify the thought or 'schema' and apply logical reasoning to 'unstick' yourself. For example, even if the car you buy turns out to be a poor choice, you're not stuck with it forever. Would keeping it for a while really be so awful if it still gets you from A to B? Resist viewing all commitments as permanent and irrevocable.

8 Prioritise action and combat vacillation. Resolve to allow a reasonable period for decision-making and resist the idea that there is only one correct option. As Mallinger and DeWyze note, 'Accept that you *can* live with something less than perfection'. Once the decision's made, refuse to question the choice or judge yourself.

9 Turn 'I should' into 'I want', and 'I can't' into 'I don't want to', so that all activities can be considered as 'wants' rather than 'moral obligations'. Emphasise needs, de-emphasise duty, and in doing so build a stronger internal identity.

10 Identify situations where you resist or don't meet a 'demand' (e.g. not completing an essay assignment for a university class on time). Identify your reluctance and its triggers, then prioritise your desired end result (e.g. passing the class to get your degree) and bypass resistance or rebellion.

11 Become less guarded, recognising that not everything in life is or can be guaranteed. Graduate your steps along this dimension slowly and progressively.

12 Focus on the 'big picture' and try to damp down chronic worry over details. Ditch ruminations about past events, doubts and self-recriminations. 'Don't sweat the small stuff'. If you absolutely must worry then engage in 'scheduled worry time', a cognitive behaviour

therapy (CBT) technique (more on that later) where a limited amount of time per day (around 20 minutes) is set aside to work through the things that you may be worried about. Worry time is scheduled not only to prevent rumination on worrying thoughts across the entire day but also so that you can become more mindful (we consider the benefits of being mindful in Chapter 19) of what you are prone to worry about and why. In addition, 'thought-stopping' techniques can be effective. One simple strategy is to wear a rubber band on your wrist and twang it when slipping into worry or rumination, and say 'stop' aloud. The brain will come to associate the sting with dysfunctional thoughts and, as the brain doesn't like pain, the ruminations will diminish.

13 Focus less on *order* in your life and more on *variety*. Start to change and vary your set activities and habits; introduce some flexibility to your orderliness.

14 Ease back from 'workaholism', where your waking hours are dominated by doing or thinking about work. Mallinger and DeWyze recommend a two-month 'leisure-reclamation' program: don't take work home, don't work at weekends, limit time at work and time spent on chores, enjoy your free time and consciously be *in the moment* when with family or friends.

Further insights about perfectionism

'No one is perfect... that's why pencils have erasers'.

Anon

In the epilogue to their book, Mallinger and DeWyze encourage those who are perfectionistic and 'in pain' to acknowledge that the source of their discontent may not, in fact, be their boss, the economy or the shortcomings of their partner, but instead their own personality. Your first instinct will be defensive. 'It's my work, my boss, my... Don't blame me!' But conceding the possibility allows the beginnings of change.

In her book *I Thought It Was Just Me (But It Isn't)*, Brené Brown claims that perfectionistic people seek to avoid shame.[4] She positions shame as reflecting fear of being viewed as flawed and unworthy of acceptance, and so a powerful strategy is to focus on developing 'shame resilience'. This suggests the need for a 'rethink', advanced by a cognitive strategy.

Brown offers four therapeutic elements, with two of relevance here:

1   Recognise shame triggers.
2   Practise critical awareness and decoding of messages that fuel shame.

In Chapter 17 we noted that CBT didn't seem to be of noticeable benefit for keeping burnout symptoms in check. This finding, however, came from a meta-analytic aggregation of studies of interventions, and we then went on to list the limitations of meta-analyses evaluating treatments for burnout. In fact, we believe that in cases where perfectionism is distinctive and a major driver of burnout, CBT is likely to be the best fix.

Observations from a clinician

Sydney psychologist Rocco Crino is an expert in managing obsessive compulsive disorder and those with a perfectionistic personality.[5] He gave us his insights and in the following allows the reader to get a taste of a sophisticated CBT approach.

> Striving for excellence is by no means a bad thing. We expect competence, ability and even excellence in ourselves and others when performing tasks and duties of all kinds and are often pleased when the result turns out well. Some individuals, however, are so driven, meticulous and perfectionistic that achieving the end result is often associated with significant personal cost in terms of happiness, health, relationships and life balance.
>
> Changing patterns of behaviour is always difficult, even more so when the person believes that the way they are doing things or the way they behave are the right and correct ways. This is particularly the case with individuals who have been meticulous and perfectionistic throughout most of their life, believing that their way is the right way, and who approach tasks with a rigid 'must be perfect at all costs' attitude. Invariably these individuals are

work-focused or task-focused to the exclusion of what most others consider important—such as family, friends, socialising, hobbies, activities and interests.

Individuals with such traits rarely present asking for help with these characteristics. Instead they most commonly present due to difficulties with work peers or superiors, work completion, procrastination, stress, sleep disturbance or anxiety associated with their work or duties, or because they're feeling burnt out and exhausted.

In treating such individuals and attempting to help them change, it is important to examine the various perfectionistic behaviours that the person engages in and, more importantly, the underlying beliefs, assumptions and imagined consequences that drive the maintaining of unrelenting standards. (For example, 'Mistakes will be made unless I check the work done by others', 'If I don't get top marks in the essay, I'm a hopeless student who won't achieve my goals', 'If I send out any imperfect goods, my business and reputation will be ruined'.) Perfectionism questionnaires are readily available online and can assist in delineating other areas of the individual's life that are affected by perfectionistic tendencies, as well as beliefs and attitudes.

Once identified, the cost of holding on to such unrelenting standards is collaboratively determined. In the first example noted above, the costs to the individual included spending lengthy periods of time after work checking his subordinates' work thoroughly, and some of his subordinates actually left work for him to complete, knowing he would do it, thus increasing his workload and associated stress further. In the second example, the student was often working through nights and sometimes submitting her work late for assessment as she felt she had to read every article, even if only vaguely related to the topic. In the third example, the individual was self-employed and manufactured items in lots of hundreds. Each had to be checked for imperfections before being sent out, resulting in high levels of anxiety and distress when finally sending the items. Invariably, there are further costs, such as time away from family, relationship strains, sleep disturbance and no downtime to enjoy other activities.

Cognitive interventions are used to challenge distorted perceptions of self-worth and that the opinions of others are based on perfect performance, and to modulate unhealthy high or unrelent-ing standards of performance as well as other irrational, inflexible thinking styles and beliefs that maintain perfectionism. Of equal importance, behavioural change in the form of exposure and behavioural experiments not only reinforce the cognitive challenging but also provide the opportunity to disconfirm beliefs and assump-tions. In the examples just mentioned, the disastrous, unwanted out-comes are ostensibly avoided by individuals' engagement in perfectionistic behaviours. Needless to say, the outcome reinforces the behaviour and beliefs or assumptions. In short, the perfectionistic behaviour works in their eyes, and if not, mistaken beliefs confirm that the individual did not try hard enough and needs to put in further effort.

Behavioural interventions provide a real-life opportunity to challenge not only the probability but also the cost of changing the maladaptive behaviour. In the first example, one of the beha-vioural experiments involved him delegating work to his sub-ordinates and not checking it. His prediction was that errors would be made, and his reputation would suffer in the eyes of his super-iors. The outcome disproved his concerns about any such errors being made, and as an added benefit, the resentment his sub-ordinates held towards him for his 'controlling' nature began to fade over time. Interestingly, when an error was eventually made, his immediate superior merely asked for a rectification, so the feared outcome of 'irreparable damage' to his reputation did not occur. In the second case, the behavioural experiment involved researching only relevant articles for the next assignment, ceasing procrastination (a function of rumination and creating an insur-mountable task for herself), writing the assignment and submitting it. Although her prediction was that she would barely pass, if at all, the result was a good mark. Not a perfect mark, but a good one nonetheless, and one that allowed her to strive for her goals. In the third example, the individual was encouraged to not check the manufactured items and to send them out as soon as they were completed. His prediction was that he would receive complaints for faulty goods and his business would suffer. Again, nothing untoward occurred. As a further experiment, once checking was controlled, he was asked to send out two faulty items in a 200-item consignment to test the hypothesis that his business and reputation would be ruined. The items were returned with a brief note outlining the fault and politely asking for replacements.

Behavioural interventions not only challenge the beliefs and assumptions that drive maladaptive behaviour in perfectionistic individuals but also give them the opportunity to increase their lived experience and acceptance of imperfection (a normal part of life), leading to less anxiety over time when faced with new goals and/or tasks.

In addition to the cognitive and behavioural techniques designed to challenge and change the identified perfectionistic behaviours and attitudes, it is important to encourage the individual to introduce a work–life balance aimed at increasing leisure, family, interpersonal and pleasurable activities. Engagement in such activities allows for the resetting of priorities so that work, study, performance or other 'tasks' are no longer at the top of the list. Care needs to be taken, however, that such leisure activities are approached with a flexible, engaging attitude rather than a 'tick the box', master and then leave it attitude.

Such observations by Dr Crino indicate how perfectionism can—if limiting the individual from flourishing—be tweaked and modified by skilled psychological interventions.

Notes

1 A.E. Mallinger & J. DeWyze, *Too Perfect: When being in control gets out of control*, Random House Publishing, New York, 1992.
2 R. Winter, *Perfecting Ourselves to Death: Bridges to wholeness and hope*, IVP Books, Illinois, 2005.
3 R. Winter, *Perfecting Ourselves to Death: Bridges to wholeness and hope*, IVP Books, Illinois, 2005.
4 B. Brown, *I Thought It Was Just Me (But It Isn't)*, Avery, New York, 2008.
5 R. Crino, 'Looking after yourself: Perfectionism', online CBT program, Centre for Clinical Interventions, Western Australia, <www.cci.health.wa.gov.au/Resources/Looking-After-Yourself/Perfectionism>, accessed September 2022.

Chapter 19

Pulling it all together

'Knowledge of what is possible is the beginning of happiness'.
George Santayana

Before we get into the nitty-gritty, we urge you (again) to recognise that burnout is the consequence of multiple connecting factors, and so its management requires a 'package' approach rather than a single de-stressing strategy. It also, for some, will require a new personal philosophy, or a complete makeover—as was the case for Grace. Her personal story, the final in this book, illustrates that sometimes the only way to keep going is to start again.

In reading the following steps and strategies, garnering wise advice, philosophy and tested remedies, consider what 'package' might best meet your needs.

First, recognise the 'need to change'

'A bend in the road is not the end of the road... unless you fail to make the turn'.
Helen Keller

The observations of our study participants and narrators have something in common: invariably their burnout experience led to a crisis (of health, relationships and/or career), which obliged intense self-reflection about the nature of their livelihood and their priorities. Grace (as you will read shortly) asks herself, 'What led me to this?' Once the noisy foreground receded all were able to recognise that they had, for example, set themselves huge targets (Sophie Scott) or prioritised work or care for others to their own significant

DOI: 10.4324/9781003333722-23

detriment (Petrea King; Grace), often continuing to give until they had nothing left.

Subsequently, each acknowledged the need to initiate change. Sophie Scott admonished herself 'nothing will change unless you do'; Grace understood that 'I had lost my way'. Their resulting decisions often involved changing their current work model—Anne-Marie Rice: 'To do less, well'; Sophie Scott: 'working differently, not working harder'—or in some cases, their actual job (Jayson Greenberg; Grace). Reflecting about yourself, your life drivers and your priorities is a vital first step.

Adopting strategies for change

While meditation and several other de-stressing salves did not benefit Dr Greenberg initially, once he changed his job he had more space and time to develop the habit of meditation and be 'more in the moment'. For others looking to alleviate their symptoms, there was some consistency in their strategies. While meditation was particularly prominent, other approaches included seeking out and relishing solitude, increasing contact with family and friends, gardening and being in nature, and becoming aware of and appreciating simple pleasures. There was an emphasis on developing their awareness and their sense of gratitude.

Following are two examples of some helpful holistic approaches adopted by study participants. The first offered a series of practical and easy-to-implement strategies:

> I was given really practical strategies last year when I'd reached the end of my tether. A cluey counsellor helped me to learn and 'settle into' some new habits. Here's a summary of what I found most helpful—and still do:
>
> • First, I dropped the belief that it was my role to shoulder the greatest share of responsibilities at home. Now, as much as we can afford, I order in easy-prepare food, favour home delivery and have a cleaner every fortnight. My family has been allocated tasks (occasional nagging/rewards involved!). Check out who else can help and for what.

- I prioritise necessary tasks, drop others forever, delegate some and do others less often. At the end of the day, I jot down a To Do list for the next day's work and home and put it aside. Before bed, I put out breakfast stuff, kids' clothes/needs and my exercise gear.
- I'm inclined to ruminate. I was told to take my worries one by one and determine if any action could be taken now, and if not, to put each aside and tune it out, like background noise.
- I have a list of stress-busting ideas to hand (I can't think if I'm cross and bothered): yoga exercises, a jog around the block, punch a pillow, calm music, a short funny video, make a healthy snack, go up and down the stairs a few times or even, at work, the fire escape!
- They are so 'not me' but I've learned some short and simple breathing and relaxation techniques. I now use a phone app to guide me. Worth doing!
- I've instituted a set time to go to bed and to get up. I never take any communication devices into my bedroom.

The second participant offered a smorgasbord of options for stress inoculation:

Here's my resilience-building list:

- Learn to switch off, set boundaries for your work, take regular breaks during the workday, think more about play.
- Attend to self-care, get organised ahead of time, lean on your support systems, disconnect from unpleasant situations, pay attention to your body signals, schedule in relaxation, stay away from sleeping pills and other 'props'.
- Plan positive activities. Read about stress management. Learn a relaxation method, make attendance at a regular (yoga, tai chi...) class your priority, drink plenty of water, buy a season ticket to the (insert sport) and barrack for your team, send the washing out, buy in a frozen meal, read a trashy book, listen to or watch a comedy show.

What Arianna Huffington learned

'Do not adjust your mind, the fault is in reality'.

R.D. Laing

Media CEO Arianna Huffington in her book *Thrive*[1] detailed strategies she found to be helpful. As you may remember from Chapter 2, in 2007 she collapsed from exhaustion and recognised from her 'wake-up call' that something had to radically change—particularly how she and society defined 'success'. She observed that those who were genuinely thriving in life emphasised *wellbeing, wisdom* and *wonder*. She added *giving* as the fourth element to her definition of success and thriving. To improve wellbeing, she recommends mindfulness, meditation, exercise, adequate sleep, rest days and avoiding technology 'overconnectivity'.

Huffington's definition of wisdom is broad, weaving together strengths and vulnerabilities, being creative and nurturing, and showing passion, discipline, pragmatism, intuition, intellect and imagination. She advocates learning to sit quietly in a room alone, not sweating the small stuff, accepting oneself with all one's faults, and ceasing negative self-talk. She also backs the need to live in a state of gratitude, trust one's gut instincts or intuition, slow down and find the positives in life and in adversity.

And what is 'wonder'? To her, wonder includes being open-minded, and giving full attention to and marvelling at the world, with nature and art being two fertile arenas for its experience. She also endorses the value of being centred, judging that all encounters, however mundane, provide an opportunity for transcendence or a spiritual element. Huffington describes regularly employing three simple practices to collect herself: focusing on the rise and fall of her breath for ten seconds; picking an image that invites joy; and forgiving herself for any negative self-judgements or judgements of others.

Huffington defined 'giving' as being loving, caring, empathic and compassionate, going beyond oneself and serving others. She believes that this is central to success and thriving, with giving and service marking a path 'to a world in which we are no longer strangers and alone'. This is a variant of Aristotle's model that has echoed down the ages: 'Happiness is the consequence of a deed'.

Huffington's recipe positions 'eudemonic' wellbeing as above transitory 'hedonic' happiness. While hedonic happiness consists of (usually temporary) feelings of pleasure and satisfaction, eudemonic wellbeing is made up of experiences of purpose and meaning, which provide the foundation for engagement, fulfilment and contentment, with Aristotle (that man again) viewing the attainment of eudemonic wellbeing as enabling the fulfilment of one's true nature. Huffington is not simply suggesting strategies for redressing burnout but reminding us that a crisis presents a tipping point for change. So, rather than simply seeking to remove burnout symptoms to achieve short-term happiness, consider how you might instead recalibrate your life course and come out of the crisis in better 'shape' so as to experience a life of fulfilment and meaning in the long term.

Huffington's strategies are ones integral to the field of 'positive psychology', an approach fathered by the American psychologist Martin Seligman and defined as 'the scientific study of positive human functioning and flourishing'.[2] In their key research paper, Seligman and Csikszentmihalyi detailed the principles of positive psychology.[3] Its focus, in contrast to psychology's more typical interest in dysfunction, is on wellbeing, contentment and satisfaction about the past, as well as hope and optimism for the future. Characteristics of positive psychology also include the concept of 'flow': being fully concentrated on a task and in 'the present', and recognising and identifying personal strengths rather than weaknesses. It aims to build strength rather than repair damage.

In the context of therapy, positive psychology seeks to advance positive individual traits, cultivate the capacity to enjoy oneself in the moment, help engender deep relationships, look for meaning in life and promote a sense of engagement. It also looks to build resilience via character strengths. Such qualities include courage, interpersonal skills, perseverance, forgiveness and originality, being future-minded (the capacity to think ahead and envisage), embracing spirituality, and fostering talent and wisdom.

Petrea King's insights about finding and nurturing wellbeing

In Chapter 11 you read Petrea King's moving account that detailed her burnout, its many causes and the strategies she adopted. As founder of the Quest for Life organisation, she has established several courses for people enduring terminal illnesses and critical problems. One course, which has now been running for three decades, is the Peace in Practice program, which is provided at her centre as well as at hospitals and in the community to doctors, psychologists, nurses and other health workers, and seeks to address burnout.

The premise of the program is that while such practitioners may be highly educated and proficient in their areas of expertise, they may not have focused on how to pursue their career or vocation in a sustainable and fulfilling manner—particularly relevant to those who feel their work *is* their vocation. Those who serve others may do so as an extension of being in service to humanity, expressed through community involvement. However, a consequence of selfless giving can be, ironically, a disconnection from people and meaning, followed by the individual responding with greater dedication to compensate, an iteration that soon leads to exhaustion.

Petrea argues that the passion that accompanies a sense of vocation may blind a person to their own needs, especially if there is already a habitual pattern of putting other people's needs ahead of their own, and thus they might neglect self-care. Those consumed by a vocation may lament that if they had more time they'd go back to the gym / eat healthier food / go for a run / take better care of themselves. Petrea King's response is: 'You don't have more time. There's just 168 hours in the week and you need to replenish yourself first. Then you will bring your well-replenished self to the task'. By replenishing wellbeing, the individual can work from a stable, healthy and integrated self, offering a more balanced and spontaneous 'self' to life and its challenges. She contends that when we reclaim our hours and ensure that self-care practices are a non-negotiable foundation for our lives, we can maintain or restore the energy needed to engage meaningfully with life and, in so doing, find deep contentment and peace.

The essential ingredients of a wellbeing program

> *'Change is hardest at the beginning, messiest in the middle and best at the end'.*
>
> Robin S. Sharma

The keystone of any wellbeing program is enabling and encouraging people to attend to their own physical, mental, emotional and spiritual needs (i.e. their self-care) both as a priority and as a foundation for lifetime resilience. Program components should emphasise the need for excellent nutrition, deep and replenishing sleep, regular exercise and lifestyle practices that are conducive to maintaining and improving physical health. Its contemplative practices may include martial arts, tai chi, qi gong, meditation and living mindfully. Such programs are cognisant of neglected spiritual needs and the imperative need for their fulfilment. These needs can be manifested in quite varying ways. Religious beliefs and practices will sustain some and provide a meaningful perspective from which to work. Others find immersion and perspective via engagement with hobbies, sport, exercise, being in nature, listening to or making music or art, massage, yoga, meditation, improved relationships and planned relaxation periods (which may be as simple as soaking in the bath). The rewards and routine of companion animals can provide a deep sense of contentment and connection with ourselves and others. A periodic check-in with a trusted counsellor helps such new and positive habits to flourish.

Beware the boiling frog!

Huffington's and our contributors' accounts are clearly success stories. For some, burnout symptoms emerged suddenly and were very severe (e.g. collapsing, being hospitalised)—a clarion call to action. Though studies are lacking, it appears that burnout more commonly emerges slowly and insidiously. Remember the 'boiling frog' metaphor that we spoke about, whereby we tend to react minimally or not at all to threats that creep up on us and we only react distinctly to acute events. So if burnout develops in increments, the individual may not be aware of the phenomenon for some time and will be unlikely to interpret their growing raft of symptoms as a 'wake-up call'. When faced with a patient displaying various 'soft' symptoms, few doctors will list burnout in the provisional set of diagnoses at that stage, so the condition is likely to continue its mission creep, undiagnosed and unmanaged.

In summary, the impact of an acute onset of severe burnout is likely to alert us to the need for change. In contrast, a gradual onset of burnout may see us quite unaware for a period. The slow build-up of distress will generally also distract from registering the need to press the 'complete reset' button. So watch out for flames that burn slowly—they still present a fire hazard and their identification is the first step to safety. And then, of course, there are the other steps to resolving burnout.

Seven basic steps to recovery

1   Identify that you have burnout. Be aware that your health professional may be quite unaware of burnout and its developmental pattern, and may therefore miss the diagnosis. Identification may well come down to *you* doing the diagnostic detective work, and we hope this book's burnout measure and clinical reasoning approach clarifies and assists.
2   Reflect on how it came about.
3   Judge the most likely beneficial corrective strategies, whether they address work, stress and/or any personality contribution. (Do not be defensive about the last aspect—it may be more fundamental to address than even work conditions.)
4   Ask for help or seek support from someone you can trust, and discuss the stressors and how they might best be corrected.
5   Change what you can in relation to work stressors.
6   Consider how personality factors may be contributing and address any key drivers (in particular, consider whether you are highly dutiful and perfectionistic and, if so, consider the strategies for modulating this trait that we detailed in Chapter 18).
7   Change any daily 'habits' that may be contributing to the stress. It takes around a month to settle into a new pattern. Be aware that too much change all at once can be hard to sustain: you don't want to set the stage for 'non-compliance' with your new regimen. Integrating changes into your life little by little can make them lasting ones. The next section is more specific about habits and provides examples.

Replace your old habits with new approaches

> *'Bending beats breaking'.*
>
> Betty Greene

In terms of habits, what to prioritise? Most people who develop burn-out do so as a consequence of relentless activity, whether work-based or due to family responsibilities. They are responding to work tasks in their usual dutiful, conscientious and reliable manner. However, on top of this, their 'activity' rate is increased even further by the current 24/7 pulsation. Overconnectivity!

In terms of 'disconnecting' consider the following:

- *Emails*: Arianna Huffington reported that the average 'knowledge economy' employee spends more than 11 hours a week dealing with emails, constantly striving to empty their inboxes and 'bailing like people in a leaky lifeboat'. Many experience 'email apnoea', holding their breath while responding to emails and consequently advancing stress.[4] Consider designing a 'flotation' system to prevent being engulfed and submerged by only checking your emails twice (max!) a day and reply, junk and delete immediately so they don't build up. Keep an old-fashioned notebook for handling email-delivered issues that will require action at some recorded time in the future and rejoice as you cross each out when addressed. Don't link your work emails to your cell phone. Don't open your inbox late in the afternoon or early evening. And if you really need to access your emails on weekends and holidays, schedule a limited time for the task.
- *Mobile phones*: Sure, phones provide convenient access and communication, but they also advance stress because you're permanently 'on' and available. Are you a prisoner? They're not called 'cell' phones for nothing. Use smartphones smartly—they're invaluable for ready communication when necessary but how much do you need them for any other purpose? Can you live without or minimise time on platforms like Facebook, Twitter or Instagram, or restrict yourself to one of them? Keep a record for one week of your phone use, and where and how long you use it for (on the train to work, walking on the street, having a meal), then consider how much access you really need and impose a limit. Avoid phone access during meals, in the company of others, or after the early evening. Remember that smartphones, iPads and related devices that emit light disrupt circadian rhythms and thus

disturb your sleep too. The moral here: if you don't turn electronic devices off, you can't turn yourself off.

- Do a *cost–benefit analysis* for each of your daily activities. How much does each benefit your functioning versus how much does it contribute to relentless activity? Like a barber, decide what to cut and what to shave—only countenance what needs to be left. Bald can be beautiful.

An eighth step: Trial several individual de-stressing strategies

If daily habits have been modified and you've freed up some of your time, it's easier to then move on to trialling differing de-stressing strategies. We list multiple tools to assist with de-stressing in Appendix D but here recommend the practical reference book *StressLess* by Matthew Johnstone and Michael Player.[5] In addition to overviewing the nature of stress, those authors provide simple and effective cognitive behaviour therapy exercises (some illustrated in the chapter on managing perfectionism), and set out de-stressing activities, including lucid examples of how to engage in mindfulness, relaxation and meditation.

But how should you choose the best de-stressing options to trial first? As detailed in Chapter 17, our two (qualitative and quantitative) studies favoured exercise, meditation and mindfulness techniques. There are numerous evidence-based studies and meta-analyses supporting the benefits of this trio for those with anxiety and depressive states. Though such 'evidence' is lacking in relation specifically to burnout, extrapolation would seem appropriate considering burnout is a stress-induced state. We now offer a few comments about each of these and link their benefits with the biological changes associated with burnout that we reviewed in Chapter 7.

Exercise: Attending to your body

What is it about exercise? Firstly, exercise releases endorphins—neurotransmitters that activate opiate receptors in the brain and create an analgesic 'feel good' effect. It also lowers stress hormones such as cortisol and adrenalin. When we are acutely stressed, cortisol levels are increased to mobilise energy for fight or flight, although (and as discussed in Chapter 7) prolonged stress-induced burnout links with low base cortisol levels, accounting for the fatigue and exhaustion. Exercise can help to counteract this as it works to stabilise cortisol levels. Exercise also helps as a distraction and it can be a form of active meditation due to a narrowing of focus. Exercise can increase levels of happiness directly and indirectly ('every golf shot makes someone happy'), improve sleep and promote beneficial socialisation (why else do people walk dogs?). The type of exercise does not appear to matter—whether aerobic or non-aerobic, martial arts or marital acts, it can range from A to Z (abseiling to Zorb football).

Meditation: Feeding your soul

And now to meditation, a practice first documented from around the fifth millennia BCE on the Indian subcontinent. Meditation involves purposeful practice of consciousness and concentration. There are different types of meditation, but the goal of each is to direct awareness towards a particular object, sensation or experience. For instance, in 'loving-kindness' meditation the goal is to cultivate love and kindness towards yourself and others, while in 'progressive relaxation' meditation the objective is to notice and release areas of tension within your body. Meditation decreases blood pressure, pulse rate, adrenalin and, you guessed it, cortisol levels. This gives the sympathetic nervous system a rest, and so reduces stress. There are secondary benefits, including improved sleep, concentration and performance. Meditation may also be of benefit in relation to ageing, specifically protecting telomeres, the protective caps on the ends of our DNA strands. These shorten over our lifetime, and exposure to stress can increase their rate of shrinkage (now that's something you didn't even *know* you had to add to the worry list!). Fortunately, however, meditation has been shown to improve the activity and length of telomeres, slowing down premature ageing.

There are many ways in which meditation can be practised, including guided imagery (with a word or thought repeated as a mantra), ultra-focus or in combination with movement and breathing exercises—as occurs with qi gong and tai chi.

Practise mindfulness: Engaging (or coming to) your senses

And why mindfulness, which has its origins in Hinduism and Buddhism? Mindfulness is characterised by an individual being completely 'in the moment', and requires awareness of the body (heightening hearing, sight, smell and taste) while maintaining continued awareness of internal and external phenomena, and accepting whatever is encountered in the present. One basic mindfulness practice is 'mindful breathing', where the focus of attention is on your breath, its rhythm and depth, how your entire body moves when you inhale and exhale, such as the rise and fall of your chest. 'Mindful eating' is another example of intensely directed attention, the exercise being to eat slowly and without distraction, focusing on how the food feels, smells and tastes, and attending to the body's hunger and fullness cues.

What are the effects of mindfulness? Well, it has been found to reduce activity in the brain's default mode network (DMN)—a constellation roused when we are worrying or ruminating—but its positive impact on the brain is far broader. Some measured effects include: decreased fight/flight activity in the amygdala (part of the brain's limbic system and principally a conduit for fear responses), increased activity in the hippocampi (which regulate emotions as well as memory and learning) and increased connections between the amygdala and the pre-frontal cortex (the 'executive functioning' part of the brain involved in awareness, planning, decision-making, problem-solving and self-control). As noted in Chapter 7 detailing biological changes, these are all brain regions that can be affected by a burnout syndrome. The practice of mindfulness can help to *reverse* damage caused by burnout to these regions!

Mindfulness can also be integrated with certain psychotherapies, for instance mindfulness-based cognitive behaviour therapy; or combined with meditation (so-called mindfulness meditation). In application, mindfulness is best practised for 10 to 15 minutes at a time and regularly—avoid going more than two days without devoting time to it if possible. Like any habit, it grows when nurtured, and although the technique of mindfulness sounds simple, it is common to find it difficult at first.

Health journalist Shannon Harvey recently documented her experiment of practising mindfulness meditation for a year while undergoing more than 100 scientific tests to determine its impact.[6] Along with improvement in psychological functioning—achieving a higher wellbeing score and with her stress symptoms (including insomnia) settling— Harvey documented many other biological changes. Brain scans (both structural and functional) indicated that four areas of her brain actually increased in size. These brain structures were related to self-awareness, memory and dealing with emotions. Connectivity between her brain regions also improved. Her C-reactive protein levels (a measure of inflammation) decreased, and a gene that activates inflammation effectively switched off. Further analysis indicated that her telomeres evidenced growth. Psychologically she felt much less stressed, but she also observed that mindfulness meditation had not made her any happier; more that it had taught her how to be less unhappy.

There is something primal about mindfulness. As alluded to in a statement by Grace, in the final personal story of the book where she details her burnout symptoms, 'I craved the simplest of pleasures—a walk in the forest… the song of a bird, the beauty of a flower, the smell of home cooking'.

So, as noted, there is a wide array of stress-reducing strategies. We also provide a resource set in Appendix D. However, what works for one individual may not necessarily work for someone else. It's wise to avoid prioritising one approach above another solely on any theoretical base. Better to adopt a 'horses for courses' model, examine the smorgasbord of options and try out (and *practise*) differing combinations. With effort and perseverance, it's guaranteed that one or more destressors will help—although this is of course subject to you identifying and addressing the key drivers of your burnout, such as work and any personality nuances.

Notes

1 A. Huffington, *Thrive*, W.H. Allen, London, 2015.
2 M.E.P. Seligman & M. Csikszentmihalyi, 'Positive psychology: An introduction', *American Psychologist*, 2000, vol. 55, no. 1, pp. 5–14.
3 M.E.P. Seligman & M. Csikszentmihalyi, 'Positive psychology: An introduction', *American Psychologist*, 2000, vol. 55, no. 1, pp. 5–14.
4 A. Huffington, *Thrive*, W.H. Allen, London, 2015.
5 M. Johnstone & M. Player, *StressLess: Proven methods to reduce stress, manage anxiety and lift your mood*, Macmillan, Sydney, 2019.
6 S. Harvey, *My Year of Living Mindfully*, Hachette, Sydney, 2020.

Chapter 20

A final note and a personal story of Grace under pressure

Before we started our studies of burnout, we had the view that it was a condition rightly labelled as 'difficult to treat'. Earlier clinical encounters with individuals who reported ongoing problems led to the belief that a significant percentage of them had lost their 'elasticity' forever. Well, we are pleased to report that we were wrong. In our studies and our interviews with the many individuals whose stories we report here, it became clear that most people do recover, subject to them addressing the drivers. Most found the right lever, sometimes by chance, but mostly by dogged persistence. In writing this book we sought to make the road to recovery easier by providing signposts, a road map and turning on the headlights.

A 'treatment' model is not the best one. It implies that an individual with complete burnout or who is somewhere on that trajectory should adopt the role of a 'patient' and that a health practitioner will prescribe a therapy to assist. Yes, some health practitioners can assist to some degree. Some can clarify the diagnosis (though that's not a common success story as burnout is hardly ever considered in health professionals' training). Some can offer guiding advice. At times they can endorse sick leave or act as an advocate for the sufferer.

But burnout resolves better with a self-management model. Burnout is often an appropriate response to a set of externally imposed circumstances. Only later, if the causes (say, unrelenting stress) continue unabated, do the physical/biological responses kick in and finally take up residence. When an individual recognises they have burnout, addresses any work triggers, selects appropriate stress reduction strategies and then both recognises and addresses any personality drivers, they almost always do very well. Not only do most recover from severe

DOI: 10.4324/9781003333722-24

burnout but a distinctive number of people (as illustrated by our narrators) come through the flames re-forged into a better shape, more resilient than they were during their pre-burnout life. Some in this group describe having fashioned a new identity, most a new way of viewing and appreciating life, and virtually all experienced a new inner peace.

Be assured: you can resolve burnout. Remember the phoenix.

A final personal story: Grace

Why is a wake-up call so shockingly painful? What was I thinking? Why could I not see where this was all going? I was amazingly fit and healthy, long-distance 40-something-year-old runner, a swimmer, full of energy, full of life, with an incredibly successful career, a supportive and wonderful family and a beautiful home in a treasured suburb. I had it all.

Sure, I worked hard, but surely not too hard, not more than many of my colleagues. We were all driven; 'AAA' personalities, we called each other. It was a dog-eat-dog toxic world, as high-flying lawyers have to battle to fly the highest. Being a woman was an extra challenge. You had to constantly watch your back, constantly be on alert. I worked long 14-plus-hour days, mostly 80-hour weeks and rarely a weekend off. I skipped meals, slept four to five hours a night. I thrived on this: I had an inexhaustible source of energy, I worked around the clock and was a powerhouse at the office and a leader in my field.

I guess I ignored the signs. We all do until it's too late. I ignored the warnings, I ignored the recurring symptoms and I even ignored the multitude of stop signs that were thrown my way. Over a couple of years, I ignored the increasingly frequent and severe respiratory illnesses. As time passed, I ignored the increasing fatigue and brain fog, and then the intolerance to cold. Over the preceding few months, I ignored the recurring palpitations, dizziness and episodes of hypoglycaemia.

Each week began to be more of a struggle. I started on energy drinks and coffee, which I had never done in my life, but it was the only way to get through the days, the work, the meetings, the responsibilities, the schedule, the stress. I consumed more and more salty foods and had binges of sweets and chocolate. My regular previously enjoyable morning runs became a torture. I was out of breath, in pain and had to drag myself through the kilometres.

Then I couldn't sleep. When I did, I was tortured by nightmares. I cried, always alone, never in front of anyone to betray a weakness or inability to cope. I didn't stop to really think about what was happening. I didn't have the time, and besides, in November I was going on a four-week holiday and would recuperate and rest then and all would be well.

It had been months since I had felt really well, weeks since I felt just okay. In fact, I didn't even know what it was to feel well anymore. In early August I started feeling a deep-seated impending sense of doom; it was deep within my heart, a physical discomfort in my chest. I named it the Gremlin; it became part of me, this horrible unease, it didn't leave me day and night.

One Saturday evening in mid-August, while in bed, I saw a vision that shook me to my core—a skull and crossbones hovering in front of me. I wasn't dreaming. I was panicked and deeply shaken. I begged my family to take me immediately to the hospital. I was frightened and became completely dismantled.

I arrived at the hospital and was admitted to the intensive care unit. I could hear muffled mutterings of cardiovascular collapse and a sense of urgency among the staff. My pulse rate was 170, irregular, and a far cry from my usual 50 regular beats per minute. My blood pressure was a reasonable 90/60 lying down but when they sat me up it plummeted to 60/40. I was shaking, trembling and sweating. My blood sugar level was 2.0 (normal levels are 4.0 to 7.8 mmol/L).

Over the ensuing days I underwent a barrage of tests and investigations. Blood tests, urine tests, cardiac echoes, brain MRI and CT scans. Everything came back normal. No one knew what was going on. The ICU specialist told me it had all the hallmarks of an adrenal-type crisis but all my hormone levels were normal and he just couldn't figure it all out.

I was weak and unable to walk unassisted to the bathroom. A shower was an ordeal. After ten days it was clear they could do nothing for me. I discharged myself and my father carried me to the car. If I stood on my own, I blacked out.

The palpitations were pounding in my ears. I was terribly ill but no one could find anything, no one could help. I fell into a deep depression; my family could hardly recognise me. I lost weight, I was a greyish tinge of white and my hair was thinning. I couldn't walk on my own, I could do nothing on my own. I had hypoglycaemic attacks throughout the day. I had to constantly eat to stave them off but was overwhelmed with nausea and episodes of vomiting. I was in constant tears and pain, a physical and mental pain as well as an emotional anguish.

My family called my office to let them know I was desperately ill and would be taking several months off. I was in a dark, dark place, and for the first time I was lost, completely lost and completely dependent.

I started to pray regularly alone in the local church. I came across the Medicine Buddha mantra and recited this all day and tried to meditate with my scented candles. I was waiting for help, desperate for help—divine help, if you like—anything that would guide me through the deep dark tunnel where I found myself.

Over the following weeks I began a journey inwards. I had more questions than answers. I seemed to wake from a maddening illusory sleep. What led me to this? How did this happen? Was it all really worth it? Why was I so driven? Why did I live for my job, my career, to the exclusion of everything else, my family, my health, my peace of mind? Where had all the years gone? Was I really irreplaceable? Was this what life was about?

During my hour-long meditations, I noticed something extra-ordinary: I was completely symptom-free. It was the only time I was not controlled by my Gremlin and did not feel the palpitations, sense the nausea and crushing fatigue. Through the despair there were brief moments of insight, of wisdom, of clarity and of hope.

One day I came across a book by Dr James Wilson, an American naturopathic physician, titled *Adrenal Fatigue: The 21st century stress syndrome*. I was intrigued and completely absorbed by this book. I believed I had found the answer to my illness. The medical profession interestingly didn't recognise this as a condition. When I mentioned it to my doctors, they rolled their arrogant eyes and mocked my words. Naturopathy had no credibility or evidence base as far as they were concerned. 'What a load of hogwash', one eloquently exploded.

I didn't care. What answers did they have for me? What did they have to offer me? One specialist told me I should try antidepressants, because after all it was 'hard being a woman in a man's world and sometimes it is too hard to cope with it all', he told me. Another one didn't even believe my symptoms, he thought I had a fervid imagination, all in my head, so to speak—what else could it be since all their investigations were normal? But then the stars started to align. Dr Wilson was coming from the US to run a seminar in New Zealand. I had to get there. But how? I was so very weak, so very frail, so very vulnerable.

My family took me to New Zealand and I met Dr Wilson, who diagnosed me with severe adrenal exhaustion. While most of the blood tests were normal, the salivary tests showed cortisol levels that were essentially unrecordable. Although he told me I was very ill, he assured me that he had successfully treated such extreme cases and gave me hope and light. I returned home and started his regimen, following it to the letter.

I now knew I could heal physically, but I knew I needed to heal mentally and emotionally. I needed to find myself again, to face my fears and find my courage and strength.

I watched documentaries on the mind and body connection, I read inspiring books on spiritual healing and the metaphysical causes of disease and ill health. I read articles on Buddhism and theosophy. I listened for the truth and for wisdom during the long silences of meditation.

I looked back at my life with regret and sadness and was often overwhelmed with grief. I had sacrificed so much. I had neglected my family, I had become a bitter, angry person, my work came before everything and everyone. I had lost my way, lost what was important and forgotten the philosophy and teachings my parents had given me.

I craved peace of mind and joy in my heart. I craved tranquil sleep and pain-free vital walks. I craved the simplest of pleasures—a walk in the forest, a beautiful movie, the song of a bird, the beauty of a flower, the smell of home cooking and comfort of a hot lavender bubble bath.

As the months passed, I gained my strength and could go on longer and longer walks, I had less frequent hypoglycaemic attacks, my heart rate stabilised and my sleep improved. I also learned not to resist the symptoms when they arrived and not to fight the illness but to accept what arose and be grateful for each day and moment. One evening, in the middle of my mediations, my Gremlin suddenly left me and I felt an enormous sense of relief and opening in my heart.

I decided to take long service leave for another nine months and at that moment felt an instant release of anxiety and apprehension. Maybe I wouldn't even go back, who knows. Curiously, I lost, for want of a better word, some long-term friends who showed their true colours. I found new friends, friends who were decidedly different from those I had had in the past.

I took up writing and painting; I had so longed for the time to do this. I started a beautiful English cottage garden and renovated the house. I cooked and baked and read a multitude of extraordinary books. I had not done these things for decades. I had completely forgotten the enormous pleasure and joy it gave me, how my mind could be at peace and my heart could sing again. It took almost four years to restore myself to perfect health and boundless energy and to find balance, harmony and peace, emotionally and mentally.

It has now been 12 years since my admission to hospital and my healing journey began. Since then I have completed another degree, a master's in journalism. For three years I worked part-time in various small jobs and then found a new job in a field of law similar to my previous position but in a completely different organisation. One where you are valued, there is mutual respect and friendly collegiality. I work part-time and spend the rest of my time freelance writing, gardening and being grateful for everything in my life.

Part 4

Appendices

Appendix A: The Sydney Burnout Measure (SBM)

Please tick the extent to which you are experiencing the following features and symptoms *currently*:

Note: Several questions below relate to 'work'. If you are currently employed, please answer these questions in relation to your formal work. If you have ceased formal employment due to burnout, please answer the questions in relation to your last job that brought on your burnout symptoms. If you are not formally employed and are primarily responsible for home or care duties (e.g. carer for a family member), please answer the 'work' questions in relation to such home/care duties.

SBM questionnaire items and scoring options

Item	Not true	Slightly	Moderately	Distinctly
1. I feel emotionally drained and exhausted				
2. My attention is less focused				
3. I wake up feeling tired				
4. I cannot concentrate or register new information because of foggy thinking				
5. I withdraw from family and friends				
6. I find it hard to concentrate on the task at hand				
7. I lack energy across the day				
8. I take longer to finish tasks at work				
9. I cannot get pleasure out of my work				

Item	Not true	Slightly	Moderately	Distinctly
10. I struggle to understand the feelings of colleagues, customers and/or recipients of my care				
11. I no longer feel as driven to meet my responsibilities				
12. I have a loss of energy which makes it hard for me to get going in the morning				
13. I keep to myself				
14. I feel slowed down mentally (e.g. hard to find words, slowed thoughts)				
15. I do not look forward to spending time with friends and family anymore				
16. I spend much of my day worrying				
17. I constantly feel tired and fatigued				
18. My capacity to remember things is not as good as usual				
19. I no longer look forward to things that would normally give me pleasure				
20. I feel self-critical and am hard on myself				
21. I have to re-read things because I was not concentrating the first time				
22. I care less about people with whom I work (e.g. colleagues, customers, recipients of my care)				
23. I am less empathetic				
24. I feel I am stagnating and that life is passing me by				
25. I feel worn out				
26. I feel like I am contributing less at work				
27. I find little things and chores frustrating				

Item	Not true	Slightly	Moderately	Distinctly
28. My work performance has declined				
29. I feel sad, empty and hopeless				
30. I feel less empathy and sympathy towards people in general				
31. I find it more difficult to take life as it comes				
32. I am less productive at work				
33. I am not refreshed by sleep				
34. The quality of my work output is poorer				

Please score each item as follows:

- Not true = 0
- Slightly = 1
- Moderately = 2
- Distinctly = 3

To calculate your burnout score, add up your scores for each item to create a total score.

Total Score: _____

Understanding your SBM scores

Total score

The most important score is the *total* score (the sum of the 34 items), with a higher the score indicating a greater severity of burnout symptoms. The highest possible total score is 102.

In Figure A.1, we plot scores generated by 622 people from our second study who judged they were suffering from burnout. Their average score was 73.8.

90% of the sample scored 50 or higher
75% scored 63 or higher
50% scored 77 or higher
25% scored 87 or higher
10% scored 93 or higher

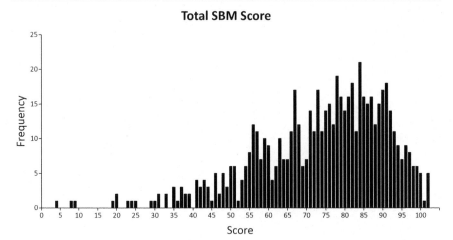

Total SBM Score

Figure A.1 Graph of SBM scores from Study 2 participants

As it is a severity measure, there is no formal cut-off score to state categorically whether you have or do not have burnout. One of our recent analyses indicated that those experiencing burnout would be expected to score 50 or more.

Scale scores

The SBM captures differing burnout symptom clusters. You may wish to calculate your scores for each of these clusters and compare them to those of our sample members. To do this, add up your scores on each item of the six symptom clusters as listed below.

Exhaustion

- Items 3, 7, 12, 17, 25, 33
- Highest possible score = 18
- Average score on this cluster from our sample members = 15.5

Cognitive symptoms

- Items 2, 4, 6, 8, 14, 18, 21
- Highest possible score = 21
- Average score on this cluster from our sample members = 15.7

Loss of empathy

- Items 10, 22, 23, 30
- Highest possible score = 12
- Average score on this cluster from our sample members = 6.5

Withdrawal and insularity

- Items 5, 13, 15, 19
- Highest possible score = 12
- Average score on this cluster from our sample members = 7.8

Impaired work performance

- Items 9, 11, 26, 28, 32, 34
- Highest possible score = 18
- Average score on this cluster from our sample members = 12.3

Unsettled mood (i.e. anxiety, depressed mood and irritability)

- Items 1, 16, 20, 24, 27, 29, 31
- Highest possible score = 21
- Average score on this domain from our sample members = 16.0

Alert, alert!

A high score on the SBM does not necessarily mean that you have burnout. Regrettably, high scores on *all* burnout measures (including the SBM) can be the result of another (or of a co-existing) physical or medical condition. Please turn to Chapter 5 where we engage you in a 'clinical reasoning' approach to clarify your most likely diagnosis.

Appendix B: Workplace triggers

Please tick any of the work factors that you experience and rate them on a 1 to 5 scale (with 5 being high relevance). Some of these factors are discussed in detail in Sharma and Cooper's book, *Executive Burnout*.[1]

MY JOB EXPERIENCE

Physical environment

I work in a stressful physical environment (e.g. noisy, poor temperature control, unhygienic). ☐

Workload pressures

My workload is excessive. ☐

I am under-loaded at work/I don't have enough work to do. ☐

My work hours are very long. ☐

I am required to be available for long and extended hours, including nights and/or weekends. ☐

I am constantly subject to demanding deadlines. ☐

Work content/quality

There are few or no rewards to my job. ☐

I have too little work to keep me interested/engaged. ☐

My work is monotonous. ☐

My job lacks stimulation. ☐

I have no freedom to decide how best to organise my day or tasks. ☐

Role conflict/ambiguity

I feel in conflict with my boss about what my job should entail. ☐

I lack clarity from my boss about my responsibilities and work roles. ☐

I am required to do more work than others with the same job description. ☐

I am required to work longer hours than others with the same job description. ☐

Job prospects and opportunity

My job provides no clear career path in the future that I can see. ☐

I feel that I am stagnating in my current position. ☐

I have no scope to exercise autonomy or creativity in my job. ☐

MY ORGANISATION'S CULTURE

Organisational responsiveness and support

My organisation is autocratic and dictatorial. ☐

My organisation does not offer me support. ☐

My organisation does not wish to hear about or address my suggestions ☐
aimed at improving work conditions.

Organisational recognition, rewards and work security threats

My superiors never praise or compliment me on my work. ☐

I feel my work is of no significance to my organisation. ☐

My organisation does not reward my job performance. ☐

I fear I could lose my job at any time. ☐

Organisational fairness and equity

I feel there is unfairness in the way the organisation judges and evaluates ☐
my work.

I am made to feel less significant than others with the same job ☐
description.

There is a lack of fairness in the way my organisation treats employees. ☐

Relationships in the workplace

My boss bullies me. ☐

My colleagues bully me. ☐

My boss treats me unfairly. ☐

My boss is autocratic and a bit of a tyrant. ☐

Match of norms, values and objectives

My expectations of my job do not match those of my ☐
organisation.

My values and objectives differ from those of my manager. ☐

My work values and objectives are not in line with my organisation's ☐
goals.

Organisational change

I find it hard to understand/adjust to constant changes in the organisation ☐
and its objectives.

Evaluation

Examine the items you have rated as most relevant to you (whether you are formally employed or a carer). Do they reflect work stress only? Or are they broader, relating to your boss and/or the whole organisation?

This checklist aims to help you identify the workplace factors that impact on you the most. By examining the triggers you have ticked you should be able to generate a personal profile which will then allow solutions to be tailored and clarified by considering recommendations in Chapter 16.

Note

1 R.R. Sharma & C. Cooper, *Executive Burnout: Eastern and Western concepts, models, and approaches for mitigation*, Emerald Group Publishing, Bingley, UK, 2017.

Appendix C: Perfectionism scale

For each of the following statements, please select the option that best describes the way *you usually or generally feel or behave* (i.e. across your adult years and *not* just during any state of burnout).

Perfectionism questionnaire and scoring options

Item	Not true at all	Slightly true	Moderately true	Very true
I try to do everything as well as possible				
I always like to do my best				
I push myself to be the best at most things I do				
I like to work to my full potential				
I work hard at most things				
I put high standards on myself and most things I take on				
I try to succeed at most things				
I commit myself fully to things I take on				
I always feel very driven to keep on meeting my responsibilities				
I am viewed as a highly responsible person				
My word is my bond and I'm somewhat perfectionistic				

Please score each item as follows:

- Not true at all = 0
- Slightly true = 1
- Moderately true = 2
- Very true = 3

To calculate your perfectionism score, add up your scores for each item to create a total score (highest possible score = 33).

Total score: _____

Interpretation

- Score of 5–11 (Group A): You are dutiful and might be mildly perfectionistic.
- Score of 12–22 (Group B): You are likely to be mildly to moderately perfectionistic.
- Score of 23–33 (Group C): You are likely to be distinctly perfectionistic.

In Figure C.1 we graph scores on this perfectionism scale returned by 566 participants in Study 2. You can see that very few were in Group A, a moderate number in Group B and the greatest number in Group C, with the average score across the whole sample being 26.

Figure C.1 Graph of perfectionism scores from Study 2 participants

Appendix D: Resources for workers and caregivers

Workplace resources

The following selection of resources includes ways of learning about burnout, how it affects you and others, the varied solutions that individuals have adopted to help themselves, and ways of reducing workplace stress causes and contributors.

Websites dealing with workplace stress and mood impacts

HelpGuide

www.helpguide.org/articles/stress/burnout-prevention-and-recovery.htm
   HelpGuide is a non-profit mental health and wellness website that aims to provide trustworthy, empowering, evidence-based information of value to those in distress to improve their mental health and effect beneficial changes.

MindTools

www.mindtools.com/pages/article/recovering-from-burnout.htm
   This UK site is mostly directed at managers. It has modules covering leadership, team management, time management, problem-solving, decision-making and communication skills.

Podcasts covering health and work–life balance

The following podcasts discuss strategies for fostering mental health and wellbeing, beneficial work–life balance and the equilibrium that meditation and mindfulness practices provide.

What I've Learned, with Arianna Huffington

player.fm/series/the-thrive-global-podcast-with-arianna-huffington-2515264
Arianna Huffington is dedicated to encouraging others to prioritise their own wellbeing. This interview-based podcast by Thrive Global details microsteps to help you advance from 'surviving to thriving'.

Safe for Work

podcasts.apple.com/us/podcast/safe-for-work/id1353460577
Podcasts that focus on finding career balance, including how to avoid burnout. Experts share insights about both the larger issues and the minutiae of the workplace.

The Pineapple Project

www.abc.net.au/radio/programs/the-pineapple-project/wait-am-i-burning-out/10860890
This podcast from Australia's ABC Radio is lighter in tone than many wellbeing podcasts but with serious subject matter: overcoming social anxiety, combating loneliness and maximising mental health. Here we link to the episode specifically addressing burnout.

Untangle

meditationstudioapp.com/podcasts
Each episode presents an expert's advice about techniques that de-stress and calm, especially meditation skills. It is billed as how to untangle from 'society's giant rule book to create a meaningful life'.

TED talks for reframing stress and self-calming

'How to make stress your friend'—Kelly McGonigal

www.youtube.com/watch?v=RcGyVTAoXEU
Practical ways to re-evaluate stress responses and 'beliefs', plus ideas about how to change your body's response to stress.

'The happy secret to better work'—Shawn Achor

www.youtube.com/watch?v=fLJsdqxnZb0

A view of how to reframe the way we see things: brain training to scan for positives and, by doing so, improve its performance.

'All it takes is 10 mindful minutes'—Andy Puddicombe

www.youtube.com/watch?v=qzR62JJCMBQ

Andy Puddicombe promotes the efficacy of mindfulness not just as 'an aspirin for the mind' but as a shield against stress. He is co-founder of the digital health forum Headspace.

Caregivers' resources

Caregivers' self-assessment tools, advice and support

Caregiver Self-Assessment Questionnaire

web.mit.edu/workplacecenter/hndbk/docs/questionnaire.pdf

The American Medical Association developed and tested the Caregiver Self-Assessment Questionnaire. It helps caregivers take stock of their behaviours and health risks so they can assess whether they need more support.

Dailycaring

dailycaring.com

Here you will find practical answers and useful tips, advice, personal stories and resources related to caregiving and ageing. The information is organised in readily accessible bites. Caregivers can also subscribe to the daily email newsletter.

Caring Village

Website:
    www.caringvillage.com/2017/10/16/top-10-caregiving-blogs-caregivers/
    YouTube:

https://www.youtube.com/watch?v=b1PvP478tsc

Caring Village lists a selection of caregiving blogs that provide resources, information and support to assist caregivers with their demanding and unsung role.

Healthline

www.healthline.com/health/health-caregiver-burnout#resources-and-support

Healthline is an organisation that overviews disorders and remedies, and shares fitness and nutrition tips, health news and practical information. Its webpage on caregiver burnout looks at burnout versus depression, the advantages of 'dialling down' stress and the different types of treatment available.

CaregiverDave.com

player.fm/series/caregiverdavecom

Dave is the caregiver's caregiver. This podcast shares insights from more than twenty years of caregiving that have qualified him to build a community of caregivers and help them to take care of themselves first so that then they can give to their charges.

Caregivers Podcasts by Player FM

player.fm/podcasts/Caregivers

This site provides a rich list of podcasts with excellent content to nurture caregivers.

Caregivers' apps for reducing anxiety and distress

MindShift CBT (iPhone and Android compatible)

www.anxietycanada.com/resources/mindshift-cbt/

The tools provided by this app reduce anxiety—meditations, coping statements and journalling help give immediate relief and longer-term learnings craft more useful ways of thinking.

Stop Panic and Anxiety Self-Help (Android compatible)

www.excelatlife.com/apps.htm#panicapp

This app helps you cope with panic attacks. Mood techniques coupled with relaxation achieve calm and reduce caregiver stress. It can be linked to journalling to track your feelings too.

Personal Zen (iphone compatible)

personalzen.com

The Personal Zen app was designed by neuroscientists to retrain the brain. It is in the form of a simple game that reduces caregiver anxiety and stress by distraction from the stressful situation.

General support

Websites (and book) with strategies to increase resilience

PositivePsychology.com

positivepsychology.com/stress-management-techniques-tips-burn-out/

A website that has ample information about what stress is and how to manage it. It has techniques, stress relief activities and suggestions for handling pressure in the workplace.

Happify (iphone compatible)

my.happify.com

Developed from the principles of mindfulness, positive psychology and cognitive behaviour therapy (CBT), Happify has science-based activities and games—via computer, tablet or smartphone—to deactivate negative thoughts and stress, and build resilience.

Thriving Mind

www.drjennybrockis.com/thriving-mind-book/

In her book *Thriving Mind: How to cultivate a good life*, Jenny Brockis examines how people can thrive in 'our brave new world'. She offers information on de-stressing and how to sustain wellbeing. Download a free sample chapter at this link.

Oprah'S Supersoul Conversations

podcasts.apple.com/us/podcast/oprahs-supersoul-conversations/id1264843400
Oprah Winfrey interviews thought leaders, best-selling authors, spiritual luminaries and health and wellness experts to highlight the best ways to look after ourselves.

Apps to help with cultivating better habits

Strides: Goal & Habit Tracker (iPhone compatible)

apps.apple.com/au/app/strides-goal-habit-tracker/id672401817
This app helps you sets goals and charts your progress as you adopt better habits, like decreasing your alcohol consumption, eating a healthier diet, increasing meditation practices and upping exercise levels.

Nudge (iphone and Android compatible)

play.google.com/store/apps/details?id=com.nudgeyourself.nudge&hl=en_AU
apps.apple.com/au/app/nudge-for-clients/id605363055
Focused on diet or weight-loss goals, this app tracks your progress and can link with other users and social clubs for added support. A personal coach is available if preferred.

Websites addressing perfectionism, anxiety, depression, grief and anger

Perfectionism

cci.health.wa.gov.au/Resources/Looking-After-Yourself/Perfectionism
The Centre for Clinical Interventions in Western Australia aims to reduce dysfunctional perfectionism. This free course helps you recalibrate perfectionism's settings: the relentless striving for extremely high standards, the fragile self-worth based on achieving such standards and the personal costs of such over-investment.

moodgym

www.moodgym.anu.edu.au

This free self-help program assists those vulnerable to depression and anxiety by teaching them protective cognitive behaviour therapy skills.

myCompass

www.mycompass.org.au

Offered by the Black Dog Institute, myCompass is a free online self-help program for people with mild to moderate depression, anxiety and stress.

Apps to help de-stress

There are time-honoured ways of reducing stress and a wide range of platforms. Depending on your preference, counselling, meditation, mindfulness, massage, breathing, cognitive behaviour therapy and relaxation techniques are at your fingertips. The most readily applicable and effective remedy is exercise.

All the apps listed start with a free trial and then give access to various features if you subscribe. They are available on both Android and Apple platforms.

Headspace

www.headspace.com

Headspace is a comprehensive meditation app that provides guided and unguided meditations focused on all life phases.

Calm.com

www.calm.com

The Calm app provides guided 'Daily Calm' (relaxation) and 'Daily Trip' (meditation) and music tracks to help you unwind. It is also focused on improving disrupted sleep. The mindfulness journal includes a gratitude check-in record.

Sanvello

www.sanvello.com

Support to improve your mental health via assistance with self-care, peer support, coaching and therapy.

SAM App for Anxiety

sam-app.org.uk

The SAM (Self-help for Anxiety Management) app helps manage anxiety via self-learning plus building a toolkit customised to your own circumstances.

Colorfy (iPhone and Android compatible)

https://apps.apple.com/us/app/colorfy-art-coloring-game/id1009442510
https://colorfy.en.uptodown.com/android

Colorfy is a free app that doesn't require any internet connection where you can colour relaxing shapes and patterns and achieve a state of flow.

Websites with remedies for poor sleep

'How to succeed? Get more sleep'—Arianna Huffington (TED Talk)

https://www.youtube.com/watch?v=BhkD6GFdJ-Y

Insights from the successful businesswoman whose burnout is described in earlier chapters and who practises sustainable mental and physical habits. Ariana Huffington especially promotes the benefits of optimal sleep and tells how to achieve it.

Somryst

www.somryst.com

Somryst is a commercial application for adults with insomnia. CBT is delivered via a smartphone or a tablet using 'tailored sleep restriction and consolidation, stimulus control and personalized cognitive restructuring' to improve insomnia symptoms. There are customer 'restimonials' in support!

Apps to control apps so apps don't control you

The apps listed below help you control your phone 'habit' or to at least be aware of how much it owns you. While both iPhone and Android have improved tools and trackers in the phone settings that help monitor and control your phone use, you might like to consider the extra features offered by the following apps.

Forest (iPhone and Android compatible)

www.forestapp.cc

Using Forest, the user can choose the amount of time they want to stay focused on a task and apps are blocked for that time. Effective concentration earns coins that grow a virtual tree; drop your task and leave the app and your tree will wither.

Freedom (iPhone and Android compatible)

freedom.to

Freedom works as a content blocker, blocking social media and other websites on Safari. Blocklists can be customised to your needs. The paid version blocks apps too.

Siesta Text (Android compatible)

siesta-text-auto-away-message.soft112.com

The function of this app is to send automatic and customised text responses to any incoming texts or calls you receive at specific dates and times set by you. It can be linked to your phone's calendar so that you won't be distracted by incoming communication when your attention is required elsewhere (e.g. while in a meeting). This allows digital disengagement without offence.

Index

Page numbers in italics refer to figures. Page numbers in bold refer to tables.

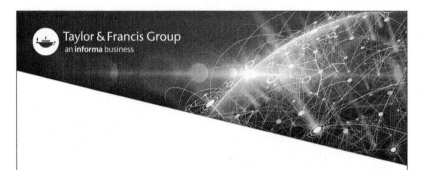